How to Rock Climb!

Lauren Lee climbing smoothly up The Crown (5.13c), Rougon, France. KEITH LADZINSKI

HOW TO CLIMB™ SERIES

How to Rock Climb!

Fifth Edition

John Long

GUILFORD, CONNECTICUT
HELENA, MONTANA
AN IMPRINT OF GLOBE PEQUOT PRESS

To buy books in quantity for corporate use
or incentives, call **(800) 962–0973**
or e-mail **premiums@GlobePequot.com.**

FALCONGUIDES®

FalconGuides is an imprint of Globe Pequot Press.
Falcon, FalconGuides, and Outfit Your Mind are registered trademarks of Morris Book Publishing, LLC.
How to Climb is a trademark of Morris Book Publishing, LLC.

Text designer: Casey Shain
Project editor: John Burbidge
Illustrations by Mike Clelland
All interior photos by Bob Gaines unless noted otherwise.

The Library of Congress has cataloged the earlier edition as follows:
Long, John, 1953-
      How to rock climb! / John Long.—4th ed.
         p. cm. – (How to climb series)
      Includes index.
      ISBN 0-7627-2471-4
1. Rock climbing. I. Title. II. Series.
GV200.2 .L66 2002
796.52'23—dc21   2002029907

ISBN 978-0-7627-5534-9
Printed in China
10 9 8 7 6 5 4 3 2 1

*Sonnie Trotter on Dream Catcher (5.14d),
Squamish, British Columbia.*

Contents

Chapter 6: The Art of Leading

215

Chapter 7: Getting Down

247

Chapter 8: Sport Climbing

273

Chapter 9: Training for Climbing

283

Chapter 10: Responsibilities and Staying Alive

299

Acknowledgments

Thanks to Bob Gaines, photographer and director of Vertical Adventures; Tom Cecil, director of Seneca Rocks Mountain Guides; and the many other climbers and instructors who reviewed the text and whose comments and suggestions were invaluable for this fifth edition. Thanks also to Keith Ladzinski (www.ladzinski.com), whose outstanding action photos bring life and excitement to what is basically a technical manual.

Introduction

When I first wrote the original *How to Rock Climb!* text, I couldn't have imagined that sixteen years later I'd be revising it for the fifth time. But while climbing fundamentals have remained basically the same for five decades, every season brings small adjustments in procedure, equipment, and style that create shifts in our general strategy. Recent testing and statistical analysis have also provided new information on the crucial subject of climbing anchors, and for any introductory book to be current, this data has to be included. What's more, the previous four editions made clear what aspects of the climbing game are most challenging for the beginner to understand and correctly carry out. Not surprisingly, these included setting protection and building reliable anchors, so this fifth edition has put special emphasis on this vital subject.

Most modern-day climbers break in at a climbing gym rather than at a local crag, where you normally must manage a full array of climbing gear and procedures—including building anchors—most every time out. While the gym continues to rapidly produce great physical climbers, it has also help foster dangerous misconceptions about what is involved and required to climb outdoors. Strong fingers can only get you so far. American climbing elder Richard Goldstone puts it this way: "It's not just that these novices have no experience thinking about the risks in traditional, outdoor climbing, it's that their initial gym training has desensitized them to critical issues and provided them with habits that will need to be unlearned. They will not be well-served by a prescriptive approach that—in spite of the demurrals at the beginning of the book about climbing being dangerous—gives the impression that if they follow some collection of codified procedures, their safety is more or less guaranteed."

Climbing outdoors will always involve too many variables for the protocols to be codified into a uniform strategy. Certainly, there are time-proven ways of doing most every procedure in climbing, but no book or instructor can predict what is correct in every circumstance, or anything close to it. Improvising on a theme will always be required owing to the rock's limitless variety. Everyone wants definitive, clear-cut answers. And everyone wants the whole shebang broken down so simply and so clearly that a total novice can grasp everything at a glance. But we've learned, after four previous editions, that sidebars and bullet points can only take us so far, and that a comprehensive, presentational style is required to accurately address climbing's infinite variety.

A little history has also been mixed in; it's often helpful to learn where things came from and how they evolved, rather than just grappling with the existing product or technique. In addition, the format of this edition has been updated to include many new color photographs, so the details are as evident and understandable as modern printing will

Chuck Fryberger on **The Skinless Arete (5.13a), Rocklands, South Africa.** KEITH LADZINSKI

allow. Basically, the book is the long-form, high-definition version of rudimentary rock climbing that assumes you know nothing at all about the subject, and breaks it all down in plain English.

Rock shoe technology, indoor climbing gyms, and the popularity of well-protected sport climbs have hastened a novice's voyage from beginner to intermediate terrain. But the cautious, athletic milieu of sport climbing has overshadowed, rather than replaced, traditional "adventure" climbing. Many climbers are still out there bagging traditional, classic routes—extreme cracks, desert towers, big walls, alpine routes, frozen waterfalls, and mixed rock and ice lines. As long as the spirit of adventure lives on, there will still be those pitting their own basic stuff against the wildest real estate nature can offer. For the vast majority of climbers, however, the main goal is to have fun and challenge themselves without compromising safety, for no sport is less forgiving if you do. More than anything, safety and fun are the focus of this book.

How to Rock Climb! is based on the "Yosemite system"—methods born out of the revolutionary climbs first established in Yosemite Valley—amply supplemented with twenty-first-century sport-climbing techniques used the world over. The Yosemite system is, in practice, much more of a philosophy, stressing safety and simplicity. As with any complicated enterprise, the more basic you keep things, the more manageable they are.

Studying this book, or one like it, is the standard first step for all beginners. Next is to take a climbing class (preferably a short, intense series of several classes), a thing no book can, or should, attempt to replace. Virtually everyone starts out this way, or is nursed or hauled up a host of climbs by a knowledgeable friend, which amounts to the same thing. The rare individual who learns the ropes completely on his own will probably later realize his learning curve was a flat line for the first few months or years. It's easier, and far safer, to get the basics worked out from day one. Again, beginner classes are now offered at most every gym and crag in America. Take one.

Statistically, rock climbing is one of the least dangerous of all the so-called thrill sports because it employs over a century's worth of refined technique and solid technology. The basic system of technical rock climbing—how a rope and specialized techniques and equipment safeguard a climber—is simple enough that most anyone can manage the basics in a few weekends (though mastery of all aspects is a lifelong process). There is no mystery, and you need not be even a decent climber to have a working knowledge of rope management. The art of climbing rock is another affair, but even this tends to be more of a learned skill, requiring less natural ability than other sports. Lastly, climbing relies more on technique and balance than brute strength (except for the more extreme, gymnastic routes), so there is no reason an enthusiastic climber cannot carry on at a top level until old age, as many do.

That climbing transcends mere sport is a conviction held by most anyone with a pair of rock shoes, and everyone who has climbed a monolith like Yosemite's El Capitan. The airy exposed routes, the spectacle of ascent, the physical and mental demands—they all give a rush to your blood that continues running rich, regardless of experience. Climbing is not an easy sport, and it has a lion's share of toil. But to thousands, even millions worldwide, the rewards are worth the struggle.

Lauren Lee jamming on **McCarthy Southwest Face (5.11c), Devils Tower, Wyoming.**
KEITH LADZINSKI

The Climbing Game

Early man was a climber. He climbed to escape predators and enemies, and to forage for food. Eons later, in the mid-1700s, man began climbing again—out of desire, not necessity. Spread throughout the European Alps, villages big and small were nestled between spectacular alpine peaks, and for a host of reasons, certain men aspired to climb the grandest peaks on the continent. The summit was the ultimate goal of these first mountaineers, and glaciers and snow slopes provided the most natural passage to the top. Following the first recorded alpine ascent, that of Mount Aiguille, the rush was on, and major peaks were climbed in succession.

After the easier routes had been climbed, subsequent mountaineers found that some rock climbing skills were necessary to open up new mountains, and they discovered that the lower cliffs and crags provided a perfect training ground to this end. To provide some modicum of safety to the falling climber, ropes and rudimentary belaying techniques were introduced around the turn of the twentieth century. At the time, climbing was effectively confined to the European continent and, to a lesser degree, England. It was in Austria, around 1910, that rappelling was invented, along with heavy steel carabiners (snap links) and pitons, the latter to provide the aid and protection required on the more difficult, modern climbs. With the new equipment and techniques and the confidence they spawned, Austrian and German climbers established climbs far more difficult than previously thought possible.

Though isolated rock summits were occasionally bagged, the endeavor was considered of lesser worth than achieving the big summits of the Alps. In retrospect, some of the training climbs on these "practice" cliffs were remarkably difficult considering the gear. The leaders had little more than hemp ropes (which routinely broke), hemp-soled shoes, and boldness to see them through. As late as the 1980s, in parts of Eastern Europe, particularly around Dresden, summitless crags were eschewed in favor of the spires that abound there; likewise, the method and style of ascent remained almost unchanged for fifty years.

Meanwhile, in pre–World War I England, rock climbing on the many backyard outcrops was being explored, albeit less aggressively than in Germany. The English discouraged the use of pitons, however, partly for ethical reasons and partly owing to the fragile nature of the "gritstone." Anyway, in the absence of big mountains, the English developed crag climbing as a sport in its own right. In the Americas, the sport's development followed the European lead, though with somewhat of a time delay—roped climbing didn't arrive until the late 1920s.

The 1930s heralded the golden age of alpine climbing, though the emphasis was still on climbing

Mike Anderson using arm bars on the first free ascent of Angel Hair (5.13a), Zion National Park, Utah. KEITH LADZINSKI

Bob Gaines on the classic **Pancake Flake on
The Nose** *route, El Capitan, Yosemite, 1979.*

Charlie Peterson on **Wheat Thin (5.10c),** *Cookie
Cliff, Yosemite, 1980.*

the major ridges and faces of the higher peaks.
During this prewar period, rock climbing standards
rose steadily throughout the world. Although most
of the glory was still found in achieving mountain-
ous summits—peaks in the Alps, North America,
and Asia were conquered in succession—in many
areas it was rock climbing standards that saw the
most dramatic development.

World War II saw little climbing activity, but
the war prompted technological developments that
greatly impacted postwar climbing. Before, pitons

and carabiners were expensive and rare, and ropes
were still fashioned from natural fibers, which were
bulky and prone to snap during long falls. "The
leader must not fall" was the unquestioned dictum
that all climbers observed if they wanted anything
but a short career. World War II changed all this
with the plentiful supply of surplus army pitons,
lightweight aluminum carabiners, and, most importantly, strong and light nylon ropes.

For the next twenty years, standards rose steadily
in both England and the United States. English

John Long, with old-school swami belt and short-shorts, following the first pitch of Hades (5.12b), Suicide Rock, California, 1984.

Climbers ascending a bolted limestone sport route at the Verdon Gorge, France, 1990.

climbers maintained their anti-piton stance and developed anchoring techniques that used runners over natural rock spikes, plus the wedging of pebbles—and eventually machine nuts slung with slings—as chockstones in cracks. Not surprisingly, the English also pushed standards of boldness. They had little choice, for their protection was often dicey at best. European standards were consolidated, but actual rock climbing standards advanced little (except some exploring of large boulders at Fontainebleau, outside Paris), because of the continued emphasis

on attaining alpine summits. European manufacturers did, however, develop new nylon ropes that were stronger and much easier to handle.

By the early 1960s, specialized rock climbing shoes appeared that didn't look too different from the all-around shoes available today. The varappe, essentially a high-top shoe with a smooth rubber sole, and improved piton design spurred higher standards. In the Americas and in England, rock climbing was pretty firmly established as a specialized sport, and routes that led, say, merely to a cliff feature or to rappel points in the middle of blank cliffs were commonly done and respected. Sparingly in America, but increasingly in England, climbers formulated strong aesthetic distinctions between pulling on pitons and artificial aids in order to ascend, and using such anchors solely to protect themselves in case of a fall. This latter practice became known as free climbing. Styles and techniques remained largely provincial until the mid-1960s, however, because few climbers traveled widely to sample various climbing areas.

This changed dramatically by 1970, due in large part to the innovative development of rock climbing techniques born in California's Yosemite Valley (during the late 1950s and through the 1960s) that allowed the ascent of the spectacular cliffs there. To learn the piton aid techniques that enabled these ascents—in splendid weather to boot—climbers from around the world traveled to Yosemite. While they learned the American techniques, they also left a heritage all their own.

By the early 1970s, American and English climbers completely dominated the development of the sport, and methods and equipment for climbing rock were becoming homogenized. Americans pitched the clunkier boots they had generally favored and adopted sensitive French and English smooth-soled shoes; in addition, the destructive and strenuous American pitoning techniques used in scaling the big cliffs were found to be less effective for free climbing than the gentler English nutting techniques. Moreover, innovative Americans started redesigning and commercially producing light and effective protection devices: first, aluminum nuts, and then spring-loaded camming devices (SLCDs). Simultaneously, rope manufacturers continued fine-tuning and improving the proper balance between strength, energy-absorbing stretch, and durability, which led to a much more relaxed attitude toward falling.

By 1980, climbers were traveling the world over to explore different areas, and climbers from many countries were involved in pushing standards. While the best climbers now trained exclusively for climbing, and the techniques and equipment were common to all, a new, pure gymnastic approach was applied to the style of ascent, particularly by the French. Inspired by the technical difficulty of the free routes in Yosemite Valley, they returned to France to begin a quest for pure difficulty, linking long stretches of bouldering moves with convenient protection afforded by bolts. With easy protection they could concentrate on difficult, gymnastic movement in relative safety, and thus "sport climbing" was born.

Today's best sport climbers sometimes "climb" the hardest routes by first descending the cliff to prearrange their protection, inspect the route for available holds, and clean away any loose holds and offensive effluvium. The subsequent ascent may take days, weeks, or even months of repeated falls, all to the goal of climbing the route—now an extremely complicated gymnastic routine—straight through without falls. This approach has further led to the development of a formal competitive circuit, where climbers compete against each other on man-made, often indoor, artificial climbing walls. Climbing competitions peaked around 1990, but they still live on in various formats, including a limited number of national meets (see http://usaclimbing.net). Small, regional competitions continue to draw participants of all skill levels, and are typically welcomed more as fun social events than as end-all competitions.

European-style sport climbing began in the United States about thirty years ago. It was accepted grudgingly at first, but is now the preferred form of climbing for most because of its secure and convenient nature. As we continue into the new millennium, sport climbing has taken center stage with most of the climbing community, and the media as well. While sport climbing has nearly become a movement unto itself, it is in fact just one more mode of ascent derived from the original contest of trying to gain the top of alpine peaks.

About fifteen years ago, sport climbing began branching out, with a few top sport climbers applying their extreme free-climbing skills to big rock walls and high-altitude alpine climbs. Over the past few years, this trend has accelerated. As predicted by Yvon Chouinard in the 1960s, the techniques and skills developed in Yosemite found their way to the most dramatic mountain ranges in the world. Huge alpine walls in Patagonia, Alaska, the Himalayas, and other wild places were ascended using the Yosemite system, further pushing the envelope of climbing and the influence of Yosemite. To the average climber, however, climbing remains an exciting means to explore the natural world and enjoy the choreography of ascent.

Rating the Difficulty

Because the vast majority of your climbing will follow established routes already rated for difficulty and recorded in a guidebook, you will, with time, need to understand the following class system. It is your only yardstick as to how difficult a given climb is, and for this reason, it is both simple and comprehensive. The American rating system that follows is one of many in use around the world (see chart on next page).

Class

The following classes are used to describe moving across various terrain:

CLASS 1: Walking.

CLASS 2: Hiking. Mostly on established trails, or perhaps slogging along a streambed.

CLASS 3: Scrambling. Angle is steep enough where hands are used for balance. A hand line is rarely used, even for inexperienced climbers.

CLASS 4: Climbing risky enough that a fall could be fatal. Pulling with your arms required. A rope, some equipment, and protection techniques are used by most mountaineers.

CLASS 5: Technical rock climbing, commonly called "free climbing." A rope and specialized equipment and techniques are always used to protect against a fall. Fifth-class climbing is the subject of *How to Rock Climb!*

CLASS 6: Rock so sheer or holdless that ascent by using hands and feet is impossible. The equipment is used directly to aid the ascent, hence the common usage names for sixth-class climbing: artificial, direct aid, or simply, aid climbing. Recall the hoary image of the intrepid climber hammering his way up the rock, his weight suspended on a succession of creaky pins. Things have changed, but the old notion still best illustrates what aid climbing is all about.

It is commonly agreed that technical rock climbing starts at fifth class, and the bulk of this book will deal with fifth-class climbing. Fifth-class climbing varies from low-angle slabs, where only the beginner will relish a rope, to 125-degree face climbs so extreme that world-class climbers might fall fifty times before they work out the entire sequence, if indeed they ever do. In the early 1950s, fifth-class climbing was designated as "easy," "moderate," and "advanced." As climbers got better and the climbs harder, a decimal system was adopted to more accurately rate the levels of difficulty within the class. Devised in the early 1930s by the Rock Climbing Section of the Sierra Club, this system is principally used as an index of difficulty. The original scale, 5.0 through 5.9, was intended at the time of its adoption to cover the whole range of humanly possible rock climbs, anything above 5.9 being regarded as impossible. Standards are made to fall, of course, and shortly that one did.

The decimal system ceased to be purely "decimal" when aggressive pioneers sought to rate climbs harder than established 5.9s. Like other rating systems used throughout the world, the decimal system has evolved into an open-ended system that now includes climbs from 5.0, the easiest, to 5.15,

World Rating Systems

West German (UIAA)	American (Decimal)	British (seriousness)	British (technical)	Australian	East German (GDR)	French
	5.5	VS	4a			
	5.6	VS	4b			
5+	5.7	VS	4b		VIIa	5a
6-	5.8	HVS	4c	16	VIIb	5b
6	5.9	HVS	5a	17	VIIb	5c
6+	5.10a	E1	5b	18	VIIc	6a
7-	5.10b	E1	5b	19	VIIIa	6a
7	5.10c	E2	5c	20	VIIIb	6b
7+	5.10d	E2	5c	21	VIIIc	6b
7+	5.11a	E3	6a	22	IXa	6c
8-	5.11b	E3	6a	23	IXb	6c
8	5.11c	E4	6a	24	IXc	7a
8	5.11d	E4	6a	25	IXc	7a
8+	5.12a	E5	6b	26	Xa	7b
9-	5.12b	E5	6b	27	Xb	7b
9-	5.12c	E5	6b		Xb	7c
9	5.12d	E6	6c	28	Xc	7c
9+	5.13a	E7	6c	29		8a
10-	5.13b	E7	7a	30		8a
10-	5.13c	E7	7a			8b
10	5.13d	E8	7a	31		8b
10+	5.14a	E8	7b	32		8c
11-	5.14b	E8	7b			8c
11	5.14c	E9	7c	33		8c
11	5.14d	E9	7c			9a
	5.15					

Though ratings vary from one area to the next, the fifth-class decimal system is pretty uniform throughout the United States: A 5.8 in Yosemite would most likely be rated 5.8 at Tahquitz Rock as well. Climbers rely on the rating system being consistent, lest they are misled by guidebooks and end up on climbs either too hard or too easy for their fancy. Once a climber travels to a foreign area, however, he must become fluent in another rating system, for every country has an individual method of rating the difficulty of rock climbs. The attending chart plots comparative difficulties relative to various national rating systems. It is reasonably accurate but not unequivocal. All rating systems are open-ended, but the differences in difficulty between various number or letter ratings vary from country to country. There are other differences also: The British system factors a seriousness appraisal into the rating that precedes the standard technical rating (E5 6a). Note that the seriousness ratings overlap each other considerably in relation to the difficulty rating, as represented in the chart by the dashed lines.

the most difficult leads achieved to date. Climbs of 5.10 through 5.15 are in the realm of the advanced or expert climber; to better shade the nuances of these advanced levels, the letters a, b, c, and d were tacked onto the rating. For example, 5.12d represents the extreme end of the 5.12 standard, whereas a 5.12a or 5.12b is an "easier," low-end 5.12 (not one active climber in twenty consistently manages this grade).

Modern routes tend to be rated somewhat softer than older routes, meaning you can normally count on an old 5.10 to be more exacting than one established last week. Convenient bolt protection, the earmark of the sport climb, at once removes much of the psychological factor while reducing the physical strain of hanging by fingertips and frantically trying to hand-place gear in the rock. Because most sport climbs are first and foremost physical challenges, they likely will seem "easier" than older climbs of the same grade that feature psychological trials as well.

The standardized rating system was intended to provide uniformity; that is, a 5.7 route at El Dorado Canyon, Colorado, should correspond in difficulty to a 5.7 route at Suicide Rock, California. This is the theory, but not the reality. Ratings should be considered area-specific only. Entire areas, such the Shawangunks in upstate New York and Joshua Tree National Park, a world-renowned desert climbing area in Southern California, are widely know to have "stiff" ratings, meaning a 5.10a route at "Josh" or the "Gunks" will likely be rated 5.10b or even harder at other areas. Other popular locales are known to have "soft" ratings, such as Red Rocks outside Las Vegas, where folks flock to shore up their self-esteem as well as enjoy the divine sandstone. A few questions to locals or, better yet, a few introductory routes at any area will generally give you a feeling about an area's tendency toward soft or stiff ratings. Either way, it's good to get straight on an area's rating biases from the get-go, especially when trying to push your limits.

There are often significant (at least one full grade) differences from area to area and gym to gym, especially at the easier levels. You must also include the "sandbag" factor, the shameless practice of underestimating the actual difficulty of a given route ("sandbagging"). The desired effect is that the sandbagger looks good and us hackers feel bad about finding a route far more difficult that it's supposed objective rating. Both individuals and entire climbing communities might systematically underrate everything by an entire grade. Unfortunately, sandbagging remains an annoyance from which the climbing world has always suffered. Inasmuch as human nature is more constant than ratings, we can expect at least 10 percent of all ratings to be sandbags. An almost certain indicator of a sandbag rating is when a plus (+) is affixed to routes in the 5.7 to 5.9 range; that is, a 5.7+ route is almost always going to be a solid 5.8.

A related point worth mentioning is that in years past you would only call yourself a 5.10 leader if you could consistently lead any 5.10 route, including thin faces, roofs, finger cracks, off-widths, et al. Today, many climbers who have hangdogged up a 5.12 sport climb tend to consider themselves 5.12 climbers. But put them on a 5.9 adventure climb, where the runouts are long and the required techniques many, and they might back off at the first difficulties. The point is: Since the rating system was first devised, climbers have been preoccupied with bandying about high numbers in the most cavalier manner. Don't be swayed by such "smack," and wait until you get out on the rock to form your opinions about potential climbing partners. Some sport climbers are fairly inexperienced and can perform only under very circumscribed conditions. The danger here is that many of them don't realize this themselves, and they subsequently can make sketchy partners outside a climbing gym or practice area where every yard of every climb is chalked and bristling with bolts. The difference between a difficult toprope climb in an indoor climbing gym and a long, complex free route in the mountains is the difference between a candle and a blowtorch. Don't get burned.

Sixth-class direct aid climbing is divided into five rating classes: A1 through A5, depending on the difficulty of placing protection anchors and their precariousness when placed. Put figuratively, this means you can hang your van from an A1 placement, but falling on a tenuous A5 thread of bashies will surely result in a harrowing 100-foot "zipper" as the bashies pull out one by one.

Grade

The decimal system tells us how difficult a climb is. The attending grade rating tells us how much time an experienced climber will take to complete a given route.

I.   One to three hours
II. Three to four hours
III. Four to six hours—a strong half day
IV. Full day—emphasis on full
V.   One to two days—bivouac is usually unavoidable
VI. Two or more days on the wall

The decimal rating is a relatively objective appraisal of difficulties inasmuch as it was arrived at through consensus by experienced climbers. The grade rating is posited as objective, but it uses the hypothetical "experienced" climber as the measure of how long a given route should take. Compare the grade rating with the par rating on a golf course. A par five means a pro can usually hole the ball in five shots, rarely less, but a hacker will smile at a bogey six. Likewise, a couple of good climbers can usually crank a grade V in one day, whereas the intermediate climber had best come prepared to spend the night. World-class climbers can sometimes knock off a grade VI in an inspired day, depending on the amount of difficult direct aid on the route. The more hard aid, the less likely that any team can "flash" a grade VI route in a day.

As you get more familiar with climbing, you will frequently read about "speed ascents" of big walls. Most of these occur on routes with either ample free climbing or aid that is quickly dispatched.

Free Climbing

There are two types of individuals who climb without a rope: the world-class climber whose experience is extensive and who knows her capabilities and limits perfectly, and the sorry fool who doesn't know any better and is courting disaster. More will be said on this topic in Chapter 6, "The Art of Leading," but let it be clear that, with rare exceptions, a rope and equipment are always employed in modern fifth-class climbing. Accordingly, the layman often assumes that equipment directly assists a climber's ascent. It does, in the advanced realms of aid (sixth-class) climbing, but not in the form known universally as free climbing.

Free climbing is the basis of all sport climbing and can be loosely defined as upward progress gained by a climber's own efforts—using hands and feet on available features—unaided, or "free" of the attending ropes, nuts, bolts, and pitons, which are used only as backup in case of a fall. Rock features—such as cracks, edges, arêtes, dihedrals, and flakes—provide the climber his holds and means for ascent. The variety is endless, and even uniform cracks of the same width have many subtle differences. It is this fantastic diversity that gives climbing its singular challenge, where each "route" up the rock is a mental and physical problem-solving design with a unique sequence and solution. Discovering what works, for what climb and for what person, is the process that keeps the choreography of ascent fresh and exciting. No two people climb the same route the same way.

It's not all ad-lib, however. There are numerous fundamental principles that apply to all climbing: The smooth coordination of hands and feet allows fluid

Bouldering is at the heart of all free climbing. Here Lisa Rands pulls down on Minky (V8), Rocklands, South Africa.
KEITH LADZINSKI

movement; balance, agility, and flexibility are often better weapons against gravity than brute strength; endurance is generally more important than raw power; husbanding strength is accomplished by keeping your weight over your feet, rather than hanging from your arms; and the best execution of any climb is that which requires the least effort. Finally, staying relaxed is half the battle. Much of climbing is intuitive, and the moves come naturally to the relaxed mind. Likewise, a relaxed mind allows you to find and maintain a comfortable pace, neither too fast nor too slow. A common situation is for the leader to tighten up and become rushed in response to the difficulty and the effort required. Learning to stay relaxed, especially in the midst of great physical and mental strain, is one of the boons of free climbing.

Climbing requires certain techniques that are not obvious and must be learned and practiced before you can hope to master them. It is one of the most primal activities a person can undertake, but unlike Java man, the modern climber usually wears shoes.

Basic Equipment

Rock Shoes

All climbing is done in rock shoes. Just as a ballerina does not dance in moccasins, climbers do not climb in loose shoes. And with anything that fits snugly, one wrong aspect (width, length, etc.) can result in blisters.

For your first couple of outings, rent a pair of rock shoes. Most mountain shops and guide schools, and all gyms, have rental shoes. Should you choose to pursue climbing, your first purchase should be a pair of shoes. Entry-level shoes go for about $70 to $100, while top-end shoes can run upwards of $160. Climbing shoes can be resoled (for about $40) when they wear out. Also, watch for notices posted on the bulletin boards of outdoor equipment stores. You can buy a perfectly good pair of used climbing

shoes for a fraction of what they would cost new. Otherwise, consider buying a pair on sale. Even world-class climbers look for shoe deals. Particularly for beginners, who can grind the sole off a new rock shoe in a matter of days, forget about getting the most advanced model (such as reverse cambered slippers) until your footwork rounds into form, usually after a few months of active climbing.

Built on orthopedically perfect lasts, with a glove-like yet bearable fit and sticky rubber soles, modern rock shoes are a remarkable innovation. Since the first super rock shoes arrived in 1982, advances in fit, materials, and rubber have paralleled advances in technical achievement. Currently, there are about a half-dozen major brands available for both men and women. The choice for the beginner is mainly a matter of price and fit. For the expert, the choice is usually an attempt to match a specialized shoe to a particular kind of rock or a specific technique. Some shoes are stiffer, good for standing on minuscule footholds but poor for pure friction. There are shoes for cracks, for limestone "pocket" climbing, for gym and sport climbing, and so forth. An expert climber will often have a quiver of shoes for various applications, much as a champion skier will have various skis for different conditions and uses.

Each manufacturer has a generic, all-around rock climbing shoe best suited for the novice—usually a board-lasted, lace-up model that provides maximum support and can withstand multiple resolings. Velcro tighteners have done away with the laces on some models, but these are usually slippers, not full-size rock shoes, which offer better support and durability for a beginner. As previously mentioned, since a beginner's footwork is generally careless, he will trash his shoes much faster than an experienced climber, so consider this when plunking down money for your first pair. Most manufacturers are continually redesigning their shoes. If you shop around, you can often buy last year's models at considerable savings.

While a general-use shoe is the novice's most practical choice, you will eventually want footwear

Shoe selection labels:
- La Sportiva Miura $140.00
- Five.Ten Moccasym $115.00
- La Sportiva W's Mythos $130.00
- Five.Ten Coyote $86.00
- Evolve Pontas $115
- Evolve Quest $95
- Five.Ten W's Siren's SALE $89.00
- Evolve Women's Electra $85
- La Sportiva Trad Master $110.00
- La Sportiva Mythos $130.00
- Five.Ten Hueco $89
- La Sportiva Cliff $90
- Five.Ten Women's Fox $86.00
- Five.Ten W's Gambit $130.00
- Five.Ten Men's Gambit $130.00

Shoe selection at the Nomad Ventures climbing shop in Idyllwild, California. Note that all models are low-tops, the long-ago favored high-top being a specialty design, normally used only in wide cracks to protect the ankles.

best suited to the type of climbing you prefer. For lower-angle face climbing, a soft sole and supple, low-cut upper is best. For steep wall or pocket climbing, you'll want a tight-fitting shoe with good lateral support, a pointy toe, and a super low-cut upper for ankle flexibility.

Many advanced climbers do most of their climbing in "slippers." While most modern rock shoes are not "boots" at all but are cut at or below the ankle, slippers have also done away with the laces (though perhaps half the models feature Velcro tighteners) and offer far less support. Slippers require strong feet, but offer a sensitivity for footholds not found in regular shoes. They are excellent for bouldering, steep sport routes, and indoor climbing. However, slippers definitely underperform on traditional routes, and can punish your feet in wide cracks—especially the reverse camber models—so many beginners stick with normal rock shoes, for that first season anyway.

Optimum performance in a slipper requires a painfully tight fit. This often results in a pronounced callus, or "corn," on top of the big toe. The only compensation here is that slippers are easy to remove, so most climbers take them off between each route. Also, to keep them light, some slippers are straight leather with no liner. Normally worn without socks (common with regular rock shoes as well), slippers—and in fact almost all rock shoes—usually take on a fierce bouquet. Air them out, clip them (dangling) onto the outside of your pack when you're out and about, and store them in a cool, dry place.

Climbers have traditionally worn shoes painfully tight to avoid foot rotation inside the shoe when standing on small holds. Climbing shoes with leather uppers will stretch with time, though many models have stitched/glued-in liners meant to remedy this. A well-fitting shoe should be snug out of the box, but never torturous. Modern climbing shoes are constructed on anatomically correct lasts and are contoured to fit the foot, but you must try them on and climb in them to know if they fit your foot.

Some brands may favor a wider or narrower last, so try on an assortment of different shoes until you find the perfect fit. As a novice it is probably more important to your climbing to have a good-fitting shoe than one that is specifically designed for the type of climbing you intend to do.

The foot should not rotate in the shoe; neither should the toes be dreadfully curled in the toe box—unless you're climbing at a very high standard. Climbers normally wear their shoes without socks for a better fit and increased sensitivity. A floppy pair of shoes are frustrating to climb in, and you don't want to spend serious money and waste all that

technology on a sloppy fit. Shoe manufacturers often run demos in climbing gyms and at bouldering competitions so you can test drive their various models. Do so and learn what you do and do not like.

Climbing magazines regularly have equipment reviews that rate shoes based on many criteria. These are usually reasonable guides in a sweeping kind of way. Just remember that despite significant advances in both rubber and shoe construction, there's no magic in shoes unless you know how to use them.

Dirt, grime, oil, tree sap, and such can affect a sole's performance, so always keep your shoes clean. Limit walking around in them to a minimum. Most climbing soles are not rubber at all but TDR—Thermo Dynamic Rubber—a petroleum-based synthetic. Regardless, the TDR oxidizes and hardens just like rubber, and though this is only a surface condition, it can affect performance. An occasional wire brushing is the solution for both grime and hardening. Hot car trunks loosen the glue bonds of the rands and soles. Superglue can fix this, but it's better to avoid excessive heat. Foot powder helps avoid stitch rot from sweaty feet.

Chalk

The use of gymnastic chalk to soak up finger and hand sweat and to increase grip, has been standard practice for over thirty years. On coarse sandstone, in 40-degree shade, the advantages are noticeable but not great. But stick a climber on a greasy, glacier-polished Yosemite crack in midsummer swelter, and his hands will sweat like he's going to the electric chair—here chalk can make a huge difference.

Though not permanent, excessive chalk buildup is not only an eyesore, but also telegraphs the sequence of holds to subsequent teams, diminishing the factor of discovery so vital to the climber's experience. Also, too much chalk on the holds can make the grip worse than no chalk at all, a common condition that has caused many climbers to carry a toothbrush to uncake chalky holds.

Chalk bag and block chalk. Gymnastic chalk (magnesium carbonate) comes in both block and powdered form.

Chalk blocks are broken down into powder once inside in the chalk bag.

Reaching into the chalk bag for a "dip." Chalk bags are typically strung on a thin sling and pulled to the middle of the back to avoid snagging on gear, the rock, or even a hand or foot.

Magnesium carbonate comes in loose and block form, and is also sold in "chalk balls," a small cloth ball full of chalk. It all goes into a chalk bag—a little bit bigger than fist-size—worn on a sling on your waist.

Helmets

In pure rock climbing areas like Yosemite, Colorado's Eldorado Canyon, Tahquitz Rock in California, or the Gunks of upstate New York, many climbers go without a helmet. The reason is that in these areas, rockfall is uncommon, and while it is certainly possible to injure your head in a fall, for some reason serious head injuries rarely happen. Most climbers have shunned wearing helmets (aka brain buckets) because they feel awkward; others consider them unstylish and gauche. These days there is not much to advance either claim. Fashioned from modern composite materials and borrowing styling from mountain biking, the modern helmet is a fashionable and functional unit. Common sense tells us that a number of head injuries (primarily from rockfall and leader falls) that occur each year in rock climbing might be avoided through the use of helmets.

Perhaps the most compelling argument for using a helmet is that, with the huge influx of new climbers, the hazard of dropped gear has increased significantly. A carabiner dropped from two pitches above you (300 feet) can have the velocity of a major-league fastball by the time it strikes your bean. Many Yosemite veterans are wearing helmets on walls. In the mountains, where the rock quality is often poor, only a madman doesn't wear a helmet. It's your choice. If you feel better wearing a helmet, do so. But avoid the tempting delusion of thinking a helmet makes you a "safer" climber than a person going au naturel. Acts of God notwithstanding, safety largely lies with the climber, not in his or her gear.

Helmet ("brain bucket") selection at the Nomad Ventures climbing shop.

Face Climbing Skills

Picture a climber on a steep wall of orange sandstone. Above her, the rock sweeps up like a cresting wave, without a single crack in which to lodge her hands or feet. From the ground you can't see one hold, just a polished face, yet she moves steadily up—high stepping, counterbalancing, reaching, ever fluid and graceful. She's face climbing, and to the beginner it looks harrowing. But you'll soon learn that face climbing is the most natural form in all the climbing game. It varies from low-angle slabs, where balance and the friction of rock shoes are all that's required, to 120-degree overhanging test pieces where strength and precise technique are required to even get off the ground.

The cardinal rule for face climbing on walls up to about 80 degrees (and oftentimes beyond that angle) is to keep your weight over your feet. They are much better suited for load-bearing than our arms, which tire quickly regardless of their strength. Keeping your weight over your feet is the result of proper body position. On face climbs less than 90 degrees (or dead vertical), your body should remain in the same upright posture as when you're walking on the beach, with your center of gravity directly over your feet. This vertical posture is the only one that is naturally balanced. If you've ever balanced a stick on your finger, you know it is only possible when the stick is vertical.

When your body is vertical, gravity forces your weight straight down onto your shoes, which is best for maximum friction and purchase. A beginner's initial reflex—to hug the rock—may feel more secure, but this actually throws the whole body out of balance; and when all the unbalanced weight is transferred to the feet, the shoes skate off. Also, when the body is vertical, the climber's face is not plastered against the rock and his field of vision is open to see how and where to proceed.

Many bad habits are accompanied by either breath holding or rapid breathing, or a combination of both. If you can pay some attention to keeping your breath slow and steady, you can avoid the frightened response to paste yourself close to the rock. So strive to breathe easily, stand up straight, stay in balance, and keep your weight over your feet. These are easy concepts to understand, but until you can consistently perform them on the rock, you will never advance beyond beginner status.

Footwork

Good footwork is one of the climber's most important assets. Except on overhanging rock, you will climb basically on your feet, your arms acting only as a support mechanism to maintain contact and balance as you step up from one foothold to the next.

Sam Elias on the thin and technical face climb **Surveiller et Punir** *(5.12c), Verdon Gorge, France.* KEITH LADZINSKI

This climber maintains an upright body posture to keep his weight directly over his feet, pressing up with the legs and hoisting with the hands as little as possible.

Even when stepping through for an "outside edge," it's best to keep a vertical posture instead of plastering yourself against the rock, which is a common impulse for beginners.

It's magical how well modern rock shoes adhere, but even so, a beginner will need some time before learning to trust her feet. Once you prove to yourself that the shoes do indeed stick, you can begin exploring the various ways to stand on holds. With practice you'll find that even the tiniest footholds can provide some support.

Gym climbing greatly hastens the overall use of feet, although on plastic holds. In most gyms and on most gym climbs, artificial holds are the only ones,

and using these requires intention. And intention—precisely placing rather than simply kicking your foot on a hold—is what skillful footwork is all about.

On actual rock, the variety of different footholds encountered is almost infinite, but aside from pure friction, where you simply paste the sole flush to the rock, there are basically two different ways to stand on footholds: by smearing and by edging.

When stretching for a high handhold, your hips, and most of your weight, should remain directly over your feet.

An admirable display of erect, vertical posture on this granite face.

Smearing

The name derives from the action of "smearing" part of the sole (generally, but not always, beneath the big toe) onto a slightly rounded hold (imagine the back side of a spoon). You will generally want to smear as much of the sole over as much surface area as possible to maximize the friction, and beginners may have to consciously push down with the toes to hold the smear. Much of the art comes from your ability to choose just the right place to step,

having a keen eye for any irregularities, rough spots, or dents.

Even the most flawless face usually has slight ripples, and above these ripples is a lower-angled spot—if only a single degree less than the mean angle. The experienced climber scours the face for these. In smaller dishes and scoops, the heel is often kept rather high, which increases the frontal pressure on the sole. On more uniform slopes, a lowered heel means more surface area of sole rubber

Smearing a big friction hold, weight over the ball of the foot.

A toe-pointing smear.

To make a smear more secure, paste a small part of your boot (typically the toe) on a rock feature.

In smearing, the foot is often weighted just as it is while edging—over the big toe.

contacting the rock. More rubber usually means increased friction. The lowered heel also puts the calf muscle in a more relaxed position. Try a variety of heel positions and find what works, and always concentrate on consciously pushing the foot against the rock to increase the friction/purchase.

Perhaps more than in any other type of climbing, keeping your weight correctly balanced over your feet is absolutely essential when smearing. Get

on a slab and, starting from the upright posture, slowly lower your torso closer to the rock. You will immediately feel that the closer you get to the rock, the less your shoes will stick. Different rock has different friction properties. Polished limestone is slick and desperate to friction on even at 45 degrees, while the coarse quartz monzonite at Joshua Tree allows pure friction well into the 70-degree realm. Given some handholds, smearing can be useful even on overhanging rock. If your foot slips, experiment with foot position: high heel versus low heel. You might also try to push into the rock more by moving your center of gravity out, away from the rock, or by pulling out slightly on the handholds.

Discovering just how steep an angle you can smear on and picking the optimum foot placement come with experience, but as with all face climbing, smearing is natural and readily learned, however insecure it may at first seem. In the bygone era (prior to 1982) of hard-soled rock shoes, particularly when many rock shoes had marble-hard cleated soles, smearing was a risky practice, rarely done. With today's sticky rubber soles, smearing has become the favored means of using ill-defined footholds.

Edging

The practice of placing the very edge of the shoe on any hold that is clear-cut—the serrated edge of a flake, a cluster of crystals, a pronounced wrinkle—is called edging. "Edge" applies not only to the shoe's running edge, but also to the "edge" that forms the top of the hold. You usually edge when the hold is sharp (many edges are wafer-like flakes on the face). The edge of your shoe is gently placed on the best part of the hold, and the sole finds purchase by biting onto the rock edge once the shoe is weighted.

On vertical and overhanging terrain, edging allows the climber to get her lower body closer to the wall and distribute more weight onto her feet, reducing the strain on the arms. Edging is the most basic method of standing on holds, but it takes practice to become precise and proficient. If you have a suitable and handy rock, the right shoes, and a knowledgeable instructor, you can get a feel for edging in half an hour.

You generally edge with the inside of the shoe, near the outside of the big toe. Both your foot and most rock shoes are designed to stand most easily on this section of the shoe. Also, when edging on dime-size holds—and you will—it is necessary to feel just how good or bad the shoe is holding, and

Edging with the inside edge of the shoe.

Outside edging with the right foot.

Face Climbing Skills **21**

the area around the big toe is the most sensitive and best suited for this work. However, it is not unheard of for people to prefer edging off the ball of the foot, which requires less foot strength, and many times it is necessary to edge with the shoe pointing straight on the hold ("toeing-in"). Toeing-in requires strong toes and is especially useful in the small pockets so common on limestone and volcanic crags.

While we normally climb directly facing the rock, many times you'll need to step one leg inside the other, particularly when traversing. Outside edging is almost always done just back from the origin of the small toe. The foot's bone structure makes that section of the foot fairly rigid as opposed to the rest of the outside part of the foot, which is fleshy and flexible and gives the shoe edge every reason to "butter off" the hold. Knowing how to edge with the outside of the shoe is often the technique that separates the intermediate from the advanced climber. No one ever reaches advanced status without knowing how to outside edge.

Edging is an exercise in precision. Many edges are so small they can't be seen until you're at them. Careful placement of the foot is essential, and once the shoe is weighted, it is equally important not to change the attitude of the shoe or you'll blow off the hold. Thus, one key to proficient face climbing is learning how to keep your foot perfectly still on the edge while the rest of your body carries on. This is especially important when extending the leg, or "pressing out" the hold, which is where it is most difficult to keep that foot rock solid. Change your foot's orientation on a really small hold, even a fraction of an inch, and you're off.

Contrary to common sense, a razor-sharp shoe edge is not ideal for standing on small holds. Because rubber stretches once weighted, a slightly round edge is less likely to "buttress," or fold off of, dinky footholds. All modern rock shoes feature a sole that is beveled back underfoot, resulting in more stable edging and less buttressing. Edge holds will appear at various angles. Here, it is critical to exactly match the shoe's running edge with the rock's edge. Again, once it is lined up, do not move it.

Since holds often slant, you will commonly find yourself applying pressure at oblique angles, which requires ankle flexibility. With extreme edging, when the holds are very small indeed ("dime edges"), many of the edges are time bomb in nature, meaning the climber cannot "camp" on them too long without the shoe blowing off from either toe fatigue or the fact that even the best shoe cannot work marginal holds indefinitely. It is sometimes best to smear an edge ("smedging"), especially if the edges are puny or the moves dynamic. Remember, you can smear an edge, but you can't edge a smear.

Backstepping

Backstepping, a technique vital and particular to steep rock, also makes use of the outside edge (see photos on next page). It increases your reach and forces your hips in, an invaluable practice on sport climbs. With a good backstep, the lower body can essentially be locked off on the holds via counterpressure, taking significant weight off the hands and arms. Believe it: Until you master this technique, many of the more difficult overhanging routes will remain out of reach.

Like all other footwork techniques, practicing backstepping on the boulders, inches off the ground—or more conveniently, at the climbing gym—will greatly hasten your capacity for what at first may feel awkward and unnatural. Many difficult gym climbs are engineered with backstepping in mind, so by and large the technique is quickly learned indoors.

Dave Mayville edging on **Solid Gold** *(5.10a), Joshua Tree, California.*

Backstepping with the right leg and foot helps you stabilize your stance.

A drop knee is simply a more pronounced backstep. Backsteps and drop knees remain the fundamental lower body techniques for all modern face climbing.

Poise

One the greatest parts of a beginner's career is realizing, after a few weeks of practice, that their footwork is starting to come together—that they are developing poise in precarious positions. Whole worlds open up after that. More about this will be discussed in Chapter 6, "The Art of Leading."

A common and practical way for beginners to gain poise and trust in their feet is to toprope (explained in Chapter 9) a low-angled slab and practice climbing with one or no hands. A no-hands climb will probably be friction all the way, but with one hand to clasp holds, you can quickly learn that edging is largely a matter of body position and precise footwork, and that when both of these factors are rock solid, your feet can truly do most of the work on less-than-vertical rock.

Rest Step

Often on sustained face climbs, your calves will become tired, or "pumped," one factor that can evoke the dreaded "sewing machine leg," where the tired limb will violently shake. To rest your calves, try the rest step: Find a good edge or hold and stand on the heel or instep of the foot, with the leg straight, the center of gravity directly over the heel or instep, and most of your weight on that foot. Use the rest step whenever you have to stop to place protection, or when you need a rest. Imaginative resting is one of the keys to efficient climbing.

Another good way to avoid sewing machine leg is fluid, relaxed breathing, a factor often overlooked by beginners and experts alike. Conscious, fluid breathing relaxes the climber and ensures the muscles get sufficient oxygen. Beginners typically climb tight, with the muscles tensed, especially in the gut and chest areas (which is where anxiety physiologically manifests). The result is shallow, rapid breathing that can border on hyperventilation, or the opposite practice of holding your breath till you're blue in the face. Direct a little of your attention to your breath, and your body will relax considerably. Shallow, panicked breathing and breath holding have probably caused as many needless falls as poor footwork.

To rest step, place your heel on a good hold, straighten your leg, and let your bones support you as you rest the calf.

Keeping your leg straight shifts the weight off your muscles and onto your bones.

Standing on the heel during the rest step.

Heel Hooking

Heel hooking is the attempt to use the foot as a hand and is rarely used on climbs less than vertical. Basically, you hook the heel of your shoe over or behind a flake, knob, corner, or any other feature that will accommodate such a move. Most often, the foot is actually extended sideways, and sometimes kicked over the head, where it is hooked behind and/or over a shelf or ledge. You then pull with the foot, folding the chest in and up until you can reach the hooked or desired hold. A heel hook is often a way to avoid throwing a risky dynamic move, and in isolated cases a climb is impossible without using this technique.

Though it is sometimes possible, even necessary, to hook something other than the heel (the toe perhaps), try not to hook anything above the shoe's rand, the strip of rubber that circles the shoe above the sole. The rand is made from the same compound as the sole and grabs the rock well, whereas the leather upper is prone to shoot off even a jagged flake.

When lateral movement is required on steep climbs, the body will often feel like it's set to hinge out and away from the face. Climbers often look for a side hold or flake at or below waist level to hook a heel on, thus holding the body in place while the hands are arranged on other holds.

Heel hooking requires good flexibility and moxie. The applications and variations are many, but

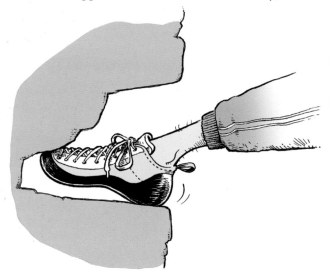

Torque between the toe and heel placed in a hole or horizontal crack below an overhang can keep the body from swinging out and provide stability and reach.

Footwork Tricks and General Technique

1. Scan the rock to find the best possible foothold. Don't move your foot until you know where you're going to put it. The size and location of the foothold determine its utility. When possible, place your feet directly beneath your hands to minimize the strain on your upper body.

2. Place the foot precisely on the best part of the foothold. "Zero in" on the foothold like an archer to a bull's eye. Concentrate on the foothold as you bring your foot to it.

3. Fluidly transfer weight to the new foot placement.

4. Hold the foot absolutely still as you stand/move on it. Use the ankle as a hinge to cancel upper body movement. Foot movement can cause the foot to ping off its hold, so focus on keeping the feet still and maintaining fluid movement and weight transference between holds. With a little experience, this will become second nature. The directions given here plant the seeds that will soon blossom into intuitive movement.

Heel hooking, the art of using a foot as a hand.

Heel hooking like this (pulling down with the leg) can basically unweight most of the lower body.

it's normally a technique used to employ a "third arm," or to stay in balance where otherwise it would be impossible. Rock gyms provide a perfect, controlled setting to practice heel hooking for the simple reason that many overhanging gym routes are unclimbable without this technique. When you have to heel hook, you will. And the more it's used, the quicker it's mastered.

Rushing the Sequence

A common problem with most novice climbers is that they rush their moves. They hug the rock; their feet are kicked toward, but aren't consciously placed on, the holds; and because they don't trust their shoes, their limbs quake and their shoes are often skedaddling all over. To climb fluidly and under control, you must settle in and relax.

The frantic climber is the first to make a mistake, to miss a key hold. You must choose your holds carefully and always follow the line of least resistance. This sometimes means passing a good hold that is off to the side and would require awkward, strenuous moves to attain. Maintaining balance often means using smaller steps and smaller holds rather than awkward, off-balance strides between larger holds. The climber should move methodically and with precision, placing his feet carefully, staying balanced, and easing up onto doubtful holds rather than jumping upon them. The aim is to climb smoothly and gracefully, and to use as little energy as possible. A good rule is whenever you reach a solid hold, pause and compose yourself, if only momentarily. Three slow and conscious breaths are often enough to steady up. And use the rest step when the chance arises.

Sloppy footwork is generally the result of impatience and anticipatory fear, most often unjustified. If fluid footwork seems impossible, if your shoes simply keep skating off even large holds, practice on slabs low to the ground. Get used to standing on marginal holds, keeping your weight over your feet. Experiment and learn. Traverse along the base of

the cliff, where a fall means slipping mere inches to the ground, and where you can try even the most improbable sequences. Practice walking over little slabs with no hands. Always aim to climb precisely, fluidly, and relaxedly. Striving to meet goals of control, rather than for success at all costs, will help build solid technique.

Always fight the initial instinct to only look up for holds. Many times the beginner will look down only to gauge the distance he is above the ground. You must pay attention to the climbing at hand. If you watch an experienced climber, you'll quickly see that she is looking down at her feet at least half the time, scanning for holds and placing them with keen eyes.

Handholds

There are as many different kinds of holds as there are ways to grab them, but five basic techniques remain: the open grip, the crimp, the pocket grip, the pinch grip, and the vertical grip. In addition to these grips, three other basic moves are often called upon in face climbing: mantling, the undercling, and the sidepull. Again, as with footwork, a calm and deliberate manner, coupled with trying different ways of using the hold, will result in confidence that you're using the hold most efficiently.

Open Grip

With the open grip, the hand functions like a claw. The core arm muscles fight the tendency of the fingers to straighten out, but if the hold isn't incut, the friction of the finger pads supplies the actual purchase on the hold. Accordingly, you try to cover the most surface area possible, increasing the friction at the power point. Chalked mitts are a must when "open handing" since the friction of your finger pad is what's securing the hold. Feel around for the most secure position, rather than just pulling straightaway the moment your hand is placed. The slightest shift in hand and finger position can make

The open grip, favored on big and rounded holds.

a huge difference. As with any handhold, if the hold is too small to accommodate all your fingers, give priority to the strongest digits, starting with the middle finger, on down to the pinky.

Experts in biomechanics insist that the open grip is least stressful on both joints and tendons and should be used whenever possible, especially when training on fingerboards. The difficulty with the open grip is that on severely rounded holds, the forearm muscles work overtime to keep the fingers from straightening out, and if the climber hangs too long, the forearms get "torched." The reason many experts utilize this grip on almost all manner of holds is that they are so honed from bouldering, sport climbing, and gym climbing that their forearm muscles are as strong as wild horses. They go with the open grip whenever possible because, over the long haul, this grip is easier on the joints and ligaments than crimping. But understand that this is a learned technique, and even those who know it well can only perform it relative to their immediate level of fitness. Even the pro who lays off for a month returns and can't begin to open hand the same holds he could before the layoff. Open hand climbing is basically strength climbing.

Crimp It

The crimp, one of the most called-upon handholds, is used most commonly on flat-topped holds, be they minute edges or inch-wide shelves. The fingers are bent at the second knuckle and the thumb is wrapped over the index finger if possible. Sometimes the thumb is braced against the side of the index finger, but whatever position the thumb ends up in, it's your best friend, as it's considerably stronger than

The crimp grip. While unnatural feeling at first, "crimping" is almost always the technique of choice for sharp holds.

Fingers aligned and crimping the edge.

any of your fingers. Remember that the thumb lies close to the rock, negating any leverage effects, while the fingers often project 1 or 2 inches away from the edge, which forces them to work counter to their own leverage. Crimping works much like a shoe does when edging. Once weighted, the fingers dig into the rough contours of the hold.

Because the second knuckle is locked off while your fingers are reinforced by your thumb, crimping allows you to apply great torque to a hold. You can also shred your fingertips on sharp edges, and possibly incur finger injuries owing to the sharp angle the tendons make and the stress the knuckles absorb. Regardless, crimping is most often the chosen technique when clasping sharp holds.

Most beginners find that crimping feels somewhat unnatural at first. It takes time for the knuckles to get accustomed to the stress. Also, you have to climb for a while to build up calluses on your finger pads, and until you do, crimping will hurt your tips. Because you don't want your fingers to rip off the rock, you'll need to feel around for the best part of the hold, which might also be the most jagged and painful. Only practice can reveal exactly how this all works, but you've got the basic notion.

Pocket Grip

The pocket grip is most often used on limestone and volcanic rock, which is typically pocketed with small holes. Many sport-climbing areas feature this kind of rock, and "pocket pulling" has long been a required technique for the modern climber. The ultimate form of the pocket grip is one finger stuck into a hole (a "mono-doigt" or "mono"). Because it is rare that a pocket will accommodate all of your fingers, the first choice is the strong middle finger, next the ring finger, then the index finger, and so on. Using the middle and ring finger in a two-finger pocket better balances the load on your hand, though the initial tendency is to use the index and middle finger for two-finger pockets. With practice, the middle and ring finger combo is generally a better option, and with use will eventually feel natural. It is sometimes, though rarely, possible to stack the fingers on top of each other for increased torque.

Feel the pocket for any jagged edges that can cut into the finger. Also, keep the pull in line with the axis of the finger, not pulling side to side, which is like bending a hinge—your knuckle—the wrong way. This is advice you will invariably have to shun, however, should you someday tackle upper-end sport routes. Just be prepared for some sore joints and a few layoffs when a tendon goes. No one who sport climbs at a high standard escapes finger injuries. It's part of the game.

Though advanced sport-climbing tricks are not the domain of this book, pocket climbing has become so ubiquitous that many beginners actually break in on volcanic and conglomerate crags, where the majority of holds are pockets (or at the gym, where pocket climbs are popular). For any number of reasons, pockets are rough on the tendons and the soft, fleshy part of the fingers, especially between the first and second knuckle (which is where the fingers usually crank over the edge of the pocket). When the pocket edge is sharp (common), you are essentially mashing both the tendons and the tissue over a blunt knife, something that takes some getting used to. Consequently, the number of finger injuries from pocket climbing far outnumbers those sustained on other venues. For the beginner, whose fingers are not accustomed to the strain, let alone to pulling on two-finger holes in the wall, caution is advised.

Some climbers, from beginners to world-class wonders, try to safeguard against bruising and outright injuries by taping their knuckles from the first knuckle down. This inhibits finger flexibility, so it's a trade-off. Many experts, however, are always nursing a sore finger or two, and these are routinely taped. Bottom line: Pockets are hard on the fingers and always will be, no matter how strong or experienced we may be.

Pocket grip utilizing the index and middle finger.

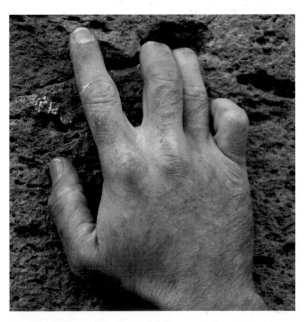

Pocket grip using the middle and ring finger, often the preferred configuration for two-finger pockets.

Pinch Grip

The pinch grip is the action a lobster does with its pincers, and what a climber does when pinching a knob, flute, rib, flange, or other protuberance. Though the basic technique is self-explanatory, a climber will often need to feel around to find just where his thumb and fingers fit best. On small knobs, the most effective pinch combines the thumb with the side of the index finger. Few people have much natural pinching strength. For the most part, it has to be developed.

Vertical Grip

The vertical grip involves bending the first and second knuckle and pulling straight down on the hold, sometimes with your fingernails behind the tiniest of edges. This grip is used exclusively on microflakes found on steep slab climbs, is painful, and is said to be the climbing equivalent of en pointe in

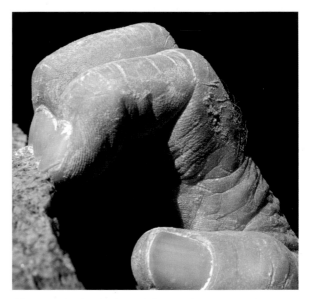

The vertical grip is rarely used.

Pinch grip.

Pinch it!

Crimping is almost always a more secure and less painful method than this vertical grip.

ballet. At 210 pounds, I've never used the vertical grip. Perhaps if you're skinny as a broom straw, your fingernails can take the strain. Mine never could.

Mantling

A mantleshelf is a rock feature, typically a small ledge with scant holds directly above, and the act of surmounting it is called mantling. Picture a young-ster heaving himself up and onto the top of a wall, then standing upon it. This is the basic form. Man-tling is often performed on shelves or knobs, but when the face offers only one hold, you might find yourself mantling—albeit gently—a mere pencil-width crease.

The technique has four basic components (see photos on next page). First, after placing both hands on the mantleshelf, inspect the shelf or hold for the best place to mantle on, usually the biggest, flat-test spot. If the spot is to the left of your face, you mantle with your left hand, and if it's to your right, you mantle with your right.

The second step involves hoisting the body up high enough to enable cocking one or the other arm on the mantleshelf. Use available footholds to get this upward impetus and to keep from yank-ing up solely with the arms. On steep mantles, it is important to get the torso as high as possible before cocking the arm. If the arm is cocked low, with your weight checked only by skeletal tension, it is beastly strenuous for the triceps to initiate upward thrust from this bottomed-out position.

The third part is the press, which is typically the most strenuous phase of any mantle. Whenever your free hand can grab a hold and pull, do so—this helps initiate the press. Keep pulling with that free hand until the mantling arm is straightened and locked out. The concern is to make sure the palm doesn't skate off the shelf, a real possibility on a rounded or slick surface. Most climbers find that the bottom, or heel, of the palm is best suited for most mantling.

Once you have pressed out the mantle, try to find a handhold above for the free hand. This makes it much easier to execute the last phase: the step up and leg press into the standing position. For balance, you'll want the foot close to the supporting hand. Often the hand must be moved to free up space for the foot. Using the knee is tempting here, but only makes it more difficult to get into the standing position and often results in abrasions. Rock your weight from your mantling hand to over your raised foot, and try to stand up smoothly and without jerking motions, which can dislodge the foot. If the wall is steep above the mantle, stepping up can be exciting, especially if there is a chance of pitching off backward. On these supersteep step-ups, your face will almost be rubbing the rock. Use any avail-able handholds to increase security.

In extreme cases, you must mantle using only your fingertips in the cling position, or perhaps with the thumb in a small divot. Many times you will step onto a hold different than the one you have pressed out. Regardless, the basics remain the same: staying balanced, utilizing footholds, not get-ting stuck in the bottomed-out position, avoiding use of the knee, finding a handhold above for the free hand, and smoothly stepping up.

Years ago, when the majority of climbing was done on granite and sandstone, top climbers were also skilled mantlers. They had to be, since mantling was a required technique on many classic traditional ("trad") climbs. As sport climbing gained popularity, mantling fell out of prominence because the routes are often too steep for it, and also because volca-nic and conglomerate rock—the common stuff of sport climbing—requires more pocket work than mantling. For this reason, skilled sport climbers have been known to get "hosed" on old climbs featur-ing hard mantles. Again, the best place to hone your mantling skill is on the boulders. It's an essential skill if you ever hope to crank the old trad routes.

1. Place both hands on the mantleshelf.

2. Next, hoist your body up high enough to enable cocking one or the other arm on the shelf.

3. Then press down . . .

4. . . . and step up!

Undercling

Anytime you grab a hold with your palm up, whether you have your fingers behind a flake or you're grabbing the underside of a small roof or step in the rock, you are underclinging. The technique is often used as a balancing tactic until a free hand can reach above to a better hold. In its pure form, it functions through the opposing pressures of the hand (or hands) pulling out from the hold under which you are clinging and the force that is directed onto your feet—counterpressure, in simple terms. The technique is intuitive and self-explanatory, but the following points are worth mentioning.

On a full-blown undercling, where you must, say, traverse under a long flake, try to keep your arms straight, as this transfers some of the load off your muscles and onto your bones. Utilize footholds as much as possible to ease the load on your guns. Rather than underclinging off your fingertips, try to get as much of your hand as possible behind the hold. Difficult underclings can involve lots of shuffling and crossovers of both hands and feet. Only experience can show you the how and why of it all. On long underclings featuring few footholds, it's often better to move briskly and without stopping. Dallying in the middle of a bleak undercling is a sure way to flame out in no time flat.

Sidepull

When a handhold is oriented vertically, or near vertically, it's difficult (if not impossible) to pull straight down, so you'll most likely use it as a sidepull. The idea is to lean away from the hold, with your hands

Rarely will you pull directly on an undercling. More often it's an oblique pull, as featured here.

Sidepull.

Sidepull on a "hueco" (pocket).

Sidepull on a vertical edge, a common technique.

and feet working in opposition, similar to liebacking a crack. If the sidepull faces right, you'll want your body to be left of the hold so you can lean away from it. Ideally you'll find some left-facing footholds below and slightly right of the sidepull to provide the opposition. You can often make a longer reach from a sidepull than you could from a horizontal handhold.

When sidepulling, strength to pull the walls down is less crucial than the ability to snake your body into a posture in balance against the oppositional force of the sidepull. In fact, most sidepulls simply keep the upper body attached to the wall, while the legs provide the upward thrust. Trying to heave yourself up off a sidepull without the aid of footholds is rarely possible.

The Upward Flow

While we have discussed hands and feet separately, the aim of all climbing is to choreograph the different moves into fluid upward movement. To settle into this flow requires combinations of holds and techniques. Looking closely at different types of face climbing—and isolating the moves—is one way to grasp the dynamics of this upward flow. Three basic ways exist for using your legs to propel your mass upward against gravity: the static step, the spring step, and the frog step.

Static Step

The static step is the most strenuous and least efficient way to move. It involves statically pressing your weight up on one leg while simultaneously bringing your other foot up to the next hold. On difficult slab and friction routes, when delicate weight shifts are required between small or marginal weight-bearing holds, the static step is almost always used.

Spring Step

The spring step takes advantage of dynamic movement to efficiently move the climber's weight. The technique comes into its own on vertical to overhanging rock. At the moment just before bringing a foot up, "bounce" off that foot to dynamically propel your weight upward. The bounce may be subtle or exaggerated, depending on the move, the individual climber's style, and the relative security of the hold. Many times it's no more than a little juke with the calf muscle.

Depending on the terrain, this move should be used most of the time for efficient upward movement. If you watch experts use the spring step, you'll note it gives them the appearance of being light on their feet. It takes practice to do this move smoothly and controlled enough that you don't shock-load the foothold and blow off it, or change the attitude of the shoe on the hold and ping off that way. Know that the spring step is rarely an explosive movement.

Frog Step

The frog step entails bringing one foot up, then the other, while the torso stays at the same level. After the second foot comes up, the climber is essentially in a crouched, or "bullfrog," position (see photos on next page). At this point both legs can work together to push the weight up. Flexible hips are required to enable adequate "turn out" of your legs and to ensure that your hips remain close to the wall, which is key to frog stepping. The frog step is useful on all forms of face climbing but is especially effective on vertical climbs.

The corn-fed male jock is likely to have as much turnout as Michelangelo's David—which is marble—and flexibility must be developed to perform an effective frog step. For this reason many climbers start each outing with a few minutes of stretching intended to loosen up those muscles. The trick is to stay consistent with the stretching. A short stretching session before each climb (make this a standard warm-up at the gym) can make a huge difference over time.

Hip flexibility is an advantage with the frog step.

When frog stepping, pull your hips in close to the wall to get all your weight over your feet.

Types of Face Climbing

Slab Climbing

Slab climbing refers to smooth rock "slabs," usually ranging from 50 to 75 degrees. It requires the application of every face climbing technique: smearing here, palming there, edging, mantling, and so on. The ace slab climber is fluid, keeps her body well away from the rock, eyes ever scanning the wall for usable features, and stops only when a good hold allows. A baseball player watches the ball all the way to where it meets the bat. Likewise, once a climber has chosen a hold, he watches the hold until he gains purchase with his hand or foot. Because you can only watch one hold at a time, you only move one limb at a time. Keep this in mind and you will naturally assume the "tripod" position, maintaining at least three points of contact with the rock while shifting your weight accordingly as you move each limb. Your feet will mostly be smearing on slabs. A series of small steps is generally most efficient, but occasionally the footholds will be far apart and you'll be forced to high step.

While slab climbing is usually thought to be more fun than toil, there are exceptions. Extreme slab climbing occurs when the angle is too steep to just friction, yet the rock is devoid of holds—the classic "bald face." On these climbs, balance, precision, concentration, courage, and a dash of magic are your ticket to ride. "Micro-edging," often painful and always nerve-wracking, remains one of the most absorbing forms of climbing. Even the expert is astonished at just how small a hold it is possible to stand on. Unlike other forms of climbing, there are usually various ways to make upward progress on grim slabs, and this characteristic has led some climbers to label all slabs as boring. In fact, slab climbing is rarely practiced by most top sport climbers, who are ever becoming more specialized and seeking steeper and steeper rock. Many advanced slab routes, however, feature protection as thin as the holds, and the critical climber might find

Slab climbing on the Weeping Wall, Suicide Rock, California.

Francisco Blanco on **Ticket To Nowhere** *(5.11c), a slab climb on the North Apron, Middle Cathedral Rock, Yosemite Valley, 1986.*

himself eating his words when facing a teetering, 5.11 high step with his quaking boots 25 feet above the last bolt.

For the beginner, there is no quicker way to learn basic climbing movement than to spend an initial few weeks (or months) doing "slab duty." Assuming the upright posture, keeping the weight over the feet, learning the various holds and grips, and moving precisely while relaxed are all essential things that are learned much faster on the less strenuous arena of slabs. Trying to break in on steep rock is a bad practice and tends to foster bad habits that are difficult to unlearn. This has been proven time and time again by my partner Bob Gaines, who runs a large climbing school in Southern California. During his longer seminars, Bob has found that spending an initial two days honing up on slabs helps students transition to the steeper climbs

considerably faster than if he straightaway threw the same folks onto vertical terrain. He's tried it both ways, and without exception, starting on slabs has provided the steepest learning curve.

Steep Face Climbing

Many modern technical advances were due to climbers venturing more and more onto the steep faces that past generations wrote off as either impossible or too contrived. Before the late 1970s, a climbing route normally followed a prominent weakness, or "line," up the cliff—for instance, a crack system or an obvious dike or intrusion. As most of these natural lines were climbed, later generations, wanting the same notoriety and thrill of exploration that past climbers enjoyed, turned to the steep and often hold-bereft faces. Climbers no longer only looked for natural lines but often chose

*Steep face climbing need not be extreme.
Here Peter Croft leads the classic face
route Figures On A Landscape (5.10),
Joshua Tree, California.*

the blankest, most difficult way up a cliff in their quest for the limits of technical difficulty.

But steep face climbs need not be extreme. Many are peppered with big holds and ledges, and they can be technically easier than difficult slabs. It's not simply the angle, but also the size and position of the holds that determine difficulty. Steep face climbs, however, even if they have bulbous holds from bottom to top, are invariably more strenuous than lower-angled climbs. They require much more from the arms and, in their most extreme expression, can involve hoisting the body up off the tip of one finger stuffed in a shallow, rounded "bullet hole."

The overall strategy of climbing long and sustained steep faces will be discussed in greater detail in Chapter 6, "The Art of Leading." For now, understand these basic principles:

Unlike slab climbing, you will often see the steep face climber sucking his hips and chest into the wall, trying to get the weight over his feet. Keeping the weight off the arms is essential to climbing steep faces efficiently, for you are often called on to make a strenuous upper body move, and if you've been needlessly hanging off your fingers, the strength might not be there when you most need it. The steeper the angle, the more the arms come into play, but try not to overpull. Try to only hang on, and rely on the legs for upward thrust. The importance of this principle cannot be overstated. The genuine expert is often not the strongest on the block, but rather the one who knows how to use the least energy to do a given move, sequence, or climb. Overpulling most often comes from impatient, ill-planned movement. Take time to recognize the best sequence for you, and then try to finesse your way over the rock.

It's often better to make two small moves than one long one. Try to avoid getting your body too stretched out, because this compromises your balance and decreases the efficiency of your muscles, making the moves more strenuous. Avoid getting

scrunched up, or any body position that requires yogi-like contortions; if this happens, quickly get into a more natural position.

Never pass up a good rest hold. If you cannot find a decent foothold to snatch a breather, stop at the best handhold and alternately drop each hand and shake out. Again, the skilled steep face climber is the one who exerts the least energy figuring out the easiest, most natural way to the top.

A beginner can benefit greatly by watching an expert climb, but in the case of steep face climbing, this can be misleading. The expert might well be hauling himself up on his arms, but what you might not know is that this expert climbs 200 days a year and has done so for a decade. As a result, he has developed phenomenal endurance and cardiovascular strength, and at the moment can't be bothered to fiddle with footholds. Put the same climber on a route at the very limit of his ability, however, and for sure he'll be observing the basic principles we've just covered. The reason is simple: The climber has not been born—nor ever will be—who can hang indefinitely on his arms. Given enough stress and enough rounded holds, even the strongest will flame out.

Overhanging Face Climbing

Owing to a plethora of new sport-climbing areas, as well as the hundreds of climbing gyms in many big cities nationwide, radically overhanging climbing long ago became the rage among most active climbers. While sustained overhanging climbing is strictly expert's turf, most climbing areas have moderate routes that feature an overhang, or a short overhanging section. In the Shawangunks in upstate New York, there are numerous moderate overhanging routes, moderate only because the holds are terrific and the climb resembles swinging around on a big jungle gym. The technique does not differ radically from that required on steep faces, save that everything is more strenuous.

Let's be frank: Overhanging climbing is

*Arms straight, hips in, shoulders back—
essential techniques for the overhanging face.*

*Keep your eyes peeled for the next hold as you
heave over a bulge.*

something you have to learn through doing, but a
few points are critical to understand beforehand.
First and foremost, always try to keep your arms
straight; when bent, the muscles are working hard
and the arms tire much more quickly. Ideally, the
hands and shoulders act only as a hinge, holding your body to the wall as your legs drive you
upward. Because this is not possible much of the
time, it is essential to return to straight arm positioning whenever you can to relieve the strain on
the forearms.

Throughout this process, body position should
be: head back, shoulders wide, hips in, legs bent,
arms straight. Constantly try to walk the feet up,

getting the lower body locked off and unweighted
via backstepping. When going for the next handhold, first choose the hold with your eyes. Then
push yourself up with your legs till you can reach
the handhold, and return immediately to straight
arms.

Try to avoid extremely long reaches, but when
you cannot, try to gently and dynamically swing
("powerglide") to the next hold. When the holds
are too poor or ill-placed to powerglide, the pulling arm must momentarily be locked off as the free
hand reaches above; and the locked-off position, on
overhanging ground, is probably the most strenuous
position in all of climbing. When you must lock off

a hold, try to keep the hand close to the shoulder and the elbow close to your side. In rare instances on exceptionally arduous climbs, you might see a climber briefly locking off a hold well to one side of his body ("flagging") and reaching up quickly to a hold on the other side. Be consoled that such a maneuver is limited to the very best and, owing to the bleak leverage required, demands a degree of strength unusual in even world-class climbers. It is also the quickest way to torch a deltoid (shoulder) muscle, or especially the rotator cuff, which requires months to heal following a thorough tweaking.

Backstepping often beats locking off when you must make a long reach on steep rock. A classic backstep move reaching left, for example, would have the outside edge of the left foot on the rock, opposing the right hand, which is ideally sidepulling. The right foot is splayed out right and propels the body as the left hand reaches for the faraway hold. As previously mentioned, backstepping is standard practice for ascending overhanging routes, and is usually first mastered in the climbing gym. In fact, many climbers first learn how to crank overhanging routes in the gym, an ideal training ground for the work.

Climb the difficult stretches aggressively, but not rushed. While you cannot get your weight directly over your feet, footwork on overhanging rock is a surprisingly crucial factor; even the poorest foothold takes more weight off the arms than common sense would tell you. When you bungle the foot sequence—often a backstep—you're left to hang on longer and harder, which on a route nearing your max will usually spell failure.

Dynamic Climbing

A dynamic move is another way to describe a lunge where a climber vaults off a hold and is propelled to another, or much more commonly, where a handhold is slapped for and clasped just as the climber's weight—briefly held in place by one hand—is starting to pull her off. Dynamic moves range from 6-inch slaps (routine) to all-out jumps (rare), where a climber is completely detached from the rock before quickly clasping holds above, at the apex of his leap. Thirty years ago, even the now-standard "deadpoint" slap was rarely seen on anything but practice rocks, but as climbs got increasingly difficult, dynamics ("dynos") became a required technique. In fact, we can look at the technical evolution of the sport as the stylistic shift from slow, supercontrolled static movement—practiced by most climbers up to about 1975—to the vigorous dynamic style displayed by virtually all top modern climbers.

A deliberate, static style is still required for climbing loose rock and routes with meager protection; only a maniac starts chucking for loose holds or firing dynos well above bunk pro. But on bolt-protected vertical to overhanging climbs—by far the norm at today's sport-climbing venues—lingering, static movement is too energy consuming, and dynamic climbing is often not only desired, but required. Skillfully performed, dynamics are climbing's most athletic expression, requiring deluxe coordination, raw power, and precise timing.

Dynamic moves are often thrown, or "hucked," to span long stretches between good holds—but not always. Oftentimes dynamics are small moves, hucked from a poor hold to a pathetic hold. On jumbo lunges, it is very occasionally necessary to generate the thrust solely with the arms, with the feet dangling in space. More often these are circus moves performed on the boulders or in the gym. Dynamics are typically initiated by an explosive pull from the arms, aided by propulsion from the feet as they drive off footholds.

For a standard upward lunge, start by hanging straight down from your arms, with your legs crouched and ready to spring. Eye the hold you're firing for and see yourself latching it, then, catlike, launch single-mindedly for the hold. Once the lunge is under way, one hand shoots up and slaps onto the target hold. Ideally the climber exploits

1. Dyno sequence by John Long at Stoney Point, 1983. First, eye the hold.

2. Pull with your arms while thrusting with your legs.

3. Stick the hold, then quickly stabilize your feet.

the moment of weightlessness that occurs at the apex of the leap—the deadpoint—to grab the hold with accuracy. But remember, the hold you're lunging for may be far poorer than it appears from below.

Rounded holds, even on very overhanging rock, are often tolerably secure when your arms are extended and your bulk is hanging directly below them. But the higher you pull up, the worse they become because your body position forces you to pull increasingly out, rather than down, on the hold. This is one reason that jumbo "dynos" are usually initiated with the arms fully extended.

Perhaps the most common situation is: You pull up to a certain height; there is a hold right above your face—or within reach—but if you let go with one hand, you'll start to fall off. So when you do let go, you slap for and clasp the hold faster than gravity rips you off the wall. This is "deadpointing" from hold to hold, basically slapping from one hold to

"Hucking" the dyno sequence on the popular boulder problem **Saturday Night Live** *at Joshua Tree.*

The free hand quickly slaps for the upper hold.

1. *Deadpoint sequence. Crouch, eye the hold, and get ready to fly.*

2. *Pull down with your arms and push up with your legs.*

3. *Here at the apex of the dyno, you enjoy a split second of weightlessness—the "deadpoint"— at the very moment when you sweep your hand up for the next hold.*

the next at the moment upward momentum hovers, for that one instant, at the deadpoint, or apex. A dynamic hoist is initiated, and again, the moment one hand lets go, the body starts to fall off, and a quick slap/dyno is needed. It can give the impression of falling up the rock. If you can get hold of a contemporary video featuring top sport climbing, or visit a gym frequented by top climbers, you will see countless examples of the deadpointing just described. That's the shape of the game in the twenty-first century.

The standard line on throwing dynamic moves is that almost every difficult dyno is "do or fly." Since there is little chance of staying on the rock after misfiring a dyno, you either stick the dyno or you fly off the rock onto the rope—or onto the bouldering mat. This is one of the main reasons why sport climbs are so well protected—because people are falling all of the time.

Practicing on boulders or in the gym can

bring to light many more examples of dynamics. Dynamic climbing requires total commitment, time, and experience to successfully hit a hold and apply instant power as your weight shock-loads down following the dyno. Practice might not make perfect, but no climber gets dynamic climbing dialed without a lot of repetition. Remember that beginner to intermediate routes never require any dynamic climbing, and the place to learn and practice dynamics is not on a long climb, but inches off the ground, or on a steep sport route with a bolt at your nose.

Moving from Your Center

One of the most obvious things about climbing is totally lost on 99 percent of all climbers. That is, in terms of the actual body mechanics, the arms and legs are serving to transport the torso up a piece of rock. What is lost here, however, is the visceral sense of moving the torso, or center, distracted as the climber is by the intricacies and toils of the movement itself and the taxing strain placed on the fingers, hands, and forearms. The center, roughly from mid-thigh to lower chest, contains the "core strength" that regulates the movement of the limbs. Core strength is key to good climbing, and is indispensable on steep to overhanging routes. With a loose core, the torso sags under the arms, and the legs are essentially moored to a flimsy base instead of counterpressuring off a taut and robust core.

Once a climber changes her orientation from hauling and thrusting herself up the rock to moving her core over the rock, technique rapidly improves. At first this takes practice and conscious effort—which is difficult to do because you get lost in scanning and pulling and stepping. The trick is to focus some attention on your core and intentionally climb as though your core is dictating what to do with your arms and legs. This way you get a feel for climbing from your core as opposed to hauling your core up the cliff. In a sense, your core leads the way. This will confound you at first, but stick with it and be amazed. The chief deterrent is that virtually all of us live from our heads and climb the same way, as though it were our heads alone that we were transporting up the rock. When you move from your core, your center of gravity shifts and so does your experience. You can practice this simply walking down the street—which is as good a place as any to start because this concept is as counterintuitive as all get out. But once you get a taste for it, you're only one step shy of a "Brave New World."

Crack Climbing Skills

The most visible and tangible weakness up a cliff is a large crack that runs from bottom to top. When you walk to the base of the rock and your partner asks where the climb is, the answer is obvious. Cracks assume two basic forms: straight-in and corner cracks. Straight-in cracks, or "splitters," are simply fissures that split an otherwise blank face, like a crack in a sidewalk. A corner crack (aka open book, or dihedral) is a crack found in the corner where two planes come together, like the crease between pages of an open book.

A climbing route is often referred to as a "line," a term derived from the line a crack forms on the cliff, though a good line doesn't necessarily follow a crack. A good crack line may pass over steep, otherwise featureless rock; be clean; and offer exciting locations, heroic exposure, and a straight, or "plumb line," topography. A bad line might wander all over a rubbly cliff, through vegetation, and up dark and dripping recesses. But good or bad, a crack line is a route waiting to be climbed, if it hasn't been already. A prominent crack system is nature's way of telling us where to climb, and when expeditions are mounted to big, faraway cliffs, or when a beginner studies a crag for the first time, eyes naturally home in on any crack system the cliff affords.

While sport climbing long ago moved away from cracks and onto the bald and open faces, a beginner's program that neglects crack climbing is a very poor itinerary indeed. The fundamentals of placing and removing equipment and establishing belays are learned on cracks. And if someday you should aspire to tackle the world's long and classic climbs—from Chamonioux to Patagonia—you will need significant crack skills because such routes are predominately crack climbs and always will be.

While face climbing might be a natural movement, few face climbs follow natural lines, and while cracks are natural lines, most beginners find crack climbing awkward and strange. Crack climbing requires subtle and strenuous techniques where the only hope of mastery lies in rote experience. All crack climbing involves either "jamming" or torquing the limbs or body inside the crack. Just as in face climbing, the idea is to keep your center of gravity over your feet as much as possible. On low-angled climbs, the hips and torso should remain back away from the rock; as the angle steepens, the hips move closer to the rock, a technique that holds true no matter the style of climbing.

There are two types of jamming. With the classic "hand jam," the hand is placed in an appropriately sized crack, and the muscles expand the hand inside the crack. The various counterpressures result in a locked, or "jammed," hand that can be very secure when properly placed. The second method involves

Brian Kimbal finger jamming and liebacking on Epitaph *(5.13a), Tombstone Wall, Moab area, Utah.* KEITH LADZINSKI

torquing and camming the appendage in a bottle-neck or constriction in the crack. In wide cracks, the limbs are often twisted or stacked, and in very wide cracks you'll find that wedging and cross-pressures are the only way to get up. Most jams use a little of both torquing and camming, so to label these as separate techniques is a bit artificial.

Since no two climbers are exactly the same size, one climber might pull fist jams, another might get wide hand jams, and so on. Again, anyone with aspirations toward big, classic climbs will soon discover such routes predominantly follow crack systems. So if you dream of the big traditional classics—from Yosemite's El Capitan to the Cima Grande in the Italian Dolomites—you must become proficient at crack climbing. No way around that . . .

The names and different techniques do not correspond to any standard crack dimension (though a "hand crack" generally refers to a 2-inch crack) but describe the method you must use based on how your fingers or hands fit a given crack. Climbers with slender hands enjoy advantages on thin finger and hand cracks, but work at a disadvantage on most wider cracks. Regardless of crack size, a smooth rhythm is preferred—hand, hand, foot, foot, repeat. In its purest form, crack climbing is a mechanical drill, with the climber repeating essentially the same move over and over, ad exhaustion.

Finger lock.

Finger Cracks

Finger cracks vary in width from shallow seams into which you can only get the tip of your pinky to a crack that swallows your fingers up to the third knuckle. Halfway between pure crack climbing and pure face climbing, thin cracks require styles from both forms. Consequently, finger cracks are often technically demanding.

Even in the Wingate sandstone found in the Southwestern desert areas—which abound in perfect, laser-cut fissures—it is the rare crack that is absolutely parallel-sided. Most cracks, thin and

otherwise, vary in size, if only barely; it's these constrictions that you look for. The knuckles are the thickest part of the finger, particularly the second knuckle. It is possible to jam the knuckles above constrictions in the crack, and when the wrist is bent and the arm pulls down, the knuckle becomes locked like a chock in a slot—the standard "finger lock." This practice may prove as painful as it sounds, and it's crucial to first briefly wiggle the fingers around to attain the best fit before weighting them. On steep thin cracks, the fingers are often inserted so that the thumb is down, but this will

Finger crack, thumb up. This crack constricts here and literally swallows the fingers.

Thumb-up and thumb-down finger jamming.

vary depending on circumstances.

As a general rule, it is preferable to use the thumb-up jam whenever possible (no matter the size of the crack). Two reasons: First, you can reach farther from jam to jam, and stretching past thin or ill-sized sections is a big part of crack climbing. As you push down on a thumb-up jam, you are not uncamming it as you do with a thumb-down jam. Second, because the hand is aligned anatomically correctly, the thumb-up jam doesn't require twisting to get the digit to lock/cam in the crack. For these two reasons, thumb-up jamming is generally less strenuous than the thumb-down variety.

Many times it is better to jam the shank of the finger—the fleshy section between knuckles. Find the appropriate slot, insert as many fingers as possible (in the thumb-down posture), then pivot the wrist and pull downward. This will naturally create a camming torque on the stacked fingers, so the fingers will stick even if the crack is parallel. Remember that the thumb is stronger than the fingers, so always try to brace it against the index finger in whatever position feels best. This reinforces the jam to prevent it from rotating out.

Finger stack seen from inside the crack.

In a pinky lock, most of the weight is on the pinky.

For ultrathin, less-than-first-knuckle cracks, you most often assume the thumb-up position to utilize the thinnest digit—the pinky—and any other parts of your fingers that you can snake into the crack. "Pinky locks" are marginal jams at best and function well only if the pull is straight down.

Though in theory the thumb-up jam is better, often a straight-in crack (a crack splitting a uniform face) requires a combination of thumb-up and thumb-down jamming. When the constrictions are slight and the jams are loose, thin, or marginal, leaning to one side or the other will often add a degree

of stability. Here, you're pulling off the side of the crack instead of pulling straight down on your jammed fingers.

Such are the basic positions for vertical cracks. But many thin cracks slant one way or another, and just as many snake left and right in the course of even a short climb. The trick is to try to keep your body in an anatomically natural position, where your limbs are not corkscrewed around each other and where you don't need excessive core (abdominal) strength to compensate for an out-of-kilter body. As the crack leans, your body will inevitably be below the crack, and this pretty well dictates that the upper hand will have to be kept in the thumb-down position and your lower hand in a thumb-up position (except when reaching through). With leaning thin cracks, it is sometimes possible, even desirable, for the lower hand to be thumb-down. But should the crack lean to your right, to place the right hand thumb-up means to crank against the knuckles the wrong way, since slanting thin cracks are usually a combination of jamming and pulling down on the lower edge of the crack.

Extended sections of finger jamming, especially if the rock is sharp, can gnarl your knuckles, so you may want to run a couple wraps of 1-inch tape around the joints. The torquing action of extreme finger jamming can result in tendon damage, so lay off if you feel your fingers getting creaky.

With all types of crack climbing, and especially so with thin cracks, quickly finding the best jams is half the battle. A wider finger lock is not necessarily the better one. The best lock is the one that best fits your fingers, usually in a constriction, so you don't have to cam the fingers and instead can slot them like tapers. Also, learning how to "milk" a jam for maximum purchase is something that requires an educated feel for jamming, a skill that is rapidly acquired.

Footwork in Thin Cracks

Even the best finger jams pump the forearms, and without good footwork, you're quickly hosed. Like face climbing, thin crack climbing is usually a matter of finding hand positions that best support the upper body, while your legs supply the upward thrust. Thin cracks get progressively more difficult as the footholds evaporate. Always scan the face for footholds. Thin cracks are strenuous, so never pass a rest spot, even if you're not tired. Leaning off the jams puts the climber to one side of the crack. If there's a foothold on that side, use the outside edge of the upper foot on that hold, as it keeps you more balanced and in a far less twisted attitude.

Jamming feet in a finger crack. Torquing action on the feet sets the shoes in the crack and provides the foundation. Often the feet have to be jammed and torqued just as ardently as the hands.

Thin cracks occasionally open up and allow a flared toe jam. Most rock shoes, especially slippers, are particularly tapered for this. Twist the ankle and get the sole of the shoe vertical, then jam the toe in above the constriction while trying to keep the heel low. When there are no footholds and no pockets for toe jams, climbers will sometimes stick the outside edge of the shoe vertically in the crack. Though marginal, this works surprisingly well because it creates a foothold of sorts and invariably

Rarely can you jam this much of a shoe into a true finger crack.

More commonly, the edges of the shoe are all that can be jammed in thin cracks.

takes some weight off the arms. The last choice is to simply use friction, with the sole flat against the rock and the foot pushing in somewhat to gain purchase. The steeper the wall, the less straight frictioning will work.

Save for a substantial shelf to stand on, "stem holds" are a thin crack climber's best friend. These are holds on each side of the crack that slant in and on which the climber can "stem," backstep, or bridge, his feet. A good stem provides a solid base for the lower torso and often allows the climber to shake out a pumped hand, sometimes both hands. On a steep thin crack, you hope for two

good finger locks within reach. Keeping your arm extended (remember, a bent arm tires quickly), suck your chest in and get your weight over your feet. Shake out one arm at a time until you've recovered enough to carry on. When climbing thin cracks in corners, it is often possible to stem between the two walls using pure friction. If you find a stem hold, look to paste one foot in the corner and backstep the outside foot onto the stem hold.

All these descriptions may sound straightforward (if a little confusing without studying the photos), but climbing a thin crack rarely is. The best—or only—workable solution is usually a subtle blend of all these techniques. The correct sequence requires patience and a certain amount of scratching around to discover what best works for you. Hasty moves can result in painful abrasions, so strive to climb fluidly.

I have broken down the variety of individual moves likely to be encountered on thin cracks. Putting these moves together, with tips on strategy and approach for all crack climbing, will be taken up in Chapter 6, "The Art of Leading."

Off-Finger Cracks

An off-finger crack is a "tweener," or in-between size—too big for the fingers and too small for the hand, where the third knuckle butts into the crack and the fingers rattle around inside. Off-finger cracks rarely allow good toe jamming—just a tad too thin—so you're doubly cursed. For most climbers this is the hardest size of crack, save for the notorious off-widths.

Everything's wrong about this size, and there are no easy solutions. One approach is to keep the fingers straight and together and stuff them in to the hilt, thumb up. You lever the fingertips off one side of the crack and the back of the fingers,

or knuckles, off the other side—sort of a crowbar effect. This "bridge" jam is terrifically strenuous, difficult, and worthless most of the time (save for transitional moves). Another way is to insert the hand thumb down, overlap the middle finger over the index, overcrank with the wrist, and pray to God that it doesn't rip out.

Far and away the best method is the thumb stack, or butterfly jam. Place the thumb near the outside of the crack, the first knuckle against one side, the thumb pad against the other. (For this to work effectively, the crack must be thinner than the link of jammed thumb.) The thumb is inserted at an angle, the pad higher than the knuckle. Curl the fingers over the thumbnail and pull down, effectively wedging, through downward pressure, the thumb between the two walls. At first this technique feels bizarre and impossible and about as reliable as a felon on bail, but it's really the only viable technique (with practice). All told, this technique is much more about "feel" than strength, and is probably one of the toughest maneuvers to master. Without it, you can bank on getting humbled on difficult off-finger cracks.

Because off-finger jams are always cammed or wedged, they're invariably less secure and more

One way to jam an off-finger crack is to stuff the fingers in as far as they can go with the thumb up, then lever the tips of the fingers off one side of the crack and the back of the fingers, or knuckles, off the other.

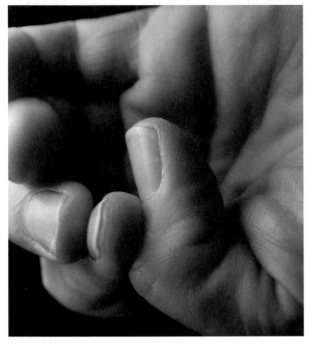

The thumb stack is a difficult technique to master.

Off-finger cracks may require a combination of thumb stacks and finger torquing.

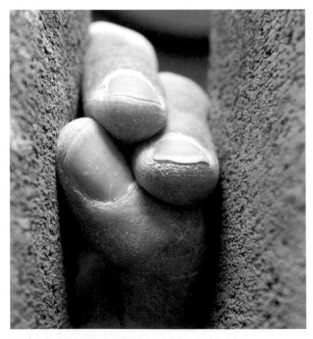

Thumb stack seen from inside the crack.

strenuous than a good finger lock. Hence, footwork, as always, is key. It will help to wear tiny (i.e., painful) slippers with a thin toe profile. The drawback is that while these might be perfect for a short pitch, they won't cut the gravy on a longer route. With luck, the crack will open up enough to allow at least marginal toe jams. If not, you're essentially face climbing with your feet. If there are no face holds, the climb is apt to be desperate.

Hidetaka Suzuki on the classic off-finger crack Phoenix (5.13a), Yosemite.

Hand Cracks

Most climbers regard hand cracks as the last word in crack climbing. The crack is perfectly suited for both hands and feet, the technique is readily learned and very secure, and vertical or even overhanging hand cracks are often readily "hiked." An added boon is that for reasons only a geologist can explain, hand cracks often bisect spectacular sections of rock, and many of the world's classic climbs involve extensive hand jamming.

Hand jamming is usually done with your fingers bent at the palm, or third knuckle. The thumb-up hand jam is a tripod configuration, with the fingertips and heel of the palm on one side of the crack and the back of the hand and knuckles pushing against the other. In a tight hand jam, increase the outward pressure by bridging the thumb off the index finger. If the crack is large enough, wedge the thumb into the palm to create additional outward pressure. The importance of squeezing the thumb

Tight hand jam.

Standard-size hand jam.

cannot be overstated. It's the expanding action of the hand and the wedging of the thumb that create the actual hand jam, which when properly performed is the most powerful jam of all. Once mastered, an experienced climber will often prefer to hang off a "bomber" hand jam than off an equally good shelf—though most uninitiated sport climbers would prefer the shelf.

When climbing straight-in, splitter hand cracks, most climbers prefer the thumb-up position, though in some situations the thumb-down jam works better. When the crack jags, or is a little slim, the thumb-down jam is normally used. With the thumb-up jam, the wrist is straight. The wrist twists with the thumb-down jam, and the result is a torquing action that can sometimes add authority to a thin or bottoming jam. As you move up, try keeping your arms straight and penduluming from jam to jam, leapfrogging each hand jam above the previous one to increase speed and efficiency. This swinging action is commonly called "windmilling." With slanting hand cracks, or in corners, you will generally jam the upper hand thumb down and the lower hand thumb up, shuffling rather than reaching through with the lower hand. When you find it necessary to lean off the crack, the top hand is most often thumb down, the bottom hand thumb up. There are exceptions to every example here, and climbing even the most peerless, splitter hand crack may require all these techniques, if only to vary the stress and to use other muscles.

A hand jam is often tight, and the back of the hand is frequently set against coarse rock. Gnarly abrasions can result from hasty jamming or rotating the hand in the crack, which is a common mistake as you pull up and past a poor or insecure jam. To avoid this, whenever possible place the jam so the fingers are pointing straight into the crack. As you pull up, rotate your wrist—not your hand—keeping the jammed hand locked tight. Even with suave technique, extended sections of hand jamming can trash your hands if you don't protect them with

Jamming a hand crack, featuring the two basic hand positions: thumb down (upper hand) and thumb up.

Foot jamming a straight-in, or "splitter," hand crack. Here the crack accepts a good portion of the shoe and provides a secure foot placement.

Sometimes the toe does not need to be torqued into the crack but can instead be positioned straight in, taking advantage of small edges on the side of the crack to stabilize the placement.

tape. Tape also adds confidence by allowing you to jam a little harder without feeling excruciating pain. Check the end of this chapter for details on taping.

With hand cracks, which readily accept feet, turn your foot on its side so your inside ankle faces up. Slot the foot in the crack—keeping the heel low—then pivot the foot toward the horizontal. As you weight it, keep trying to rotate it tighter in the crack. Properly set, such foot jams easily support the bulk of your weight. The foot jam does not improve the deeper you set your shoe. Keeping the foot as far out of the crack as can be easily secured allows

quick removal and keeps your center of gravity away from the rock and a bit of your weight off your arms. You rarely have to stick the shoe in past the ball of the foot. Any constrictions make foot jams that much more secure.

Try to keep the feet low, hips into the rock, and the legs somewhat straight while crack climbing. The higher your feet, the more your rump hangs out and the more you hang on your arms. The low heel position lays more rand and sole rubber along the crack, resulting in added friction. Also, the increased surface area available for contact on the rock minimizes the pain quotient (and to be sure, jamming can be painful).

Lastly, understand that at first it feels like you might break a foot bone or the foot jam might suddenly blow out. Neither are true. As with all jamming, learning to be comfortable and secure with jammed feet is a matter of feel, which readily comes from experience. Like riding a bike, once you learn how to climb cracks, the technique is yours for life.

Cupped and Cammed Hands

As the crack opens up too wide for tight hand jams, the security of the jams begins to diminish, peaking at the point just before a fist jam fits in the crack. For these wide hand jams, try "cupping" the hand by pushing the fingers forward into the crack and stuffing the thumb into the palm, or "camming" the hand by rotating the hand sideways until good purchase is made on both sides of the crack—a sketchy technique to be sure. For cammed hands, it is necessary to keep the hand torqued to maintain the stability of the jam. The hazard here is that the more radically the hand is cupped, the less of the hand (back) is contacting the rock. Pushed to the max, the back of the hand becomes convex, and only the bit of flesh just back from the base of the middle finger will be catching the rock. Accordingly, that small area can be abraded down to the wood with a single ill-placed jam or slight shift or pivot. For that reason, if you are cupping at the max, tape your hands. I can look down at my hands and see white marks that bear painful stories, some twenty-five years old, of ripped flesh from cupping.

"Cupped" hand jamming.

Fist Cracks

Most climbers find fist jamming a little sketchy. It's seldom used for more than a few moves because, again for reasons only a geologist can explain, there are comparatively few pure fist cracks out there. You can climb for fifty years and never scale a crack that features pure fist jamming for 100 straight feet. It takes a lot of practice to totally master this technique, which is easy enough to learn but a strangely elusive skill to develop to the point to where fist jamming feels as natural and secure as hand jamming.

The jam is set by clenching the fist, which enlarges the small fleshy muscles on the outside of the hand; since these expand very little, the best fist jam is usually a matter of matching fist size with crack size. When the fit is snug, the fist jam can, with practice, be made very secure.

Look for a constriction to jam above. If the crack is parallel-sided, choose the spot where your fist fits snugly. Sometimes you will slot the fist straight in, like a boxer throwing a slow-motion jab. The fist is then flexed as the hand is rotated into the vertical position. Other times the fist is placed vertically and the hand flexed. Depending on the crack, the fist, once slotted, can assume several basic forms.

With a glove fit, the thumb is wrapped across the index and middle finger. The thumb may be tucked across the palm on a tight fit. On an ultrathin fist jam, let the middle and ring finger float above the index finger and the pinky, which narrows the profile of the fist. This ball jam can be expanded very little and is only bomber above a constriction. (A wide hand jam is usually preferable here.) An even less reliable position is very rarely used when the crack is too wide: keeping the thumb on the outside of the fist, braced over, or against the index finger. This is a painful, makeshift jam that won't bear much weight but might work as a transitional move. Sometimes the flex of a forearm inserted into the crack will add security to a loose jam.

On straight-in fist cracks it is often possible

Fist jamming.

to jam the entire crack with the back of the hand facing out. However, most climbers prefer to jam the lower fist palm out, finding the strain is distributed over a greater range of muscles. Picture yourself picking up a beer keg, then tilting the keg horizontally. Your arms would form a circle, with your lower hand palm up, supporting the keg. If your lower hand was palm down, the keg would be resting, no doubt precariously, on the back of your hand. Turn your hand over, and you kick in

Faculty

Crack climbing faculty depends more on technique than strength, a truth frequently proven by gym-trained climbers who devour 5.12 plastic like so much layer cake but who get perfectly spanked on, say, a 5.9 fist crack. Clearly, the strength is there, but not the craft. Without practice you cannot develop a feel for the jams—what works best, how to quickly set reliable jams, keeping your body long, plus coordinating all the movements into a liquid flow. Understanding that few cracks are a uniform size, bottom to top, you can count on encountering stretches of those pesky in-between sizes on a crack of any length—in between finger and hands, between hands and fist, and up through the dreaded off-size cracks and flares. You can also count on your in-between size being different than someone with different-size hands. Mastering these in-between sizes is key to developing crack climbing skills; stretches of "bad" jams is where we all struggle and where most falls occur. While you cannot cheat your way past any section of poor jams, there is every reason to want to get through them quickly and efficiently.

Once more, crack climbing is mostly about feel and rhythm, learning how to place your fingers and hands in ways that allow you the most energy-efficient, secure, and least painful jams that a given crack affords. In face climbing, a keen novice can often make valiant strides, sometimes skipping entire grades. Not so with crack climbing. Proficiency comes from rote learning, which means mileage. Without exception, no climber masters cracks without his share of pain and failures, and without logging many miles up cracks.

Two routines can drastically hasten your learning curve, if you're willing to put in the work. First, you must log enough crack time to feel comfortable with the moderate grades, perhaps up to 5.9. Most dedicated climbers can accomplish this in a year or a little less. Once you are fluent with the fundamentals, spend a day or two each month trying to climb as many cracks as you can in one day. Obviously you need to climb at an area featuring crack climbs, hopefully ones that are centrally located. This practice caught on at Joshua Tree in the late 1970s, and quite a few climbers joined the "Century Club," having bagged at least a hundred crack climbs in one day.

Another drill, one especially effective as you broach the upper grades, is to first lead a difficult crack, then drop down on toprope and lap it to failure. Take breaks. Rest and eat between "burns." Even leave and come back. It's amazing how what seemed like death on the lead will (if you're in shape) seem pretty casual after a few laps—or be totally impossible once you get totally pumped out. When I used to frequent Yosemite, I must have climbed *Butterballs* and the last pitch of *New Dimensions,* two wonderfully classic cracks, at least twenty times apiece, mostly on toprope. The technique and confidence I picked up doing this was invaluable. Most world-class climbers use this approach to their advantage. It takes a massive amount of mileage to attain top form, and toproping and "working" a route is an especially efficient way to log that mileage. You can also learn a lot of subtle technical tricks in figuring out the easiest way to do a given climb.

By normal climbing standards I have large fingers, and through doing laps on these test pieces, I learned to compensate for finger size, discovering easier, or at least possible, ways of doing things. I rarely bothered pulling this drill on hand or fist cracks because few of these ever gave me much pause. Do the laps on the size that gives you fits, and improve by leaps and bounds.

When fist jamming, squeezing the fist tighter expands it to create a more secure jam.

the full power of your shoulder, back, and biceps. With extreme fist cracks, by jamming the lower fist palm up, you form a ring of power; using this configuration, many grim fist cracks have been tamed. When the crack leans, you will invariably use this technique.

Unlike jamming thinner cracks, it's generally too awkward to reach above the upper fist with the lower one. Instead, shuffle the fists up the crack, locking off the lower jam and reaching above for the next one. However you set your fists, strive to keep your body long, in an anatomically natural position, rather than bunched up, with your butt hanging out and your knees up at waist level.

Since the breadth of your hand and foot is roughly the same, if your fist fits, so will your feet. Look for a constriction. Otherwise, the foot goes straight in. If it's loose, torque it laterally for stability. Again, try to keep the feet low and the weight over them. Resist the temptation of booting the shoe into the crack or jamming it too deeply. The shoe can get stuck, and it's scary trying to crank it free.

Fist cracks are often quite strenuous, and even crack masters are inclined to rotate their jams. Some of the worst hand abrasions I've ever seen—and gotten—were a result of battling overhanging fist cracks. For this reason, tape (and sometime the use of thin leather gloves) is a common aid for hard fist cracks.

Off-Width Cracks

Off-width, or off-size, cracks are too wide for fist jamming and too narrow for anything but the knee, if that. The extreme off-width crack is questionably the most feared, and unquestionably the most avoided, prospect in all of climbing. There is simply no easy means to climb off-widths, and success often involves more grunting than elegance because very few climbers have put in the time to master this, the most awkward technique of them all.

Among the reasons for this is that few climbing areas feature many off-width cracks, and if you can't practice, you'll never get them "dialed." The technique is more battle than dance, and in today's world that makes off-width cracks about as popular as standing in a campfire. History also plays a part in the disdain climbers have for off-widths. In the early 1960s, many of America's greatest climbs were in Yosemite Valley, and most featured off-width climbing. When up-and-coming climbers wanted to bag the big-name routes, they had no choice but to tackle these off-width test pieces. The first few encounters were desperate, thrashing, villainous affairs, but they stuck to it, and one long summer was usually enough to get comfortable with the technique. As the newer generations turned toward thinner cracks, the nasty off-widths were gratefully overlooked, and today most climbers simply avoid the technique because they lack the requisite experience for the climb to be anything but a pitched battle. If one of the international climbing competitions were staged on an overhanging, 5.11 off-width, we'd probably see contestants trying to paw up the bald face on either side of the crack.

The most arduous off-widths are typically about 4 inches wide, too thin to slot a knee in. Upward progress involves locking off the upper body, moving the legs up, locking them off, and then jackknifing the upper body back up. Repeated ad nauseam, this sequence can make the Eight Labors of Hercules seem like raking leaves.

You must first decide whether to climb with your left or right side in—and it's often hard to change sides halfway up. In a vertical crack, if the gash is offset, you will probably climb with your back against the raised edge, which may provide a little extra leverage, allowing you to stem outside of the crack. If the crack edges are uniform—a flush splitter—find what side of the crack has the best edge and/or footholds, and keep the opposite side leg in the crack. While the outside arm grips the

Pratt's Crack, *Pine Creek, California. This super uniform, 7-inch-wide crack requires practiced off-width technique for safe passage.*

Arm bar.

outside edge, the inside arm is locked inside the crack.

In thin off-size cracks (normally 4 to 5 inches), the back of the upper arm is held in place by pushing the palm against the opposite side—the classic "arm bar." The outside arm adds torque and counterpressure by pulling out on the crack's edge. For optimum leverage, place the arm bar diagonally down and away from the shoulder, with the elbow higher than the palm. This kicks in the front deltoid and upper chest muscles, and adds to the fulcrum effect of the arm bar.

If the crack won't accept your knee, jam your inside foot (and if necessary your calf), usually by torquing it horizontally. If the crack is slightly larger than the width of the foot, torque the foot diagonally across the crack so the toe jams against one side of the crack and the heel wedges against the other side ("heel-toe" jam) to create opposition

across the crack. The heel is placed on the side of the arm bar.

Usually it's best to use the outer foot to propel the body upward, driving the weight off the heel-toe jam; the inside leg and arm stabilize the body in between thrusts. Use any edges or stem holds for the outside leg. Once the feet are set, the outside hand moves up and pulls hard against the lip of the crack, then the arm bar is quickly shuffled up, reset, and locked off, usually level with, or just beneath, the outside hand. Then the process is repeated. If the crack is overhanging and you can't get the knee in, the hardest part is usually moving the arm bar up. Sometimes this is only possible with little dynamic hops, shuffling the arm bar up and quickly locking it before you pitch out backwards.

Many consider true-blue off-width cracks to only be those that are too wide to fist jam and too thin to set a knee inside. It is impossible to get this technique wired without pretty intensive practice on either a route that features exactly this kind of jamming, or on a practice crack, such as the fabled *Generator Crack* in Yosemite Valley. This approach touches on what I've mentioned earlier—that to get good at climbing, some time must be devoted to working on specific techniques as opposed to simply climbing routes. Note that professional golfers don't just play the course. They spend hours on the putting green and at the driving range. I trust the idea is clear.

Once the crack opens up enough to get a knee inside, off-width technique is much more manageable. While the jackknife motion may still be necessary to move your upper body, your lower body can now be more securely jammed. The inside leg is in a vertical version of the arm bar, with hip, thigh, knee, heel, and toe all torqued and counterpressuring. Both the outside and inside foot should be in a heel-toe jam. Keep the toes lower than the heel, which allows the toes to be smeared for better purchase. The outside leg is usually set above the inside leg, with the knee pointed up and out of the crack.

If you are either wafer thin or super flexible, or if the crack opens up enough, the arm bar can be replaced with the arm lock, or "chicken wing." Much like the arm bar, you simply fold the forearm back and palm against the opposite side of the crack. If the crack is tight, your elbow will point into the crack; with a slightly wider crack, the elbow will be pointing nearly straight up, with the triceps resting against the rear crack wall. Often the natural muscular tension in your arms and a little upper body English will make the arm lock so snug that it's hard to even move it. Some climbers swear

Heel-toe jam. Both feet are in the crack and jammed at the heel and toe.

This heel-toe jam takes advantage of the rock's natural features to create a more secure platform.

by the arm lock and use it whenever possible, others only use it to augment the arm bar, and some find it too awkward and only use it to rest. Some don't use it at all. When the crack widens too much to use the heel-toe jam, you must start foot stacking, the most called-upon stack being the "T-bar."

The best sequence of when to move what is a matter of what the crack dictates, and what process works best for you. Difficult off-width climbs require you to fluidly bust out all the techniques we've just described, and to transition from one to the other as the crack subtly or dramatically changes size over the course of a pitch. Experience is the best and only teacher, but remember the following points: Resist the natural temptation of sticking your body deep into the crack. It may feel more secure, but it inhibits your mobility, so stay outside of the crack as much as possible. And don't thrash (advice that, to the beginner, is impossible to follow). Set each limb solidly, and keep it locked

Knee in and knee out of crack.

Use footholds on the edge of the crack to supplement your knee jam.

as the others shuffle up. Don't rush, pace yourself, rely on small movements rather than drastic lunging, and never skip the chance to rest. Always scan for face holds inside or outside the crack. Often a couple of face holds will get you around the nastiest part of an off-width.

A hard off-width will exploit the slightest form break and can swallow more energy than a black hole. It's common to see a novice thrashing like mad and getting nothing but exhausted on rugged off-width climbs. Always wear sufficient clothing to protect against the inevitable abrasions. Anyone heading off to climb a difficult off-width crack wearing shorts and a T-shirt is in for a rough afternoon. Especially for those cracks requiring foot stacking—and for most all off-widths in general—a proper boot (not a low-top) is almost always the best choice. You can probably thieve your way past a few off-width moves wearing slippers, but they'll kill your feet if the off-width is hard and covers any distance.

As a beginner you may find even a moderate off-width climb the hardest thing you've ever done. Most climbers do. After you have a few under your harness, go back and see what a huge difference experience and technique make.

Lastly, this writing will make little sense till you have checked the photos and thrashed up a few off-width climbs. After that, return and reread this, and laugh at yourself. We all went through the same ordeal with off-size climbing. No exceptions.

Hand Stacking

Also known as "Leavittation" (after Randy Leavitt, pioneer of this clever technique), hand stacking supplants the strenuous arm bar with a variety of two-handed jamming configurations: fist against hand, hand against hand, fist against fist.

This technique should work anywhere that hands can be stacked and the lower body can at least momentarily support the whole body via knee jams and/or calf locks. Leavittation is particularly

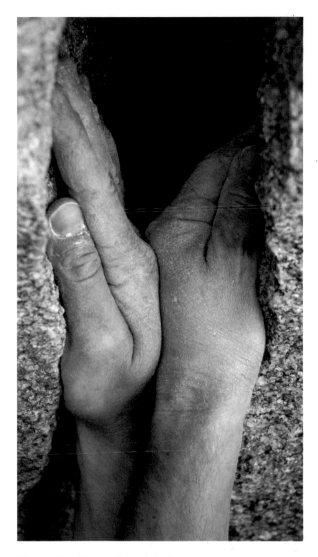

Hand stacking—Leavittation.

efficient on straight-in, off-width cracks so desperate or overhanging that a pure arm bar is prohibitive, if not impossible. Leavittation has also been used, repeatedly, on horizontal roof climbs. Only practice can show you what kinds of hand stacks actually work—there are no rules or "best jam" guidelines. It's the jammed legs that are the real trick.

The basic sequence: Find a hand stack, then a knee lock as high as possible below the hand stack. This "active" leg will soon bear your full bulk, so work it in as securely as possible. The "passive" leg is heel-toe jamming below and is mainly a balance point. You must then release the hand stack and establish another above, the high knee jam supporting your weight while your abdominals—locked in a withering crunch—keep your torso upright. Then repeat the process.

The knee lock is key, though tough to master, and is usually where even world-class climbers fail with Leavittation. The secret is to keep it as high as possible. For optimum torque, once your knee is completely inside the crack, bend the lower leg back till the knee expands and locks tight, the foot now hanging outside the crack. Your "active" foot is in turn placed against the outside of the crack, supplying a sort of brace effect allowing you to let go with both hands and set up the next hand stack. A straight-in crack allows a choice for the active, or jammed, knee; the leaning crack does not. If the crack leans right, jam the left knee; if left, jam the right one.

Leavittation is the most complex and counterintuitive technique in all of climbing. Its normal application is on off-width cracks at the top of the scale and in a fairly narrow range of size, though the technique is occasionally fitting on moderate routes and in cracks that fluctuate between sizes. One thing is for sure: No one has ever mastered Leavittation without a lot of practice in a controlled (usually a toprope) situation. There literally are only a handful of climbers in the world who are capable and willing to climb the hardest off-width cracks, and each of them has made the art a special study.

Squeeze Chimneys and Flares

By definition, any crack too wide to heel-toe jam but only wide enough to barely accept the body is a squeeze chimney. They may be easy to slide into, but usually are strenuous and claustrophobic to ascend. A bottoming, or shallow, squeeze chimney is a flare. Once it is too wide to use an arm lock, or "chicken wing," it becomes a chimney. These techniques typically overlap on a given climb, but we'll look at them separately to focus on the various methods of climbing these types of cracks.

Oftentimes the inside leg seeks a heel-toe jam while the outside leg basically chimneys between the flaring planes of the crack.

Squeeze chimneys are climbed using off-width techniques with a few additional antics and variations. The arm lock is the standby for the upper body, though a wide arm bar and even an inverted arm bar (elbow higher than the palm) is often used. You can typically get inside a squeeze chimney, so the arm lock and arm bar variants can be used with both arms. The normal setup sees the arm lock for the inside arm and the inverted arm position (chicken wing) for the outside arm. Sometimes, both arms are using the inverted arm bar.

Foot stacking (the T-bar) should be used if at all possible. If the chimney is too wide, press both knees against the front wall, with both feet torqued flat against the back wall. The opposing pressures between knees and feet keep the lower body in place. Like off-width cracks, the lower and upper body move up alternately.

Many squeeze chimneys are so slim, you have to exhale to move up. Most chimneys narrow the farther you enter them, so fight the urge to work

Chicken wing (arm lock).

Chicken wing used in conjunction with a heel-toe jam.

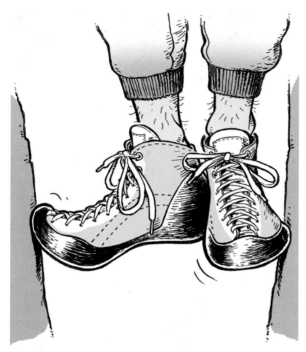

The T-bar.

deeper—albeit more securely—into the bowels of the crack, and instead stay toward the outside, where movement is easier. You'll probably find that staying lodged is easy, but moving up is tough duty. Just climb slowly, work it out, and never get frantic—which is sage advice no novice can ever seem to follow. But at least bear it in mind as a future goal. Also, consider wearing knee pads if the squeeze is long and sustained. I remember my first season in Yosemite, thrashing up the *East Chimney* of Rixon's Pinnacle, and feeling as though my kneecaps were turning to powder.

Flares are wide enough to get inside, but too shallow to enter very far. They can be nasty undertakings, strenuous and insecure, and technical riddles. At once grueling and confounding, grim flares have humbled many world-class climbers. Because every flare is a little different, they defy much generic explanation. The main challenge is the lack of flat or opposing planes to work off. Instead, the

walls of the crack flare outward like a V on edge, so regular counterpressuring techniques become extra precarious, with everything slowly or rapidly buttering outward. Still, almost every flare requires the inside arm to be arm locking, and often the purchase of elbow and palm is marginal. The outside hand needs to exploit any handhold, or at least vigorously palm off the flare to augment the doubtful arm lock. The feet are bridging—inside foot backstepping the back wall, outside foot pressing off any footholds available—or simply frictioning flat against the face. Sometimes you alternate these tasks between the outside and inside feet. The outside foot is key, for it presses the butt and back against the back wall, so the decision on which way to face often depends on where the footholds are. Many times you won't know which way to face until you try (though with notorious flares, there is usually a traditional direction climbers face: toward the wall or with their backs to the wall).

If the flare is unusually shallow, very steep, and devoid of footholds, you're looking at a nasty piece of work, where anything goes. Routes with these characteristics, like *Edge of Night* in Yosemite, might only be rated 5.10, but without the right technique, they are impossible.

Though difficult flares often require considerable fitness, you cannot simply muscle them because the purchase of the various arm locks and foot stacks are so marginal. Protection is often lacking, rests are few, and five moves might be required to gain a few precious feet. The good news is that once you acquire a feel for the work, you have the technique for life and don't have to continuously work at keeping your edge, as you do with face climbing. But gaining that technique in the first place is, for most climbers, so difficult and frustrating that many don't bother at all. The drawback with this is that many of the great classics require fluency in this technique, and if you're ever interested in establishing big new routes, what will you do when you encounter a grisly flare?

Duo heel-toe jams.

Like grim off-width cracks, very few climbers ever make a special study out of climbing flares. Most experienced adventure climbers have bagged just enough flares to understand the technique should they run into a flare on a classic big wall or a new route.

Chimneys

When cracks widen enough so that they are easily entered, they may lose some degree of security, but they are usually much easier to climb. Knee chimneys are just that: Bridging is done between knees and back, and different sizes are accommodated by flaring the knees to varying degrees. Movement is a ratcheting affair, with the arm usually in the inverted arm bar position. Knee chimneys are almost always secure. Knee pads can prevent hateful bruises (and pain) to the kneecaps, and a long-sleeved shirt will protect the shoulders.

When the chimney is wider than the distance between your knee and your foot, you push your feet against one wall and your back against the other. To move up, one foot backsteps off the back wall so your legs form a bridge via opposing pressures. The hands are either pressing off the far wall or bridged between both walls, like the feet. In either case, the back is released and the legs

climbers have done this for a couple of moves somewhere—but not for long.

Chimneying is a pretty natural technique that is easily learned and often used on classic adventure climbs from Yosemite to the Towers of Paine. There is hardly any long climb that does not involve a little or a lot of chimneying, so working the technique to an advanced intermediate level is essential for all those with dreams of climbing the great walls of the world.

Liebacking

Hanging on for dear life is often the description given for the full-blown, all-out lieback (or layback). Fortunately, few liebacks are all-out, but most are athletic and strenuous. Liebacking is perhaps the most exhilarating technique (outside of roofs and big dynamics) in the climbing game. You can span amazing sections of rock. It's also the quickest way to find hell in a handbasket because, owing to the great opposing pressures, if your hands fail, you fire off like you're spring-loaded. In its pure form, the technique is used to climb arêtes, cracks in right-angled corners, or cracks that are too shallow for jamming. In its partial form, anytime you lean off a hold, you are liebacking, for you are lying back off the face hold, the jug, the edge of the crack, or whatever your hands are on. It's a means to use holds that are other than simple horizontal edges.

Liebacking is known by some as "the technique of no technique" because it is often possible to swing into a lieback and muscle over sections that would otherwise call for more complicated jamming maneuvers. That's why you sometimes see climbers trying to straight lieback off-width cracks, flares, and other highly technical obstacles. It is almost always more dangerous to do so, for stopping to place protection from a lieback position is doubly difficult (it's almost impossible to look directly into the crack when liebacking), often leaving the committed liebacker no choice but to simply go

*Leading **Elmer Fudd** (5.11b), Joshua Tree. The holds on this lieback are thin and insecure.*

*Liebacking a flake. Patty Kline on **Hair Lip** (5.10a), Suicide Rock.*

for the next rest hold, be it 10 or 30 feet above. In other words, a climber can quickly lieback their way into real trouble, and the beginner should be especially leery about doing so till they know their strengths and limitations.

The basic liebacking motion is pulling with your hands and pushing with your feet, one in opposition to the other. A typical layback will find your side flush against the wall. Your hands are clasping the near edge of the crack, and you are liebacking off them. Your feet are either pressing against the crack's far edge, balanced on small holds, vigorously pushing off a corner's far wall, or maybe even jammed in the crack. There are many quasi forms of liebacking, but all involve the upper torso leaning off to one side and the arms pulling to create opposing pressure against the feet.

The purest and most typical lieback occurs on a flake leaning against the wall or in a crack in a 90-degree corner—a dihedral, or "open book." Here, your hands are pulling directly out, and your feet are pushing the opposite way, directly against the face or far wall. Since the technique is strenuous, try to keep the arms straight, which again lets the skeletal system, rather than the muscles, absorb at least some of the strain. Many times it is possible and desirable to leapfrog the hands, one over the other, but often the top hand will remain on top throughout, with the lower hand shuffling up to it, and then the top hand reaching above. On steep laybacks, you'll want to limit the time the hands lose contact with the liebacked edge, so in some cases the hands are slid up. Also, leapfrogging your limbs can sometimes get you crossed up, throwing your balance out of whack. Try to keep your feet as low as possible, using any footholds. The closer your feet are to your hands, the more strenuous the layback becomes. Of course, the feet stick best when they are up high, close to the hands, as most of your weight is counterpressuring off the soles of your shoes. However, that same weight is also taxing the daylights out of your fingers and arms. It is much

Liebacking a flake, making sure to keep the arms straight.

Liebacking a flake, with much of the climber's weight taken by her left foot.

Working up a finger crack in the back of a corner. The lack of footholds might require you to smear your feet up by your hands—always a strenuous drill.

Liebacking a corner that is usually jammed via off-width techniques. This is often possible on wide cracks but makes placing protection extra difficult.

less strenuous with the feet lower, but with the decreased pressure, they will skid off much easier, so watch out. There is a fine line—often a matter of a half inch—between just right and too low.

The full-blown, or "Frankenstein," layback is most often found in a steep or overhanging corner. The crack's edge might be rounded or the crack is so thin it will accept only fingertips. The opposite wall may be overhung, slanting away and smooth as polished marble, so your feet gain purchase only through the friction of direct pressure. The Frankenstein layback entails drawing your feet up by

your hands and swinging into the all-out, liebacking posture. The problem is, not only is this extremely strenuous, but there's often the tendency to swing completely out, like a door opening on its hinges. This "barn door" effect can be countered either by increasing the torque to both hands and feet (which makes things more strenuous still), or by bridging the outside foot out and pushing obliquely off the far wall, hoping to stall the swing and regain equilibrium. Sometimes you must momentarily palm off the opposite wall to halt the swing, and sometimes it is possible to jam the inside foot in the crack, keeping the other foot stemmed wide to provide a hinge-resistant base. If you're fortunate, the opposite wall will be flecked with footholds. If not, it's you and Frank all the way.

Most liebacks require a clever mix of many techniques; when to use what is fairly intuitive once you've swung into the layback. Your body responds automatically to changes in equilibrium and variations in angle. As much as you can, strive to keep the arms straight. Feel the edge of the layback as much as possible, and crank off the sharpest, most defined spot. Look for any stem or rest holds, but don't stop if it's more strenuous than carrying on. Climb aggressively, and don't hang about looking for footholds that aren't readily apparent. The exhortation "Go for it!" was invented for the climber swinging into a layback. Once committed, don't hesitate: Power over it quickly.

As mentioned, physically fit beginners can quickly lieback themselves way over their head, so again, a special caution must be given for the technique. Because there are high counterpressuring forces at play here, if a hand or foot suddenly blows, a climber can fire out of a layback position as if shot from a cannon. So striving for control and measured, fluid movement is key to keeping the exercise safe and sane.

Stemming

"Stemming," or bridging—essentially backstepping off two planes of rock—normally occurs in right-angled or oblique corners, where the crack is nonexistent or so thin as to be of little value. Many times it is necessary when the crack momentarily pinches down. Even when the crack is good, your lower body may stem the whole way. In any case, stemming is essentially face climbing in a corner.

By crosspressuring your feet against opposing planes of rock, your lower body creates a momentary platform that takes some or even all the weight off your hands. Many difficult climbs involve stemming, and the extreme stemming problem can require creative sequences and improbable, marginal counterpressures. Consider the stemming corner as an ultra-flared chimney. In its pure form, the feet are pasted on opposite walls, perhaps frictioning, maybe backstepping and smearing on footholds, but always counterpressuring against themselves and/or the hands. The hands may also be crosspressuring, palming off the slightest irregularities or pawing holds.

Essentially, your body is like a spring lodged between two sloping walls. The only thing keeping the spring in place is the purchase at both ends and the tension between. Moving the spring up, then, is the hard part, for this requires the tension to go lax, at least momentarily—yet it never can. Usually it's the diagonal pressure of one hand and one foot that keeps the climber in place, and the climber alternates this bridge in moving up. This can involve a dozen little moves to gain even a meter of upward progress.

Sometimes you may actually chimney the corner, back against one wall, feet smearing off the other. You may backstep with one shoe, edge with the other, palm with one hand, and mantle with the other. The possibilities are endless. Flexibility, balance, and the ability to exploit any and all features are a stemmer's best tools. For some reason, many climbers forget to breathe when stemming. This can not only make things more strenuous, but can freeze you up after only a few body lengths. Staying fluid and loose is key to this technique.

I mentioned earlier that once you learn jamming technique, you need not relearn it. Crack climbing, however, is a matter of feel, and you can lose that feel if you haven't climbed cracks in a while. The intuitive, no-thinking movement that earmarks great crack climbers is attained by familiarity. If you're out of crack climbing form, take a few days to get dialed back in, and the feel will quickly return.

For both crack and face climbing, movement is the name of the game. But paradoxically, perhaps

Stemming with both hands and feet. Body position is maintained by the crosspressure between limbs.

the most crucial aspect of efficient movement is when you stop moving and attempt to rest between spurts and sequences of moves. Remember that husbanding your strength, not overgripping or overjamming, and resting whenever possible is paramount to fluid, controlled movement. There's little technique involved in resting on a big hold. Learning how to pause for quasi-rests while, say, pumping out a long hand crack or pulling up a vertical wall of pockets is very much an acquired skill best learned by watching top climbers in the gym or on the cliffside. Believe it: Conserving strength is absolutely crucial on routes close to your limit, and the ability to rest and shake out whenever possible, if only for a moment, can spell the difference between success and failure. Bottom line: Put as much thought into trying to obtain rests—in the middle of a climb—as you do in executing moves, and your technical limit will invariably increase.

CHAPTER FOUR

Ropes, Anchors, and Belays

We have reviewed the salient points of physically climbing rock. The psychology and strategy of putting it all together, in concert with the process of safe rope management, can be done only after we have a working knowledge of equipment. No climber ever gets "honed" without falling, and the falling climber is quickly killed without a solid, dependable protection system. The protection system combines bombproof anchors, ropes, connecting links, and alert partners to provide a sort of safety net that, in the event of a fall, keeps him from hitting the ground. When a layman sees a climber lashed to the cliff, all the odd-looking widgets and knots and whatnot appear complicated. Actually, the system is quite basic and largely intuitive once you understand what the gear is and how it all works.

We see the climber moving up the dark cliff, secured by a rope and partner above. Who got that line up there? Somebody had to go first, and had he fallen, he would have died a horrible death—right? Wrong. The whole point of the rope and the attending gear, along with the hundred years that went into refining both technique and equipment, is to safeguard the climbers in the event of a fall. Rock climbing is not the pastime of nihilists or madmen, at least not in the mainstream.

When an ace climber starts an extreme climb at the limit of her ability, it is likely she will fall, perhaps dozens of times. And she doesn't expect to get hurt. When the beginner starts up her first climb, the aim is entirely different than that of the ace. She is not looking to push her limits, rather to comfortably learn how to move over rock and to bone up on what the gear is and how it is properly used. But for both the ace and the novice, the larger aim is to have fun, not to cheat death. Of course, both climbers can only do so if they are confident the safety system is fundamentally reliable. And it is.

In a nutshell: Two climbers are tied into their respective ends of a 165-foot rope (200- and 230-foot ropes are standard tackle at sport-climbing areas). Starting from the ground, one climber secures (anchors) himself to a tree or a big block, or perhaps arranges an anchor with some of his specialized gear fitted into a handy crack. In any case, the anchor is not "good enough" unless it cannot be wrenched loose no matter what happens on the cliffside. The climbers then double-check themselves and each other to make sure harnesses, knots, and anchors are properly arranged. Having decided on a particular passage, or "route," up the cliff—say, a prominent crack—the "leader" starts up, scaling the crack using hands and feet. The person on the ground (the "belayer") is meanwhile paying the rope out ("belaying") through a lightweight mechanical device that can stop the rope cold if need be.

Lauren Lee slotting pro on **Inner Chi** *(5.11d),*
Tombstone Wall, near Moab, Utah.
KEITH LADZINSKI

Now the leader has gained a difficult section. She removes an appropriate piece of gear from the gear loops on her harness, places said gear in the crack, tugs it to get a good seating, clips a carabiner (snap link) through the gear, then clips her rope through the carabiner. The leader now has an anchor, or piece of "protection," that protects her for the climbing just overhead. On sport climbs the anchor is usually a permanent bolt, drilled and set into the rock. Say she climbs 3 feet above the anchor and falls. The belayer locks off the rope, and the leader falls twice the distance she has climbed above the anchor, or 6 feet. Since the rope stretches, she might fall a few inches more, but the belayer, lashed taut to his anchor and holding the fall, doesn't budge. The leader gathers her wits and tries again.

A question: If the leader was only 3 feet above the anchor, why did she fall 6 feet plus the odd extra inches? First, for several reasons, the belayer cannot effectively take in the rope when the leader falls, which happens in a flash. His duty is to lock the rope off, so when the leader's weight comes onto the rope, the rope is held fast. If the leader is 3 feet above her anchor—or protection—she must first fall 3 feet to that protection. She still has 3 feet of slack out, so she falls 3 more feet, past the protection, for a total fall of 6 feet plus, depending on rope stretch. Hence the equation: The leader falls twice the distance above her last protection—and then some.

Carrying on, the leader places protection (commonly called "pro") as she sees fit, always placing something before a difficult section. Sixty feet up the crack, she might have placed six or eight pieces of pro, depending on the difficulty and how secure she feels. Once the leader gains a convenient place to stop—say, a ledge or a stout tree—she arranges an anchor that is absolutely fail-safe. In this case, that means an anchor strong enough that, no matter what the other climber does, no matter how far he falls, he cannot cause the anchor to fail or come out. On popular climbs in established climbing

areas, secure anchors are readily built, used, and removed many times over a weekend.

Now it is the leader's turn to belay, or to take the rope in, as the other climber (the "second") follows the "pitch" (rope length). As the second follows, he removes, or "cleans," all the pro that the leader placed so that it may be used on the next pitch. Since the belayer is taking up the rope as the second climbs up to her, the second can only fall as far as the rope stretches.

The amount a typical rope will stretch depends on the amount of rope that is "out." Body weight stretches a standard, dynamic climbing rope about 6 to 8 percent of the length in use, though this ratio will increase slightly as the rope ages. In other words, say you are the second (following) on the rope and are presently 100 feet below the belayer overhead. If you fall, the rope could stretch as much as 8 feet, meaning you could fall 8 feet. This rarely happens, however, because rope stretch is reduced by the various frictions along the rope—namely, the assorted protection devices the leader has placed and through which the rope runs. Generally, though not always, the above scenario would result in the second falling only 2 or 3 feet. The point to remember: The more rope that is out (the distance separating the second from the leader), the greater the rope will stretch when weighted and the longer the potential fall.

Once the second reaches the leader's anchor, or belay, he in turn takes over the lead while the previous leader continues belaying, and the process is repeated until the team finishes the route.

This is free climbing—note that the gear is not used for upward progress. The leader does not hang from the gear she places; rather, she climbs using only hands and feet. In free climbing, the gear is used only to safeguard against a fall—the sport is to climb the rock using your own physical abilities. Rope and gear are what make the process sane and allow you to push your limits, saving your life should you fall off. Since falling has become an integral part of sport climbing, both the system and the gear are very reliable, but, once again, it's all in how you use them, and the most fundamental item, the rope, is no good if you're not on it or it's not anchored.

The Rope

The rope is your lifeline, the primary piece of equipment for any climber. There is not a single serious climber whose life has not been saved by the rope many times over. Climbing ropes are extremely dependable. Modern ropes have evolved a long way from the horsehair cords of the Carthaginians and from the dicey hemp lines the climbing pioneers used around Zermatt and other alpine villages, where accounts of ropes snapping were many and tragic. Those early hemp ropes were replaced first by flax, then with cotton varieties from European-grown fibers. Philippine manila and sisal from Mexico in turn succeeded these, and by World War II a dense, three-strand "balloon" manila and a similar four-strand yachting rope (white line) were the only choices for an alpinist. During the war, Arnold Wexler of the U.S. Bureau of Standards concluded that for strength, elasticity, and durability,

An assortment of modern climbing ropes on display at Nomad Ventures climbing shop, Idyllwild, California.

climbs), she will simply use a smaller-diameter and substantially less durable line.

"Static," or "working elongation," basically refers to how much a rope stretches when weighted with an 80-kilogram iron block. The leading ropes vary little here. "Impact force elongation" (IFE), how far the rope stretches when fallen on, is far more important but seldom listed in the statistics. The longer a rope stretches, the farther you fall, which increases the likelihood of hitting something. Conversely, more stretch means less impact force on the line, so it's a trade-off. The available specs from most leading manufacturers vary from about 6 to 7 percent IFE. Negligible, you say? Maybe, but the difference might be 6 inches in a 40-foot fall, and as rope physicist Dennis Turvill has pointed out, "A fall 6 inches longer can mean the difference between a good bar story and a compound fracture." Hopefully, impact force elongation will soon be a required statistic for all ropes.

"Impact force" pertains to the degree of shock the body receives at the end of a fall, a crucial factor since a greater force means a more jarring, painful stop. The UIAA specifies that the maximum impact of force on the climber must be less than 2,640 pounds for a single rope. Different brands can vary as much as 25 percent, so some thought should be given to this statistic.

Another, less important factor is whether a rope has been treated with a waterproofing compound. Compounds differ among manufacturers, and most of them rub off after a rope has been used a few dozen times. The better and now-standard coatings are silicone or various fluor chemicals, the latter being the best for durability. Though nothing can keep a rope dry in a deluge, tests indicate that coated ropes are approximately 33 percent more abrasion-resistant than uncoated ropes. Also, coating greatly reduces the ability of the rope to absorb damaging ultraviolet rays. For these two reasons, coatings do more for a rope's longevity than the number of falls they allegedly can sustain.

Different sheath characteristics—the tightness of the weave and whether the sheath, or "cover," moves much—directly affect how a rope handles. Sheath slippage is the result of core and cover balancing/stretching, not the core and cover shifting. The cover works like a Chinese finger lock, meaning it is not going to shift when loaded. Remember that the UIAA spec calls for less than 1 percent sheath slippage, which is less than 2 feet for a 60-meter rope. Whenever a little sheath creeps off the end of a rope (which happens), cut off the excess and reseal the end with a hot knife.

Ropes that are prone to excessive kinking, that are stiff and hold knots poorly, and that twist and spin a suspended climber are really dastardly things to use. Unfortunately, it is difficult to determine a rope's handling characteristics (the rope's "hand") when it is brand new, and there is little objective information that honestly pegs these qualities. Moreover, a rope in the retail shop that handles like silk might prove to be a "corkscrew" once you have used it. The sheath might stiffen or soften up after only moderate use. Ultimately, a climber is left to review the available literature and experiment with various ropes, drawing conclusions accordingly. Fortunately, most of the ropes currently available work very well.

Since any UIAA-approved rope is stronger than you'll ever need, most climbers tend to buy the cheapest UIAA-approved rope they can find. The majority of climbers don't understand, or care, about all the attending statistics. Ropes range in price from around $130 to $200. In decades past, most of the ropes sold in North America were imported from Europe. However, the popularity of sport climbing has, over the last twenty-five years, spawned a plethora of American and Canadian manufacturers who fashion top-quality climbing ropes, usually at a lower price than the continental articles.

Despite the astronomical tensile strength of kernmantle ropes, they are made of supple nylon, which is easily damaged when even slightly abused.

Since you're hanging your all on the rope, you'll want to pay extremely close attention to the use and care of your lifeline.

Regarding a rope's life expectancy, the following general rules are worth considering. Retirement guidelines recently issued by the UIAA give a modern rope ten years of life if it's used rarely or not at all. Traditionally, for normal weekend use, you chuck a rope after two years no matter how good it looks or feels. For multi-fall use, retire a rope after three months of constant use or up to a year of part-time use. Any rope suffering a long fall of great severity should be retired immediately. Howard Wright of Maxim Ropes nods to these rules but stresses that the primary criterion in determining a rope's condition "is accomplished through visual inspection [look for wear, cuts, discoloration, and chemical exposure] and tactile inspection [feeling for damage to the core, including lumps, twists, or breaks]." And beware of rope fattening: Remember that nylon absorbs water and will fatten. In short, the best retirement guidelines are visual inspection and feeling the line in your hands. And remember the Slinky metaphor: The more you use a rope, the less it stretches back to its original length and the less it is able to elongate and absorb energy.

A rope bag is a great way to keep dirt off your rope and prolong its life.

Rope Bags

A rope bag is an inexpensive and practical way of storing and protecting your rope till the moment you start climbing; the rope is re-bagged once you're done. Some climbers use them to store the slack during a climb—a good habit to acquire. In extreme instances—say, climbing just above a wind-whipped ocean—a rope fed out of a rope bag is a saving grace. For sport climbing, a rope bag (one that rolls out into a rope tarp) protects the rope from dirt and harmful UV rays and makes it convenient to move the rope from route to route, as you commonly do when sport climbing. Rope bags have been standard gear for many years.

Rope Care

- Never step on the rope. Debris can work through the sheath to cut and abrade the core. Stepping on someone's rope is a serious violation of form.

- Never lend your rope to anyone. Never buy a used rope. Used ropes don't fetch much money, and there's probably a good reason why someone wants to deal it. It may have been used to tow a backhoe out of a ditch.

- Protect your rope from unnecessary exposure to the sun. Save for huge falls that result in sheath damage and careless abuses, UV rays are the single most destructive force your rope is exposed to, so the more time spent in sunlight, the faster it will deteriorate. Always store your rope in a cool, dry, shady place.

- Contrary to common opinion, alcohol, gasoline, and other hydrocarbon solvents do not affect nylon chemically; and though you should avoid exposing your rope to any foreign substance, a little gasoline is not disastrous to your rope. Battery acid and other corrosives spell instant death to your line, however.

- A certain amount of grime is unavoidable. When the rope becomes obviously dirty, machine wash it in cold or warm water and mild soap. Use the delicate fabric setting and rinse it for two cycles, then pull your hair out trying to untangle it. Avoid the dryer. Instead, string it up in a shady place, or flake it out on a clean floor and let the water evaporate naturally, normally accomplished in a couple of days.

- Periodically inspect the rope for frays and soft spots by folding it carefully between your fingers and working it from one end to the other.

Webbing (Sling Material)

Since World War II, nylon webbing has been widely used in rock climbing. Invented to batten down gear on PT boats, climbers have found nylon webbing (flat rope, or "tape") useful as gear slings, runners, and tie-offs. For fifty years standard nylon webbing was used to form slings of 1 or ⁹⁄₁₆ inch diameter, the latter for tying off pitons. The ⁵⁄₈-inch sling was introduced about thirty years ago. The strength of the material was more than adequate for its applications, but the shortcomings of pure nylon are that it weakens with age and use, and as is the case with all webbing, it is adversely affected by exposure to sunlight's ultraviolet rays. The great

majority of nylon webbing is manufactured for the military, and the government has set minimum requirements, or specs, that the webbing must meet for use in life-support situations. "Mil-spec" refers to these government, or military, specifications.

Though nylon is still a viable, and often preferable, material for slings, other materials have come to replace it in some situations. BlueWater Spectra is a molecular-weight polyethylene developed by Allied-Signal, Inc. It is the strongest fiber ever made, roughly ten times stronger than steel. It is also about ten times as expensive. Spectra-sewn runners are available in various sizes and are ideal for those who want half the bulk and weight of other runners with no significant reduction in strength. Spectra's wear resistance is excellent. When cut, it will not tear through. Spectra was for a time the sling of choice throughout the United States. However, Dyneema and the new Dynex (which the engineers at Black Diamond assure me are essentially the same thing as Spectra), also manufactured by Allied-Signal, have come to replace Spectra as the favored sling material. These fibers are fifteen times stronger than steel and are now available in 10mm width as the standard runner size.

Aside from the price, Spectra/Dyneema/Dynex do have shortcomings. They can be up to 19 percent less resistant to UV damage than regular mil-spec nylon and too slick to work as well as nylon for the friction knots used in self-rescue situations (Prusik knot, Klemheist knot, etc.). These materials weaken when repeatedly flexed under moderate loads, whereas nylon does not. In fact, after about 200 flex cycles with a 40-pound load, a Spectra sling is no stronger than a nylon one, and only gets

weaker with more flexing. They also have a low melting temperature, so a rope running across can burn them easily. And since they do not stretch at all, they can heat up when directly weighted in a dynamic fall situation. Spectra/Dyneema/Dynex can actually be weaker than standard nylon webbing under these conditions, because standard webbing will stretch. In this sense, the biggest strength of these superfibers is also their biggest weakness. As we will discuss later, the reliability of anchors and the overall safety system depends on the dynamic qualities of the components to slow down the loading curve so peak loading doesn't occur all at once.

Despite the drawbacks of these new fibers, and others like them, many climbers consider them superior to standard mil-spec nylon for use as sling material. Mil-spec runners also have some drawbacks of their own. There have been isolated cases of mil-spec runners tearing over razor-sharp edges. And nylon does wear out, so it is not unheard of

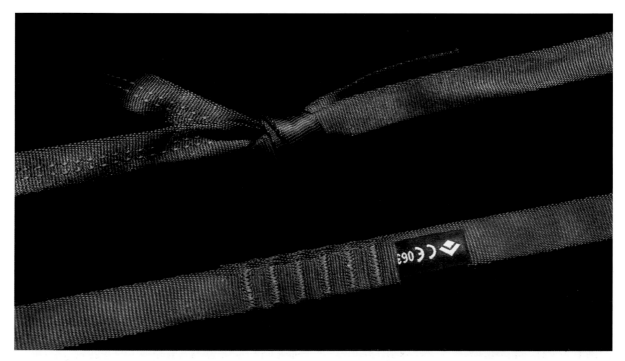

⁹/₁₆-inch nylon webbing, tied vs. sewn.

The water knot (aka ring bend) is commonly used for tying runners.

for old runners to break under the impact of a fall, though I've never heard of a nylon sling in good condition breaking when the system has been properly rigged. Consequently, the far cheaper mil-spec webbing remains a viable, and in some cases favored, choice for slings—provided the climber keeps a sharp eye on their condition and retires them when signs of wear are obvious. If the nylon feels stiff, it probably has been affected by sunlight—the webbing may be weakened but show no such sign. If there is any doubt, retire your runners after using them for a period of, say, a hundred days, remembering that the relatively inexpensive nylon is far less precious than your life.

Sewn webbing loops are stronger, lighter, and less bulky than knotted ones, so most climbers usually use sewn slings. Nylon slings equipped with a water knot can come in handy for tying around trees, flakes, and tunnels in the event of a retreat,

but you should check the water knots frequently, as they have a tendency to come untied.

Quickdraws and Runners

The most common use for webbing is for quickdraws and runners. Quickdraws (or simply "draws") come pre-sewn with a carabiner loop on each end and are used to connect the rope to chocks or bolt anchors. Runners are tied or sewn in single loops (about 4 to 6 feet of 1-, ⅝-, or ⁹⁄₁₆-inch webbing) and are often carried over one shoulder and under the opposite arm. (This is often a problem, however, as the loop length in doubled slings is always changing and entangling with other slings and gear, one loop hanging down to your crotch, the other tight as a noose. Many climbers prefer to triple the sling, tie it in a knot, and clip it onto the gear sling or side of their harness.) The length will vary according to your size. The runner should never be

High-Tech vs. Nylon

R ecent testing strongly suggests that old-style nylon sling material (and cordage) is superior for general use in rock climbing. The mega-strong "tech webbings" (such as Spectra/Dynex) were originally produced for the military, generally for securing static loads. Static forces in climbing are basically body-weight loads, far too small to require sling material "stronger than steel." More importantly, in a climbing context, the strength of sling materials is significant only during falls, when dynamic, not static, forces are generated. Since climbing's roped safety system acts as a peak (dynamic) force load limiter, nylon with just a little bit of stretch helps to absorb peak forces, while the virtually static tech webbing translates dynamic forces directly to the carabiners and protection devices, which can blow apart under high-impact dynamic loading. Moreover, recent tests from several sources indicate that nylon webbing and cordage can absorb (without breaking) greater dynamic forces than high-tensile-strength cord and tech webbing.

so long that the bottom hangs below your waist, where it can easily snag on the rock or even on your foot during a high step.

Runners and draws are used somewhere on virtually every climb, and it is a common error not to have enough. Most climbers consider ten to twelve quickdraws and four or five runners more than adequate for all but exceptional cases. On short (one pitch) sport climbs featuring bolt protection exclusively, the leader will usually count the bolts and take the exact number of draws needed for the route.

Sewn slings and runners are the norm. The sewn joints dispense with the knot, which is sometimes a hindrance. The disadvantage is that they cannot be untied and connected with other slings to form a king-size runner should the need arise, and it will. Be cautious when using any sewn gear. In their original state the stitching is stronger than the webbing; however, the stitching abrades with use, and the overall strength is then significantly reduced. It is a good practice to inspect any sewn webbing periodically. Most climbers carry a collection of both sewn and tied slings.

There is more on runners in Chapter 6, "The Art of Leading."

Most climbing stores offer a large selection of quickdraws and carabiners.

Cordage

Accessory cord comes in several styles made from different materials. Cordage is mostly used to fashion cordelettes and Prusiks. It comes in a range of diameters up to 9mm and can be bought in any length desired, custom cut off a spool at your local climbing store.

The differences between standard nylon accessory cord (aka utility cord) and newer high-tensile cords (such as New England Ropes' Technora and BlueWater Titan/Spectra cord) are fairly simple to sort out. Nylon stretches a small amount because it's made strictly of nylon; the newer cords combine materials such as Aramid, Dyneema, and Technora with nylon and do not stretch as much as nylon,

if at all. The newer cords are lighter, less bulky, and, most importantly, stronger—but this strength advantage can be lost depending on which knot is used (up to a 40 percent loss of strength on high-tensile with a figure eight knot), whereas knotted nylon hardly loses any strength at all.

Which cord works best for what situation is a matter of debate, but the most up-to-date thinking recommends 7mm nylon, with its attending stretch, for use in rigging cordelettes. The increased stretch equals decreased force on the anchor, meaning more security in the event of a fall.

As far as knots go, it is generally accepted that a double fisherman's knot is sufficient for nylon cord, while a triple fisherman's knot is best for high-tensile cord.

"Tech" and nylon accessory cord. Top to bottom: 6mm nylon (Prusik) cord, 6.5mm Sterling PowerCord, and 7mm nylon Sterling cordelette cord.

Knots for Slings and Cordage

The ring bend, or water knot, has been the traditional knot to tie runners together. Nylon webbing is slippery, however, particularly when new, and it's not unheard of for the ring bend to loosen with time and come untied. A good practice with any gear is to routinely check your knots, especially the ring bend.

A much more secure (albeit permanent and bulky) knot for both rope and webbing is the double fisherman's, or grapevine, knot. Since the grapevine knot is a "cinch" knot—meaning the tighter you pull, the tighter it gets—once the knot is repeatedly weighted, it is more or less impossible to untie. Should any knot prove difficult to untie, roll the knot quickly between your palms or under a foot. If the knot has been sucked down to the size of a pea, however, this method won't work. Try some gentle taps with a smooth rock, which will often loosen the knot enough to get your fingers in.

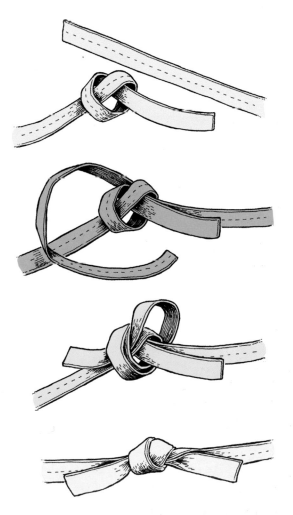

The ring bend (water knot).

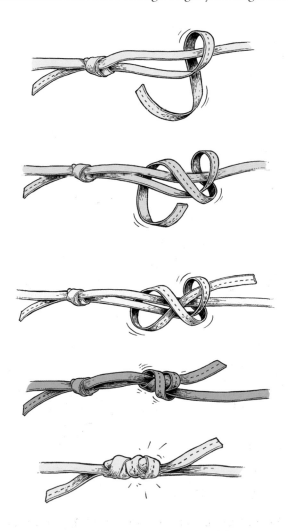

Double fisherman's (grapevine) knot.

Connecting the Climber to the Rope

For decades, climbers tied the rope directly around their waists. It was a simpler era, and climbers also avoided taking falls. The main disadvantage with the bowline-on-a-coil, the standard knot used years ago for tying in, is that when weighted or fallen on, it cut into a climber's vitals or worked up the rib cage like so many pickaxes. Other disadvantages: The knot uses a lot of rope, is a hindrance on long pitches, and cannot, by definition, be used if there

is a need to rappel or anchor to the cliff independently of the rope. Particularly as falling became an accepted side of the sport, and with the advent of tubular webbing and sewn harnesses, the bowline-on-a-coil became obsolete and is almost never seen. Still, it is absolutely secure and works dependably in a pinch. For those reasons alone, it is essential to know for emergency situations. But in most circumstances a much better option is the figure eight follow-through (see sidebar on page 102).

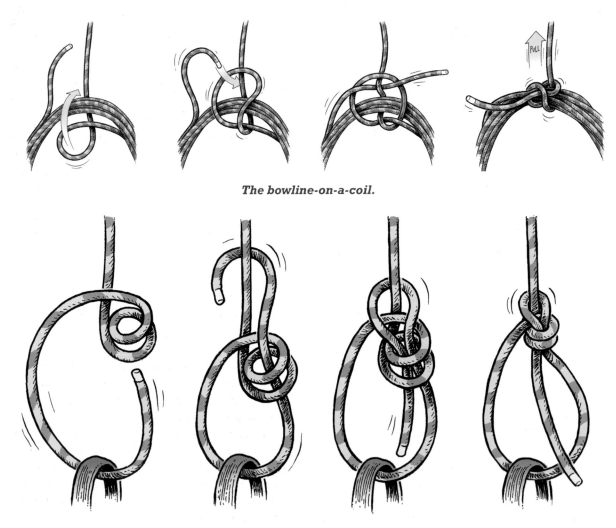

The bowline-on-a-coil.

The double bowline.

Bowline-on-a-coil with a backup knot for added safety.

Swami Belt

A swami belt consists of four or five turns of wide webbing around the waist, secured with a ring bend. Like the bowline-on-a-coil, the swami has for thirty years been supplanted by the modern harness, and its only viable use today is in an emergency or when you choose to go superlight on, say, an easy alpine route. Either way, you'll need to know how to tie a swami belt.

The wraps should be snug but not constricting. It takes some practice to tie the ring bend while keeping the swami snug. A loose swami belt is hazardous, as it can creep up your torso, inhibiting breathing and doing the pickax number on the ribs. The basic swami was originally constructed from

1-inch webbing, but as soon as 2-inch webbing became available (circa 1974), everyone switched over to the wider, stronger, and more comfortable webbing. Tie the ring bend with a generous tail—plenty of extra webbing beyond the knot. Once tied, slide the knot around your back, occasionally inspecting it for peace of mind. Falling on a swami or simple bowline-on-a-coil is not necessarily as uncomfortable as it may sound; with the tightening rope, the swami pulls up snugly underneath the rib cage. Hanging for very long on a simple swami is distinctly uncomfortable—even dangerous—and is a poor and perilous substitute for the comfort and safety of a sewn harness.

Clearly, the swami belt has no place in today's

Tying In

There are several knots suitable for connecting the end of the rope to the harness, but over the years, from Bulgaria to Baton Rouge, the figure eight follow-through (or more commonly, double figure eight) has become the industry standard. And for good reason. The figure eight has one of the highest strengths of all climbing knots, it does not have a tendency to come untied, and it is easy to visually inspect. Like the majority of knots used in climbing (there are only about six primary knots, and another ten or so specialty or trick knots), the double figure eight is a cinch knot: The tighter you pull, the tighter the knot cinches on itself. Like all knots, the figure eight follow-through must be double-checked before relying on it. If you later decide to go with another knot, do so only after you've mastered the double figure eight.

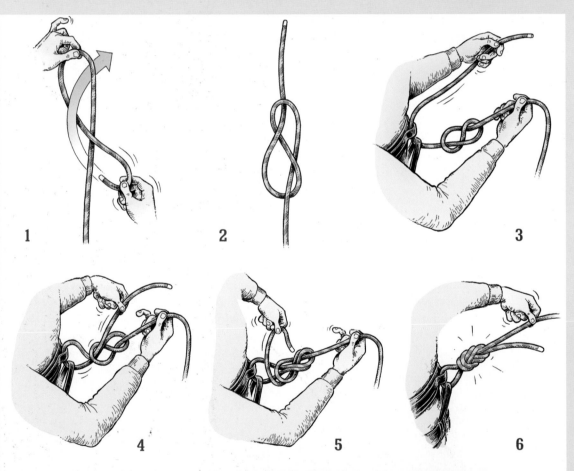

1   **2**   **3**

4   **5**   **6**

The standard tie-in is the figure eight follow-through. Be sure to loop the rope around both the waist belt and the sling that bridges between the leg loops. You can use the remaining tail to tie a backup.

climbing world as anything but a stopgap device. Modern harnesses are superior in every way, save strength (several wraps of 2-inch tubular webbing is good to beyond 20,000 pounds!). As an emergency measure, however, a swami is viable. I climbed more than twenty big walls with nothing more than a swami. If the angle is steep or overhanging, you'll need to fashion a pair of makeshift leg loops out of 1-inch-wide runners. You can only free hang from a swami for about twenty minutes, max, before passing out.

Harnesses

Anyone who plans to climb regularly must invest in a quality, properly fitting sewn harness. A harness features a waist strap and leg loops that are sewn into one unit. Present-day harnesses are featherweight, stronger than necessary (when in proper working shape), and fit so well it's hard to remember you even have one on. There are dozens to choose from, and with a little shopping it's easy to find the right one. Most manufacturers make several models—for alpine climbing, general rock climbing, and sport climbing; the latter two styles are the lightest and most comfortable.

A good fit is critical to the performance of a harness, but it might be difficult if your physique is even a little off the norm (although manufacturers currently make harnesses specifically for men, women, and children). You might have to try on several to get the right one. A harness is a very personal, specialized piece of gear, so general craftsmanship should reflect this.

Gear-racking loops are necessary, but if possible, avoid adjustable harnesses, which are often overbuilt and feature superfluous buckles and doodads. Adjustable harnesses are primarily used as rental rigs in climbing gyms, where one harness can be adjusted to fit a variety of physiques. If you're going to buy a harness, get one that perfectly fits you, not one that you must adjust to acquire that glove fit.

Many harnesses have individual methods of threading the rope through them for the best tie-in

Sewn harness without adjustable leg loops.

Harness with adjustable leg loops.

Dwight Brooks free climbing using a swami belt on the Lost Arrow Tip (5.12b), Yosemite, 1984.

Many harnesses require some special buckling procedure in order for them to be secure, perhaps similar to the double pass-through illustrated here.

knot. Likewise, most harnesses have some safety procedures that, if neglected, render the harness potentially dangerous—a double pass-through buckle, for example. Read the instructions carefully, follow them to the letter, and always double-check your harness setup before you leave the ground.

One other issue: bladder relief. Most harnesses are pretty free in the front—aside from the tie-in knot—and a male's plumbing can usually navigate these obstacles, even on a wall. For women, special harnesses are available where the leg loops can drop out while the waist belt stays fastened.

Another type of harness—the chest harness—bears mentioning, though in more than three decades of climbing, I have never seen anyone but kids using one, in either sport climbing or rescue work.

Carabiners

Also known as biners (*bean-ers*), a carabiner is an aluminum alloy snap link used to connect various pieces of the climbing chain. Biners come in three basic designs: oval, D, and asymmetrical D. The D and asymmetrical D have the advantage of greater strength, they open easier when weighted (important in artificial climbing), and the rope flows easier through them. Many climbers always position any D or asymmetrical D biner so the gate opens down and away from the rock. That way, the rope feeds through the bigger end. The oval can be positioned with gate up or down, but it's easier to clip the rope in if the gate opens down. Ovals are becoming less and less prominent, but they are still superior for racking wired tapers and are favored by some aid climbers.

Many popular brands of quickdraws are sold as composite units, with two biners and a connecting draw. Another popular innovation is a biner that has dispensed with the solid gate and replaced it with a stiff wire-like gate. This technology was fleeced from industry and has proven a boon as a lightweight, easy-to-clip alternative to the standard, solid-gate models. Sometimes during a fall or when the gate is quickly loaded and unloaded, the gate on a standard biner can "flutter" and possibly open, but wire gate biners supposedly eliminate this remote possibility.

Spikes are pointed flakes or blocks that are usually, but not always, part of the main wall. On well-traveled routes, most of the loose rock has already been stripped away by previous parties, but don't bank on it. The adage is: Never trust anything outright. Always assume it's poor, test it with caution, and only use it when you're convinced it's good. Guides at trad areas report that many accidents are the result of beginners aggressively grabbing loose rock features without first cautiously testing them. Assume such features are poor.

A boss is a rounded spike or knob; a chickenhead is a knob that often resembles a protruding mushroom; and a bollard is a hummock of rock. The bigger they are, the more probable it is that they are sound—but not always. Depending on the shape of the knob, the hardest part might be figuring out how to tie it off. The more rounded, the less secure. The slipknot is usually helpful here.

Approach all chickenheads with wariness. They usually consist of a mineral or rock type that is more resistant to weathering than the underlying stone. Carefully inspect the base of all chickenheads because many are shot through with thin cracks. Thump them gently, then harder. I've had more than a few chickenheads come off in my hand, and several have popped the moment I stepped on them.

Common sense and skepticism are your best weapons when dealing with all natural features.

Big block slung with double rope loop.

Girth-hitched block.

Whatever the rock feature:

- Look out for sharp edges.

- Test the security of the feature by thumping it with the heel of your hand. Anything that wiggles or sounds hollow is suspect.

- Look for surrounding cracks.

- Tie off as close to the main wall as possible, to reduce leverage.

- Tie off with runners, slipknotting if the form is rounded.

A flake slung with a double sling. If the direction of pull changes much from straight down, this sling might slide off the flake.

Single sling on the tip of a flake. Better than nothing, though probably not by much.

A selection of straight tapers (background), micro-tapers (foreground), and a wired Hexentric (lower right), circa 1981. These days most tapers are curved and color coded.

chockstones in the cracks. This led to placing chock-stones in the cracks and stringing runners over them. Next came machine nuts (found along the railroad tracks below the British crags), through which rope was slung. Sometime in the 1960s, someone began making nuts particularly for rock climbing. As mentioned, the first nuts were crude and had limited applications, but once the wide use of nuts caught on around 1970, the designs steadily improved to where now, in most cases, nuts can provide better anchors than driven pitons ever could.

When weighted, a nut will lodge in the narrowing slot in which it is placed. Obviously, a nut is placed with a certain direction of pull in mind, usually straight down. In some instances, a nut is placed so the direction of pull is straight out, or even straight up (explained later in this chapter). Whatever the placement, the loop of sling or cable issuing from the nut can be considered an arrow that,

when extended from the nut, clearly shows where the direction of pull should be.

Developing good hardware-placing skills is crucial for safe climbing and requires diligent practice; the best way to start is to get a grasp of the material from a book like this, practice placing pro low to the ground (preferably with your feet on the ground), and then take an anchor-building seminar from a qualified guide. Such a multipronged approach increases the odds that the material will thoroughly be understood, and that it will stick.

The family of climbing nuts can be split into two categories—passive nuts, which emphasize simplicity by having no moving parts, and active nuts (spring-loaded camming devices, SLCDs, or "cams"), which achieve a high degree of utility through their geometry and moving parts. Passive nuts can be further divided into two categories: tapers and all the rest. Passive nuts wedge into constrictions inside cracks, with the notable exception of Tricams, a sometimes fussy piece of specialty gear—loved by a few, never used by all the rest— that can wedge in a constriction or cam in a parallel-sided crack. The greatest asset of passive nuts is their simplicity. They are light, compact, inexpensive, and easy to evaluate when placed.

Tapers

Tapers are basically six-sided aluminum wedges. Smaller tapers also come in brass and steel. They are light and fairly cheap. Present-day tapers are fitted with a thin, swaged wire cable. There are three basic variations on the original straight taper: the curved taper, the offset taper, and the micro brass or steel taper. In addition, designers have altered the sides of these various tapers. The variations are many, but all are meant to be slotted in a crack whose contours approach the symmetry of the nut, with the cable or sling pointing in the anticipated direction of pull. Most manufacturers have discontinued making the straight taper in anything but the smallest sizes, having found that the curved model is more stable when placed.

Tapers often are the easiest nuts to place because their design is the most basic. The crack must pinch off in the direction of loading—usually down—to accommodate the taper. Simply try to place the taper that best corresponds to the geometry of the

Functional art. This color-coded wired Black Diamond Stopper is a modern curved taper.

crack where it pinches (the "bottleneck"). Ideally you want a match-fit, in which the contours of the crack are precisely those of the taper. Imagine a pea in a pod. Best of all is when the crack pinches somewhat in the outward direction as well. Here the contour of the rock will resist a slight outward tug that could be created by a falling leader, or a

Placing Passive Gear

- Developing efficient hardware-placing skills is an applied craft requiring diligent practice.
- Practice placing pro (protection) low to the ground, where the risk is zero.
- Cleanly aid climb a steep 5.10 crack to see how your placements respond under full body weight.
- Study how more experienced climbers place pro and fashion anchors.
- Ask questions whenever you encounter a setup you don't understand.
- Take an anchor-building seminar from a qualified instructor.

When the rock matches the symmetry of the taper, as it does here, the nut is often bomber. With plenty of surface area contacting the rock, this is an ideal nut placement.

Poor placement. The right side has only about 50 percent surface contact. It might hold body weight but should not be trusted to hold a fall.

belayer shifting about to rubberneck the leader. The ideal placement may be elusive, but good placements are generally plentiful.

The more surface area you contact between the rock and the nut, the better. Sometimes, you will have to slot a nut deep in a strangely formed, flaring crack, but if you have a choice, place the nut where you can see exactly what it is set on. With straight tapers you go after placements where the nut fits like it was milled just for that slot—the proverbial match-fit. Always go with the bigger taper whenever possible. The cable is probably stronger, and the larger nut will afford more surface area contact and more security. But the principal concern is the placement—be sure the taper fits the crack.

In shallow or flaring cracks, even pros have to tinker around to find the best placement, and this is where endwise placements are most often used. An endwise placement offers less surface-area contact with the rock, but go with it if the fit is superior. You might have to, because some cracks are too shallow to accept a normal placement. At times

you will have to try various tapers to find one that will fit at all, then have to jockey the nut around to locate the best placement, or any placement. On some climbs the hardest part is placing the gear.

Curved tapers are a bit trickier because they present options that straight tapers never did. The actual curve is slight—just a few degrees—and normal placement usually attains an adequately flush fit on the face sides. You should always try to get this match-fit type of placement, but accept the fact that sometimes you cannot.

A straight taper works much like a fist jam in a constriction, where both sides of the fist are lodged between the walls of the crack. A curved taper sets in the crack like a hand jam, with three points of contact; a downward pull achieves a rocker effect that further locks the nut in place. There are several things to understand about curved taper design.

(The following discussion can best be understood if you have a curved taper on hand for reference.)

Like a banana, you can place a curved taper two

ways on the tabletop, so it curves one way or the other. You have a "left" and "right" option simply by flipping the taper over. In a V-slot, or uniform constriction, the curved taper is placed the same way as a straight one, and the curved design plays no meaningful role. Most any nut will do in a true bottleneck. If a bottleneck or obvious constriction is unavailable,

search out that section of crack that best corresponds with the taper's curve, and place it left or right as necessary for the best fit.

When the crack is truly even-sided, you have to utilize the camming action of the nut. The crack still has to constrict, if only slightly, and you must go after that place where you can get a good three-

Rules for Setting Safe Tapers

- The primary rule is that no rock climbing anchor is 100 percent reliable. Appropriate backups are essential for secure climbing.

- If you haven't used a certain type of chock before, practice (extensively) placing it on the ground before trusting it out in the field.

- Before setting a chock, look around to find a strong, quick placement, considering all possible directions of loading. Always go for the easiest, most obvious placement.

- Try to slot nuts in constrictions where, in order to ever pull through, the nut would be reduced to something as thin as beer can aluminum. Try to get the most surface area of the taper in contact with the rock.

- Always visually inspect the placement. If the situation requires, set the piece with a tug.

- Any climbing protection is only as strong as the rock it contacts. Manufacturers report that nuts pull out under frighteningly small loads during testing in poor-quality rock. Chocks create a large outward force when holding a fall. Avoid setting anchors behind a shaky flake or block rather than risk pulling it down if you peel off—it's always best to fall alone!

- Try to place the gear in its primary position. A taper can be placed endwise, but usually it is not as reliable as one placed the primary way.

- Be especially careful not to dislodge the taper with your body, rack, or rope after you have placed it—especially as you climb past.

- If you have a choice, go with the bigger taper, as it is generally more secure, with more surface area contacting the rock.

- Whenever possible, set the taper where the crack not only pinches off in the downward direction, but also in the outward direction.

- No climbing gear lasts forever. Inspect your gear frequently. Retire hardware if you observe cracks or other defects in the metal, or if the cable becomes kinked.

Well-set endwise taper placement. Taper fits the symmetry of the crack with maximum surface contact.

Endwise taper placement. Too much of this taper is not contacting the rock. Poor.

point setting—a fix on the top and bottom of the concave side, and a firm lock on the convex side. You may have to try both left and right placements before you achieve the best fit. The security of the nut, however, usually is determined by how much and how well the convex face is set. If the concave side has a decent two-point attitude, if much of the convex side is set snugly, and if the rock below the point of contact narrows even slightly, the placement is likely sound. If the convex side is barely catching, or if its point of contact is either high or low, the nut is almost certainly marginal. Often you can simply flip the nut around and get a better placement. If this doesn't work, try another type of nut.

Beware that the crack doesn't open up on the inside, where the chock could pull through and slip out below like so much sand through an hourglass. In horizontal cracks, try to find where the crack opens in the back to accept a taper, but pinches off at the lip to hold it securely. Otherwise, place two tapers in opposition (discussed later in this chapter). Tugging on a precarious nut may set it and improve its stability, but yanking every piece will drive your partners mad as they curse and dangle from their fingertips, trying to remove your jammed gear. That much said, one of the most common novice mistakes is to not properly set nuts and have them rattle out as the climber claws past.

The business of placing nuts in horizontal cracks requires special attention. For now, understand that nuts are routinely placed this way, but for various reasons, horizontal placements, alone and in groups, present special challenges and require all the judgment we can muster. Several recent anchor failures, which killed outright all involved, were owing to failed nuts in horizontal cracks.

Offset Tapers

These nuts are tapered in two directions, creating a shape that improves security in flared cracks. The best and perhaps only way to understand this design is to get an offset taper and look at it. You'll find that one edge is thicker than the other—or "offset." Offsets are ideal for flaring cracks that narrow toward the back—like pin scars—where a normal taper would find scant purchase. Be warned, however, that though the offset will work well when properly set, unless you've got most of the surface area firmly locked, offsets can pop unexpectedly. Offsets have a very limited place in the protection game—virtually no one carries them for normal free climbing—and are likely to remain a specialty item rarely used in normal climbing situations.

DMM Alloy Offset in use. Here the nut was placed so the shape of the taper matched the shape of the crack (flaring outward in this case).

DMM (formally HB) Offset Taper.

Micro-Tapers (Micro-Nuts)

The limitations of micro-nuts are matters of strength—the strength of the cable, of the actual nut, and of the rock in which the micro is placed. Cables on the puniest micros are rarely good beyond 500 pounds, if that much. Most manufacturers don't recommend micros for free climbing, as even a short fall can snap the cables. But sizes beyond the smallest featuring silver-soldered cables are good beyond 1,500 pounds and are adequate to survive small to moderate falls. The cables are fragile, however; frays and kinks denote weakening and are sure indicators that the nut should be retired. The cables are particularly prone to fray just beneath the body of the nut, a consequence of the wrenching they take when cleaning them after a climb. Place and remove them gently if you want them to last.

A couple things to remember when placing micros: Anything but a match-fit, where most all of the nut's surface area is flush to the rock, should be considered marginal. The four sides of some micros are nearly symmetrical. For those that are not, endwise placements should be slotted with a prayer. The smaller micros are used almost exclusively for aid or artificial climbing. Whenever a small micro is used on a free climb, it's always a provisional

Black Diamond brass micro-taper.

nut, something to get you to the next good placement—the sooner, the better. There are well-established accounts of micros holding good-size free-climbing falls, but the reason these accounts live on is because they are so improbable, or more likely, made up.

Tips for Using Micro-Nuts

- The clearances of every micro are quite small, so only ideal placements are secure.

- Owing to the small surface area, micros are reliable only in good rock.

- Lateral forces easily pivot micros out of cracks; always slot the micro directly in the line of pull. This also prevents tweaking the cable.

- Always extend the placement with a quickdraw. Rope drag can easily displace the micro.

- Avoid placements where the wire is running over an edge.

- Avoid jerking the micro too hard, either when setting or removing it, lest you prematurely bend, weaken, or even break the wire.

Perfect placement of a micro-taper.

This endwise micro-taper placement looks solid.

All the Rest

Tapers are designed specifically for small cracks and are indispensable for cracks up to about ¾ inch wide. The smallest are about ⅛ inch thick, the largest about 1¼ inch thick. Beyond these dimensions, the design becomes prohibitively heavy, and other designs—all the rest—take over. In real-world climbing, most climbers only use tapers in the smaller sizes and go with camming devices on everything else. The exception is in areas featuring seamy, incipient cracks too shallow for cams, and where tapers placed endwise are the only pro available.

Tricams

Aside from at places like the Gunks, in upstate New York, and a smattering of other areas (mostly in the southeastern United States) featuring a lot of seamy horizontal cracks and shallow pockets, Tricams are seldom seen or used these days. The beauty of the Tricam is its ability to work in both parallel and constricting cracks, and its uncanny knack for fitting where nothing else can. The Tricam design is meant to create a stable tripod with the two parallel camming rails flat against one side of the crack, and the fulcrum or "stinger" point contacting the opposite side, preferably in a dimple or small feature in the stone.

For placement in parallel-sided cracks, Camp USA, who took over manufacture of Tricams from Lowe Alpine, advises: "Cock the Tricam by running the sling down the cam channel. Look for a rugosity of some sort on which to position the fulcrum point. [This is not absolutely necessary, but often makes the placement more secure.] Give a good jerk on the sling to set the nut."

Rock hardness and crack taper and flare will affect the security of a given placement. If the placement is prone to sideways or outward pull, sling the Tricam or extend it with a quickdraw. Practice is necessary to judiciously place the Tricam with one hand; it is almost impossible to remove it

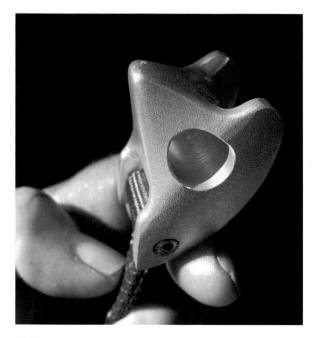

Tricam

A second Tricam orientation uses the camming action of the nut to create a secure placement.

Using Tricams requires familiarity. Here the piece is placed like a traditional taper.

with one hand, however. Most climbers consider the unit a somewhat screwy specialty item, though as mentioned, on rock heavily featured with horizontal, seamy cracks or pockets and huecos—and for other weird, one-off placements—a Tricam might be the only pro you can get.

Even Tricam fans generally only carry the three smallest sizes, featuring white, black, or pink slings. One reader put it well: "You can get some truly bizarre yet bomber placements with them in pockets and horizontal seams. Nice and light for alpine routes, where you get mostly good stances. I'm not selling mine, but they don't get to come along very often."

Hexes

Says Black Diamond Equipment: "Classic, simple, lightweight, functional pro, Hexes shine in rapidly-widening cracks where cams might walk out. With a subtly asymmetrical cross-section, flat sides and slight end-wise taper, they offer three different

Black Diamond Hex, color-coded by size.

Hex set in a bottleneck. Bomber.

widths when turned on their axes and another when placed end-wise. Easy to rack and place in bottlenecks, Hexes come equipped with durable, galvanized steel cables."

Since Chouinard Equipment (now Black Diamond Equipment) introduced them in 1971, hexes have steadily evolved. Several companies produce their own version of the basic design, with names like Rockcentrics, Curved Hexes, etc. They all work the same way and cover the same dimensions (crack size).

Since the introduction of camming devices, hexes have almost disappeared. For sure, hexes remain old-school protection; they were called "obsolentrics" as far back as the early 1980s. And yet for the true bottleneck placement, a bomber hex is still the strongest nut in town. Not one has ever broken in use. They are relatively inexpensive and sometimes can find better purchase than the high-tech camming devices that have largely replaced them. They are usually lighter than the

This solid placement accomplishes some camming torque when weighted downward.

same-size camming unit and are most often taken on backcountry and alpine climbs—or on any climbs—where there is a chance of gear getting left behind. Most manufacturers offer hexes in five sizes.

Because the sides of a hex (both regular and curved models) are angled similar to the opposing faces of a taper, you generally can place them using the same rules of thumb that apply to tapers. You want that match-fit, in which as much surface area as possible is flush on the stone. With four possible placement angles, chances are one of these attitudes is going to work if the crack constricts at all. When the crack is especially uniform, the hex works best through the camming action on the convex side. In those rare cracks that are perfectly parallel-sided, you're hexed and have to go with camming devices.

For big adventure climbs, two or three hexes are sometimes helpful. This allows you to build a belay anchor around a hex in a bottleneck (if such a placement is available, as it usually is), and an anchor like this is often strong as Gibraltar. Hexes are especially welcome in junk rock, where a camming device can sheer away the surface bad rock and blow out of the crack.

Big Bros

The Trango Big Bro is a spring-loaded, telescoping cylinder of 6061 aluminum for use in wide cracks. Its minimum breaking strength is over 3,200 pounds. Six color-coded sizes provide an expansion range from 2.7 to 18.4 inches. The Big Bro is virtually the only mode of protection for cracks

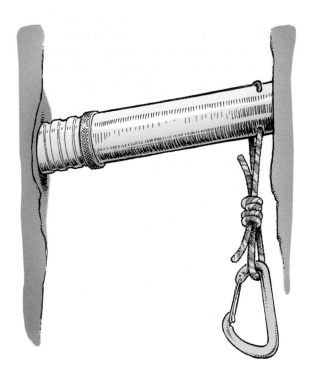

The Big Bro is available in six sizes to fit cracks up to 18.4 inches.

bigger than 6.5 inches. Though it takes some preliminary fiddling to get the knack of placing a Big Bro quickly and correctly, each unit comes with a pamphlet on use, and a climber can get the hang of it in a matter of minutes. The only significant drawback is that Big Bros are worthless in flaring cracks, and need two parallel-sided rock planes to achieve reliable purchase.

Aid It

One of the best ways to understand how good, or bad, your placements are is to grab a big rack of nuts and aid climb a popular 5.10 splitter crack (make sure it's a steep one). If you don't know how to aid climb, go with somebody who does. It is one thing to practice slotting nuts and eyeballing them on the ground, but the real learning begins once you start loading the same placements. The exercise is self-evident the moment you put your weight on the nut.

A set of Big Bros will set you back about $500, but under the right circumstances (parallel-sided cracks), they work like magic, and the alternative is nearly always no protection at all. The #2 Big Bro alone provides nearly the same expansion range as an entire set of the old Chouinard tube chocks, and the #4 has a greater range than a whole set of traditional cams.

Removing Passive Nuts

To remove passive nuts, first try a gentle approach, wiggling the piece out the way it went in. If a taper is stuck, you might try a slight upward tug. But remember, jerking in any direction other than straight down from the bottom of the nut (which you rarely, if ever, do to remove or "clean" passive pro) may kink or even break strands of the cable, resulting in hateful "wild hairs," little filaments of sharp cable that can and will prick your chafed fingers like porcupine quills.

If the piece still won't come out, try loosening it with increasingly harder nudges from a nut tool, a standard item on many climbers' racks. If a taper is apparently stuck fast, place the end of a nut tool against the wedge itself, and tap the other end of the tool with a large nut, fist-size rock, or other object. If the piece still won't come free, better to leave it before you completely trash the cable, so it will be of use to future parties.

Oppositional Nuts

Imagine yourself climbing up a thin flake, but presently you must traverse off right. You find a nut placement at the top of the flake, but see straightaway that the traverse will put a sideways pull (to the right) on the nut, which is slotted for downward pull. In short, the sideways pull could jerk the nut right out, no matter how many runners

Removing a taper with a nut tool.

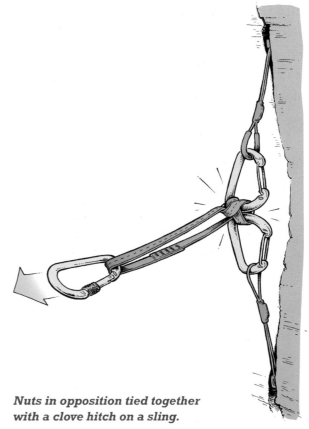

Nuts in opposition tied together with a clove hitch on a sling.

or quickdraws you attach to it. And a camming unit (explained shortly) won't fit the crack. The normal solution is to place an up-slotted nut and lash it tight to the down-slotted, load-bearing nut. The up-slotted nut keeps steady tension on the down-slotted nut, keeping both securely lodged and providing a multidirectional setup. The hardest part of this operation is almost always attaching the up-slotted "keeper" nut to the other one, while still hanging onto the holds.

Rigging Oppositional Nuts

Opposition can be rigged in vertical, horizontal, or even diagonal cracks. Essentially four situations can arise in establishing opposition:

1. You can't find adequate placements at the right distance, and the nuts are so close together that they can't hold each other taut. In this case the best you can do is clip both the nuts together with a carabiner. When possible, use two carabiners with gates opposed, because of the dangerous triaxial loading on the carabiners caused by this arrangement. Each of the placements must be fairly stable, as no real tension will be placed on the nuts to hold them tightly in place.
2. The ideal situation: The nuts are at the right distance from each other, so they provide natural tautness when cinched with two clove hitches on a ⁹⁄₁₆-inch or ⅝-inch sewn sling. After rigging this setup, clip into the sewn loop or one of the pieces, whatever best suits the overall anchor setup.
3. The nuts are very secure and don't need to be held taut (rare), so the easiest solution is to simply clip both pieces into the same sling to create a multidirectional anchor. It might be best to arrange the sling to equalize the load with a sliding X (described in Chapter 5).
4. The available nut placements are too far apart, so the pieces must be held together with clove hitches in a longer section of cordage or a sling.

This works, but make sure you analyze the setup well, and crank those clove hitches tight so the nuts hold each other in place.

There are many other possible configurations for opposing nuts—far too many to run down here. The important thing is to understand the few rules of thumb we have laid down: opposition, tautness, and adjusting the length of slings. Exactly how you rig any anchor is always case dependent.

Horizontal Opposition

For a nut placed in a horizontal crack to be any good, it must be capable of withstanding some downward pull on the cable or sling, which will result in an outward pull on the nut. Generally, the loading will be straight out on a nut placed in a horizontal crack. Therefore, some part of the crack must taper at the lip, allowing you to wiggle a nut into place, set it with a yank, and hope it doesn't shift around and work loose from rope drag. It's often hard to clean these types of placements.

When the crack does not taper at the lip, one option is to place oppositional nuts. This setup appears much more in climbing books and articles than it does in the field, however, because unless you have two ideal slots closely positioned, it's exceedingly tricky (and typically time-consuming) to rig horizontally opposed nuts that are worth the hassle. The advent of camming devices has greatly reduced the need to consider horizontal oppositional nuts, but has not eliminated the technique altogether (in quirky circumstances). In over thirty years on the rock, I haven't placed horizontally opposed nuts more than a few times, and never in an anchor array.

Whatever the setup, horizontally opposed nuts are only as good as the weakest nut. Ultimately, the only way to be sure is to test them with as violent a tug as is prudent, which, in fact, is but a mere fraction of the forces exerted by a fall. However well we explain things here, placing horizontally

Rigging oppositional nuts horizontally using clove hitches.

opposed nuts takes a lot of practice. You're off to a reasonable start, provided you understand and heed the basics.

Spring-Loaded Camming Devices (SLCDs)

The only way to get a clear mental image of an SLCD is to get one and start pulling on the trigger. Currently SLCDs—commonly called cams, or camming devices—are made by many companies, each with slightly different features. The similarities are far greater than the differences in design; all involve a stem, or two, and cam lobes. Popular brands include Black Diamond Camalots, Wild Country Friends, Metolius Power Cams, DMM 4CUs, Trango FlexCams, and CCH Aliens.

Most cams are shaped similar to a capital T. The top (horizontal) part of the T features a solid axle on which are arranged two, three, or four opposing teardrop-shaped lobes. The vertical, lengthwise part of the T is the stem (there are both rigid and flexible-stemmed cams), featuring a triggering device that allows you to adjust the span of the spring-loaded lobes. Each unit has a minimum and maximum degree of latitude, and each is adjustable (via the trigger) within those parameters. With a full selection of cams (including Wild Country's Zero Cams, the Z1), you have a rack that can be micro-adjusted to perfectly fit most any size crack from about $^{13}\!/_{64}$ inch to 6½ inches. All popular cams have color-coded slings, but since each company uses a different color for a given size, you're left

Metolius Power Cam, with color-coded dots to assess cam placement.

Black Diamond Camalot.

Black Diamond Camalot with cams at mid-range. Solid placement.

This Camalot fits into this pocket like a pea in a pod. All four cams have flush surface contact, and the range of retraction is about 50 percent.

to memorize your gear to know sizes at a glance. Once you grasp the basic principles, cams are perhaps the simplest, most adaptive, and easily the most expensive pieces of equipment on your rack.

Basically, cams work by translating a downward/outward pull to an even larger force against the walls of the crack. That is, a fall on a camming device pulls on the stem, which in turn pulls on the axle(s), forcing the spring-loaded cams to spread farther apart, converting the pulling force along the stem of the unit into outward pressure as the lobes dig into the rock. Get one and look at it, and all will become clear.

The chief advantage of cams is the speed and relative ease of placing them. The majority of cam placements are sound and straightforward, but for those tricky placements, it is essential you know their limitations, as well as some general rules of thumb that apply to all camming units.

Three or Four Cams, Flexible or Rigid Stems?

Most cams are four- and three-cam units; two-cam units are also available but are used far less. Four-cam units have two sets of opposing lobes, or cams, situated along the axle, whereas three-cam units (TCUs) feature a single middle cam opposing the two outside cams. Four cams provide the best strength and stability, while three-cam units reduce the unit's profile to allow placement in shallow cracks.

Any camming device is "flexible" if the stem is not rigid. Flexible stems are fashioned from thick, semi-stiff cable. There are several reasons why flexible camming devices were invented, and why they have more or less supplanted the rigid-stem units. First and foremost, a rigid stem is a liability in pockets and in horizontal, diagonal, or shallow placements. When odd angles or torque is involved, a fall can wrench the unit in strange ways, bending

Three- and four-cam units.

Old-style, rigid-stemmed Friends. These units were state-of-the-art several decades ago, but are rarely used today.

or even breaking (though very rarely) the rigid stem, or—more commonly—ripping the unit from the rock. In thin placements a rigid stem is sometimes thicker than the crack, making placement impossible. Overall, a cable stem gives the unit a thinner profile and greater placement utility.

Flexible-stemmed units generally will work fine in wider cracks, though arguably not as well as rigid units. The issue becomes more involved with flexible units that feature a double stem. Though indeed flexible, they offer more stability than a single-cable stem, but still are less predictable (in terms of loading the cams) than a rigid stem. All told, double-stem units are not designed for shallow, vertical cracks, where the stems of the unit protrude horizontally from the crack. The single flexible stem is much better suited for this and other situations.

In terms of use, differences between rigid- and flexible-stemmed camming devices are obvious. Performance differences are less obvious, and debatable. What's not debatable is that in real-world climbing, most rigid-stem units are quickly becoming museum pieces. All American- and

Always use flexible-stemmed units like this in horizontal cracks. Rigid stems can break over the edge.

British-made SLCDs employ quality materials and craftsmanship, so the relative strength of rigid stems versus flexible stems is often overstated.

As noted, the primary difference is that rigid-stemmed units cannot be placed where the impact of a fall will stress the stem, other than along its vertical axis—for instance, in a horizontal placement where the stem is set over an edge, and where a fall will bend or possibly (though doubtfully) even break it. Wild Country warns against placing its rigid-stemmed Forged Friends in horizontal placements, but offers some suggestions that can make the prospect more acceptable if you have no alternative: First, place the unit as deeply as possible in the crack. Second, if the stem runs over the edge, use a Gunks tie-off, which consists of 5.5mm cord tied through the stem up near the cams.

Finally, Wild Country warns that any friend, rigid- or flexible-stemmed, placed in a vertical shallow (bottoming) crack where it is impossible to align the stem in the direction of anticipated loading "will have its holding power seriously compromised." In other words, a unit placed like this will almost certainly get wrenched from the crack if fallen upon.

Camming devices very rarely break. Most often the unit has simply ripped out of the rock for any number of reasons. The Metolius company contends that "rock strength accounts for what is probably the most common mode of failure in the real world. Even in very hard rock types it is not uncommon for the surface layer of rock to pulverize under the force of the cams, forming a loose layer (like ball bearings), which allows the cams to pull out." Thus, when you read claims of stronger cams, this usually refers to the component parts, and not the unit's effectiveness under the stress of a fall out in the field.

Each cam on every camming device is individually spring-loaded—regardless of the axle configuration, whether it's a three- or four-cam unit, or is equipped with a rigid or flexible stem. The degree of expansion or contraction of one cam is not affected by the position of the other cams. This allows the unit to accommodate size irregularities inside the crack with little loss in stability. Here, when the lobes are deployed at different attitudes, certain things must be remembered to try to ensure sound placement.

The most secure placement is usually when the cams are retracted as far as possible while still leaving 10 to 25 percent unretracted to allow removal. Be careful not to stuff a piece into the tightest placement it can fit, lest you sacrifice a $60 (at least) piece

Know this about flexible camming devices:

- They are less durable than rigid units. Under the impact of a fall, the cables can sometimes kink and/or become permanently deformed.

- The action of the flexible units is less positive because of the inherent flex. This can make placement and removal slightly more difficult, particularly when a climber is tired.

- It is impossible for a flexible cable to load the cams as predictably as a rigid stem does—or so it would seem. Wild Country claims to have overcome this problem on their Technical Friends, using stronger springs and incremental increases in cam-head width that resist rotation as a climber moves past the placement. This, they say, combined with the single axle and frame that supports the stem, ensure the cams are always loaded in the best possible plane of rotation.

of gear. In an irregular-sided crack, maneuver the unit around so the cams are deployed as uniformly as possible. Remember that even moderate rope drag can cause the unit to walk, or move around in a crack. Because a camming unit will often auto-align to accommodate a new direction of pull, some climbers consider them multidirectional. The problem is that rope drag can also auto-align the unit into an unfavorable position. Remember this. In a wavy crack, even meager movement can radically alter the position of the cams and render the placement poor, or even useless.

While Wild Country recommends its cams be placed between 25 to 75 percent retracted (the middle half of the expansion range), Black Diamond suggests 50 to 90 percent retraction for their Camalots, which reflects the difference between a double-axle (Black Diamond is the only one) and single-axle design. Other manufacturers have recommendations specific to their own devices. Read the guidelines that come with the unit.

Dangerous Cam Placements

There are several configurations a camming unit can assume that spell danger—or at least trouble. As mentioned, one of the most troublesome positions is when the cams are fully closed inside the crack. That means no matter how hard you pull on the trigger, you can't suck the cams in any tighter, you can't loosen the unit, and you probably can't get it out. This usually happens when a panicked climber shoves too big a unit into too small a crack. Removal, if possible at all, probably will entail holding someone on tension so both hands are free to spend minutes jerking the unit this way and that. So whenever placing cams, leave some room in the range for removal. Because micro-camming units feature a limited expansion range and must be placed near full retraction or they might pull out, particular care must be taken to avoid getting these units stuck.

Offset cams are another dangerous placement and should always be avoided. This occurs when

one cam is near minimum range, and another near maximum. (Don't confuse the concept of unintentionally offset cams with deliberately manufactured offset cams, which are made for flaring cracks.) Beware of this happening in wavy cracks, when the cams must adjust to extravagant differences in crack size. If such a placement is your only option, try a passive chock. Offset cams can also occur in parallel-sided cracks. Remember, if you split the difference, the cams would be at 50 percent—or optimum range—so it's not a problem of size. Instead, the cams have been forced or wrenched into offsetting positions, which renders the placement worthless, or nearly so. Most all modern SLCDs have cam-stops to prevent the lobes from totally inverting, but the best policy is to consider placements worthless when the cams are radically offset, or nearly inverted.

A third kind of dangerous placement is when you have "tipped out" cams, where the cams are fully, or nearly fully, deployed. No camming device is capable of functioning correctly when the cams are at maximum expansion, except the Black Diamond Camalot, which has the requisite strength but virtually no stability in this position, and is never recommended to be placed this way. Other units are simply too small for these placements. A fall and the unit will either blow out, or the unit will walk to an opening in the crack and become utterly worthless.

As mentioned, the security of a camming unit is only as good as the position of the cams combined with the relative soundness of the rock. When the unit is placed too deep, the trigger is hard to reach and the unit is that much harder to remove, hence the need to place the unit near the outside of the crack, or as near to that as placement allows. In soft desert sandstone, however, it's best to set the SLCD somewhat inside the crack so an impact on the piece won't blow out the edge of the crack.

It is commonly believed that an SLCD will swivel toward the direction of pull, once weighted. In many cases this is true, and the cam then

Too tight. This Camalot's lobes are pulled so tight that removal might be difficult.

Offset cams. One set of cams is retracted to minimum range while the other is near maximum. This placement is prone to "walking" out of the crack.

becomes a multidirectional anchor. The swiveling action will often align the cams for maximum strength and stability. But the fact is, you should avoid letting your protection swivel, because sudden and violent loading may swivel the unit straight out of the crack, especially if the crack is wavy. Take special care to anticipate the direction of pull, and to align the unit accordingly when you place it. Basically—as is the case with all protection that is not hammered into the rock—place the unit with the stem pointing in the anticipated direction of pull, and do whatever is necessary to ensure rope drag won't set the unit to walking inside the crack. Even nominal rope drag can change the unit's position, so virtually all camming units come with sewn slings.

Tipped out cam placement (cams almost fully deployed, caught on the "tips"). Doubtful it would hold a fall.

The Basic Essentials of Placing SLCDs

- Always align the unit with the stem pointing in the anticipated direction of pull.

- To keep the unit from "walking" because of rope drag during a lead, clip a quickdraw into the sewn sling of the unit.

- Try to place the unit near the outside edge of the crack, where you can eyeball the cam lobes to determine their position. This also makes it easier to reach the trigger to clean the device.

- Strive for the ideal placement, with the cams deployed/retracted in the most uniformly parallel section of the crack, so the cams cannot open if the unit walks a bit. Metolius puts color-coded dots on the cams to help with lobe positioning, but with others you'll have to eyeball it. Read and follow the manufacturer's recommendations for cam deployment.

- Use a larger device over a smaller one, but unless you are absolutely desperate, never force too big a unit into too small a hole. Once the cams are rolled to minimum width, removal, if even possible, is grievous.

- Never trust a placement where the cams are nearly "tipped" (the cam lobes almost fully deployed). In such a position there is little room for further expansion, and stability is poor.

- Never place a rigid-stemmed unit so the stem is over a lip. A fall can either bend or break the unit.

- Take some time to experiment with marginal placements on the ground. Clip a sling into the device and apply body weight to discover just how far you can trust it. But remember—body weight testing is far milder than a lead fall!

Placing Cams in Flaring Cracks

Camming devices work in flaring cracks if the rock is sound and the flare is not so radical that the cam lobes cannot attain adequate bite. When a crack nears the critical flare angle, a fall will load the unit in an unstable manner. If the rock is poor as well, the placement will sheer ("track") out. Even in dense granite, the unit will rip out if the flare is too great.

With outward flaring cracks—where the lip of the crack is wider than the depths—jockey the unit around to find that spot where the difference in cam expansion is the least. If the rear cams are rolled tight, and the outside cams nearly tipped, you're looking at sketchy pro. Though two cams actually can hold a fall, the unit tends to pivot when the other cams fail, and this pivoting can dislodge the unit altogether. For tapering cracks—where the crack is wider below the placement—a couple of hours of tinkering with placements on the ground are advisable to fully understand where the critical taper angle starts. The offset cams made by several manufacturers can help attain more secure placements in flaring cracks.

Camalot C4s feature a double axle. The design means the Camalot can cover a significantly larger expansion range than other, comparably sized devices. I will not attempt to describe why this is so. Simply get a unit, fiddle with the movement, and you'll understand the mechanics. The added camming range is also beneficial in flaring cracks, where the disparity of crack width is more pronounced. One drawback of the added range is a slight increase in weight, but technology is making up the difference: The newest, third-generation Camalots are about 20 percent lighter than the previous generation, with only a slight strength decrease in the components of the larger sizes (.75 and up).

Stuck Cam

Once you realize a camming unit might be stuck, be careful how you work with it. Frantic jerking can turn a mildly stuck SLCD into a fixed one. And brute force is a poor removal strategy. Pull hard on the trigger to retract it as far as possible, and try to pull the piece straight out. This may seem obvious, but you wouldn't believe how often a novice has claimed a cam to be hopelessly stuck, only to have an expert remove it in a few seconds. If that doesn't work, look in the crack for an opening to move the unit through, carefully working the unit toward the edge of the crack. Clever and delicate maneuvering is usually required to free the unit. As a last resort, clip a sling to the cord with a carabiner and give it a good jerk. If the first tug or two doesn't free the piece, you're usually hosed. Nut tools can often be used to snag the trigger of a stuck SLCD.

Wild Country offers some specific recommendations for removing stuck cams. First, focus on one pair of cams at a time, and try to feel or see if there is any play. Another solution is to use a pair of bent wires looped around the trigger (as if anyone carries such things on rock climbs). Use the loops to fiddle with the trigger while you tap the end of the stem. Another technique is to move or tap the cams sideways, in the direction the axle is pointing (perpendicular to the stem). Finally, don't give up too early, because most cams can be removed with patience.

It takes a little time using SLCDs to develop a feel for how they work. Placement is easier than removal for most climbers. It took me a month or so of daily use to get good and fast at cleaning cams from cracks, including those thorny placements where the lobes keep snagging on the crack walls. Over time you develop subtle ways of twisting the unit around and applying just the right pushing and tugging action, as well as feathering the trigger, to place and remove them quickly and efficiently. It's mostly rote and acquired feel.

Maintenance

Kolin Powick, quality assurance manager for Black Diamond, says this about Camalot maintenance, advice that applies to all camming units: "Periodically clean your Camalots with warm water and mild detergent. Swish the cam head in this solution while working the trigger bar and keeping the cam sling dry. A stiff bristled brush will help clean around the springs and inside the cam lobes. Don't use corrosive substances like acetone or petroleum-based solvents that can cause irreparable damage to webbing and plastic. Rinse in clean, warm water, shake off excess water, and dry at room temperature. Once dry, apply a graphite- or silicone-based lubricant with a long-stem applicator. Spray in and around the head of each camming device, being careful to NOT get lubricant on the cam lobes themselves. Wipe off any excess lubricant. Avoid using heavy-viscosity oils or greases that attract dirt. Repeat the above steps as often as necessary."

Summary

Almost without exception, all commercially available protection devices are first-rate in terms of design, materials, and construction. Selection, then, is best decided by determining the climbing situations you will most likely encounter, and knowing what gear is specifically suited to them. In other words, buy the gear you're going to use, and what you might use will vary considerably from area to

SOS

SOS is an acronym devised by Tom Cecil of Seneca Rocks Mountain Guides. It stands for solid, orientation, and surface area. Beginners often find it helpful to keep SOS in mind when placing most any protection device, especially tapers.

S (solid) tells the climber to check the rock and make sure it is solid, using a sight, sound, and feel approach. You first look around (sight) and determine that the rock is of good quality and the area is clear of loose flakes and obvious choss. This helps break the tunnel vision many beginners experience when first learning to place gear. To determine the "sound" aspect, you beat on the rock to see if it's hollow, holding a hand on the rock to "feel" for vibration. You have to start with solid rock to get a solid primary placement, and climbers should examine the rock in macro and micro terms. In macro terms, what you're looking for is the proverbial straight-in crack set in massive, solid rock, as opposed to a flake crack, or worse, a crack under a block. Micro structure refers to what's inside the crack. Ideally you want a fairly uniform crack devoid of hollow spots, flakes, grit, or decomposed sections.

O (orientation) means the placement must be aligned to withstand loading in the anticipated direction of pull. In the event of a fall, you cannot count on the gear holding if it changes direction or must adapt to an oblique angle of pull.

S (surface area) ensures the placement is well seated, with sufficient surface area contacting the rock and everything touching the way you want it. For instance, the most common mistake with SLCDs is that climbers don't look closely at the back cams.

area. Even so, if you can get one brand of nut to fit, other brands will probably work just as well. That assumes, of course, that the nut is either American or European. American- and European-made products are, by any engineering or manufacturing standards, far superior to all others.

Gear manufacturers now have the option of having their equipment tested and CE (Conformité Européenne) certified, and all the top brands do so. All of our strength ratings have so far been discussed in pounds, though in recent years the industry has shifted over to rating everything in kiloNewtons (kN). I've converted everything to pounds for easy comprehension (for Americans), but the time is nigh to deal with kNs as the prevailing system.

Ultimately it's not the gear but the person placing it that makes the difference. Considering that forty-five years ago British climbers used to protect their most difficult leads with machine nuts found on the railroad tracks, the present-day climber should respect having such wide choices among what 95 percent of the time is fabulous gear.

An active trad climber needs to consider equipment in terms of an ongoing education, much as an attorney is required to take annual courses to keep his license up to date. The trick here is not to try to learn everything at one exhaustive session every year or so, but to casually keep abreast via the gear reviews featured in climbing magazines and online analyses. Information is like insurance, and with rock climbing, you want as much as you can get.

Fixed Gear: Pitons and Bolts

Fixed gear refers to any piece of equipment that you come across on a climb—a nut, bolt, piton, camming unit (very rare), sling, et al, be it permanently placed, stuck, or left behind for any number of reasons. One rule of thumb about fixed gear: Never trust it outright. Because it's fixed doesn't mean it will hold a fall, only that it's stuck. Fixed nuts tend to be more reliable, but not always. Always check the placement. Since everybody and his brother have tried to clean it, the cable is probably damaged. Fixed micros are almost always abused and worthless. The maxim is: Eyeball and test any and all fixed anchors, and presume they are suspect even if they look good. And back them up whenever possible.

Pitons

Pitons ("pins," or "pegs") are tapered steel devices, usually spike-shaped, that are hammered into cracks to secure anchors. The shapes are many, but every modern piton has an eye through which a carabiner is clipped. A recreational climber today might frequent a popular sport climbing area for five years and never hear the ring of a piton being driven. Chocks, camming devices, and bolts have made pitons unnecessary in almost all cases; but for big artificial climbs, and now and again in free climbing, pitons still have their place. Regardless, the ranks of climbers experienced in placing pitons is shrinking, and the number of accidents as a result of misplaced trust in fixed piton anchors shows the need for developing pitoning skills.

As mentioned earlier, prior to World War II pitons were made of malleable soft iron so they could conform to the crack. Even one placement would maul their shape, and they were usually left in situ, or "fixed," since removal would usually destroy them. You might very occasionally run across a soft steel ring-angle—a pin of channel design with a welded ring—if you frequent classic old trad climbs. Obviously these pins are going on half a century old, and in addition to being of very questionable security, the welded ring design may fail at relatively low loads. There really is no practical way to test such pitons, so it's best to assume them to be worthless.

In 1946, Swiss expatriate John Salathe hand-tooled pegs from Model-T axle stock for the first ascent of Lost Arrow Spire in Yosemite Valley.

Pin scars in a Yosemite crack might make convenient finger jams, but altering the rock in such an ugly manner should always be avoided when possible.

Pitons, left to right: Lost Arrow, angle, Leeper Z, knifeblade.

Knifeblade and RURP.

Tradition says these Salathe pins were the first ever made from hard steel. In the 1950s, Chuck Wilts invented the "knifeblade," a wafer-thin peg he fashioned from chrome molybdenum (chrome-moly) steel. Like Salathe's, these hard steel pins could withstand repeated placement and removal, enabling climbers to scale multiday climbs and carry a limited selection of pins, rather than lugging a pack full of soft iron.

Yvon Chouinard began manufacturing chrome-moly pitons in his mom's backyard in the late 1950s. He quickly expanded, and by the early 1960s any climber could purchase state-of-the-art chrome-moly pitons. That the first ascent of Yosemite's mightiest walls corresponded with the availability of good pitons was no fluke. While every other facet of climbing technology has steadily evolved, pitons have changed little in the last forty-five years—either in design or construction. Chouinard had it down by 1960.

Various European manufacturers still market pitons, but in the United States, what was Chouinard Equipment—now Black Diamond—has totally locked this limited market and is the only company making them on any kind of scale. Black Diamond Equipment makes pitons in four different shapes. Each model is either stamped or forged of alloy steel, and for better or worse, all are far more enduring than the hardest granite or limestone.

There are four basic piton designs. Knifeblades (called Bugaboos in the larger sizes) come in six sizes, from ⅛ to ³⁄₁₆ inch in width, and from 3 to 4⅞ inches in length. Precision grinding ensures a uniform taper. Lost Arrows (aka horizontals) come in eight sizes, from ⁵⁄₃₂ to ⁹⁄₃₂ inch in width, and from 1¾ to 4⅝ inches long. Angles come in six sizes, from ½ to 1½ inches. The RURP (Realized Ultimate Reality Piton), a postage stamp–size peg with a thin, ½-inch-long blade, is for aid only. For merely thin cracks, knifeblades usually work better than RURPs, which come into their own in incipient cracks, where their hatchet-like blades can burrow into the rock.

Again, pitons are rarely used in sport climbing. The one exception is climbers making first ascents. It is rare even for them to use pegs, but in the case of a hole or a thin, parallel-sided crack, sometimes only a piton can secure the desired protection, although in most cases nowadays, leading climbers just place bolts where they can't get in good chock protection (dreadfully, sometimes even where they can). To preserve the rock and avoid future climbers having to place the pin, it is always left fixed. Never remove a piton from an established free climb. It's there for a reason.

To adequately judge the security of a fixed piton, however, you must have experience in placing them, and a hammer. Most piton hammers have a forged steel head attached to a wooden handle. Steel- and aluminum-handled piton hammers are also available. The vibrations from hammering travel up your arm; over the course of a big wall (several days), they can deaden your arm; over the course of a career, they can cause pesky elbow and wrist problems (a condition that essentially retired Yosemite legend Royal Robbins). A wooden handle absorbs the vibrations better than a metal handle. Hammers weigh in at around 24 ounces and generally last for many years.

Placing Pitons

First, use a piton that fits the crack and enters about 75 percent of the way in before you start hammering. Both the spine and the two running edges of the peg should have good bite in the crack, and the peg should ring as you drive it home—like the rising ring of a xylophone. Try to bury it to the hilt, but don't overdrive it, or you'll either never get it out or ruin it trying to. In soft rock, particularly desert sandstone, you can virtually create your own placement by blasting an oversize pin into an undersize crack, but it still might come out with your fingers. Piton use in any rock causes such vile scarring that it is always best to use nuts whenever possible.

Set the pin in the crack by hand. Ideally about 75 percent of the pin should fit in the crack before you use the hammer.

Pound it in the rest of the way.

Learning to Drive Iron

The best way to learn piton craft is to grab a handful of pegs, a hammer, and aid slings; go to some junky crag where nobody climbs; and experiment low to the ground. Bang in a few, and stand on them to see just how much or how little various placements will hold. After dinking around for a couple of hours, you'll catch on. There's a barbaric joy in slugging steel into the rock, no question about it. Since pitons are rarely used to protect free climbing anymore, the standard method to acquire piton craft is to venture onto a beginner wall climb. Over the course of a dozen or so pitches, you might place and clean fifty or more pitons, plenty to get a journeyman's feel for the work.

Fixed Pitons

Again, never trust any fixed gear outright. Assuming you have no interest in big walls, have no hammer as you approach a fixed piton belay station, or must rely on fixed pins for lead protection, how do you gauge the security of your anchor? First, inspect the pins. How rusty are they? Do they move? Are they fully driven, or do they hang halfway out of the crack? Are they creaky knife-blades, funky soft-steel European pegs, or beefy Lost Arrows or angles? As with tapers, the bigger the better. Do they cam into a hole in the crack, or will a hard pull likely twist them from their placement? At best, it's still a crapshoot, so back up fixed pins whenever possible.

In years past, pitons were often used for communal anchors at the top of popular climbs. Now pitons are so expensive, they are never left as modern anchors; rather, someone will simply drill a couple bolts. Know that if you come across a fixed piton anchor, it's probably at least twenty-five years old.

Fixed Lost Arrow.

Fixed angle.

Fixed Leeper Z.

Bolts

For more than fifty years, the bolt was the bane of sportsmanlike climbing, though it always played an important role. First ascensionists justified the judicious bolt, but risked much and scared themselves stiff to avoid placing it. In the 1980s, the attitudes of sport climbing changed all that, and presently the majority of the most notorious routes are predominantly, if not entirely, bolt protected. Since bolts play such a leading role in climbing—at all levels—it's best we go into some detail about them.

Bolt History

Before the early 1980s, no company manufactured bolts specifically designed for climbing, leaving folks to rummage through hardware stores for whatever might work as a rock anchor. These bolts were devised as hardware fasteners and construction anchors for concrete, block, brick, and stone. Because there were so many varieties of these bolts, if you should ever climb an old, obscure route in a seldom-visited area, you might clamber upon some curious, seldom-seen, and almost certainly rickety bolts. On well-traveled routes, local activists have generally replaced the old construction items with bomber, made-for-climbing bolts, hangers, and anchor setups.

In the mid-1980s, when sport climbing and rappel bolting took over the U.S. climbing scene, the quality of bolts drastically improved. The modern standard calls for expansion bolts of ⅜ to ½ inch diameter. The Rawl 5-piece and Rawl Stud

Top: Royal Robbins homemade hanger cleaned off **Unchaste, Tahquitz Rock, California, circa 1957.**
Bottom: Star Drive nail and homemade hanger from the **Sling Swing Traverse, Tahquitz, circa 1951.**

Contraction bolts, left to right: ¼ inch, ⁵⁄₁₆ inch, ³⁄₈ inch.

Expansion bolts, left to right: ³⁄₈-inch Fixe Triplex, ³⁄₈-inch Powers, ½-inch Powers.

were the most popular bolts in the United States throughout the eighties and nineties. The Rawl 5-piece is a "pullout"-type bolt that pulls a cone into an expanding sleeve by cranking on the bolt head with a wrench.

The Rawl 5-piece (now sold under the brand name Power-Bolt) is one of the best rock bolts available. It has good strength (7,900 pounds shear strength for the ³⁄₈ inch), is suitable for a variety of rock surfaces, and is relatively foolproof to install. Modest cost, availability, straightforward installation, and general reliability have made the Rawl 5-piece the bolt of choice. Over the last decade Petzl, Fixe, Raumer, and other companies have started making bolts specifically for rock climbing, and the 5-piece Rawl has not only stood the test of time, it seems to be as good as all the others.

We purposefully have neglected the business of how to place bolts. Establishing routes that require bolts traditionally has been, and should remain, in the realm of the expert, and therefore is beyond the scope of this book.

Modern hangers, left to right: Petzl, Mad Rock, Metolius Camo.

Stainless Powers ³⁄₈-inch bolt with Petzl hanger.

A newly placed stainless Powers ³⁄₈-inch bolt with Petzl hanger. Bomber.

rusted condition and trapezoidal shape. Thankfully, these relic hangers are only to be found on aging classic face climbs. Most have been replaced with modern gear—but not all.

Homemade hangers are seldom seen, but they are out there and run the gamut from sawed off and drilled angle iron to double links of chain. Some are good, some are bad—it's anyone's guess. Some of the older homemades, nicknamed "pop-offs," feature a design that twists the downward pull of a falling climber into an outward pull on the bolt stud, which could prove disastrous with an old ¼-inch contraction bolt. Beware of any hanger that levers the bolt outward. Always eyeball suspect hangers for cracks or other deformation.

Metolius and Fixe have led the current trend to minimize the visual impact of fixed anchors by offering camouflaged stainless steel hangers. If not using these, responsible first ascensionists often paint their hangers to match the color of the rock. Petzl and Raumer also make excellent hangers, along with a handful of other companies.

American Triangle

A triangular sling configuration, often called the American Triangle, is commonly seen when two fixed anchors are side by side—two bolts on a smooth wall, two pitons driven into a horizontal crack, etc. A sling is fed through the two anchors, which form two points of the triangle. The third point of the triangle is where the rope or biner passes through the sling, at the bottom of the setup.

In years past there probably wasn't a cliff in America that didn't sport this configuration, most likely as a popular, fixed rappel point (cold shuts have largely replaced this configuration in many areas, but not altogether). Considering that the physics are all wrong with this setup—the triangle increases the load on each anchor—it's a wonder more of these rigs don't fail. As with other fixed anchors, you may well find an abundance of slings threaded through the anchor, climbers not realizing

American Triangle. Beware of this setup because the triangle configuration increases the stress on each anchor.

that it's not so much the slings that present the danger, rather the triangular rigging that so stresses the anchor.

Obviously, when any anchor is built from atomic bombproof primary placements, it doesn't much matter how you tie them off—provided the slings are good and the knots properly tied. But anything shy of big new bolts should not be subjected to such inward loading as caused by a triangle. Even the stoutest fixed pins will work loose after a while, and to use the American Triangle to connect passive anchors is to invite disaster.

The solution is easy. Tie the anchors off individually and rappel or belay from two or more slings, or equalize the force on them with the sliding X and back it up. Remember, the sliding X (explained in Chapter 5) yields no redundancy.

Cold Shuts

A trend at some sport-climbing areas is to use cold shuts (hooks)—either open, closed, or welded—for hangers. Cold shuts used in climbing are generally borrowed from heavy construction work, where by and large they are used for anchoring as well as interim links connecting two large chains. (The cold shut is slid between the end links of two chains and is then beaten "shut," thus connecting the chain.) Because said chains are often hauling around bulky industrial loads, the larger shuts are usually quite strong—some test-rated to upwards of 3,000 pounds. However, because cold shuts are borrowed from construction, they are not UIAA-tested or approved. While they may, or may not, meet established climbing standards in terms of strength, they have been a staple in California climbing for over fifteen years, and to a lesser extent, at many other sport-climbing areas.

Even the strongest shuts are not used as protection; rather, they are doubled up at the top of clip-and-go sport routes and serve as fixed anchors for the leader to lower and then toprope other climbers wanting to follow, but not lead, the route. One handy feature of cold shuts is their relatively large diameter and rounded surface, which allows the rope to be placed directly through the shut for lowering. When two open cold shuts are fixed at the tops of some routes, at the end of the climb, you simply drape the rope through the open shuts and lower off. Though some people still swear by them, others are leery to toprope off such hangers. Reportedly, it's slightly easier for a quickdraw to accidentally unclip from a welded cold shut than from a traditional hanger, but the cold shut offers easy retreat from any point on the route, and it's easier on carabiners.

Convenience has made cold shuts popular top anchors on routes that see massive traffic, especially on sport climbs that people "lap" for workout purposes. The problem is that with all those ropes running through the shuts, coupled with the abrasion caused when lowering, a beefy cold shut can, after a few seasons (or less), thin to the breadth of a paper clip. Once a shut is visibly grooved, its holding power is significantly reduced and its temper shot from so much heating and cooling. Inspect shuts for wear and tear, and avoid those that are clearly eroded from use. I've seen some shuts in Malibu State Park (a popular sport crag in Southern California) that were worn almost entirely through. Locals usually replace shuts on trade routes, but not always, so keep your eyes open and don't trust the well-worn shuts. If and when you come across sketchy shuts, you might have to climb down to the last protection and lower off from there. Do whatever is necessary to avoid trusting untrustworthy gear, and use quickdraws whenever toproping off cold shuts.

Cold shut anchor backed up by a bolt.

Though hardware store–variety shuts are still used in many areas, Fixe and Raumer (distributed by Climb High) now sell a variety of sport-climbing hardware, including stainless steel cold shuts, sport anchors, and ring anchors that meet the standard for lead climbing, lowering, and toproping and that will last far longer than the hardware store items described above.

Knots for Tying into the Anchor

Before you begin a climb, you must first uncoil, or "flake out," the rope. Find the end, then feed out the line in a neat stack, making sure not to bury (hide) the ends. You now have a bottom and top of the pile, and to avoid tangles, you always draw the rope from the top. Most every rope bag features two short loops into which the respective ends of the line are tied. Usually, the white or black loop marks the bottom of the pile, with the top ("live" or "business" end) tied to a colored loop.

Now you're at the bottom of the cliff, harnessed, booted up, tied in to the rope, and chomping at the bit. Beginners should always tie into an anchor when belaying. Later, when you know the ropes, you might dispense with the ground anchor, but never if the belay site is at all exposed or if the leader significantly outweighs the belayer. Here, you will always want a solid ground anchor. Look for a natural anchor—a stout tree or a large block. You could use the rope to tie these off, but go with slings. Better to get tree sap on a $5 piece of webbing than the rope. And the anchor is often weighted, pulled on, and jerked about, so let the sling take any abuse. The rope is plenty strong for this, but why scuff it up if you don't have to?

Two Biners at the Power Point

Though we will dive into this later, and in greater depth, whatever knots you use, many experienced climbers avoid arranging the power point with only one carabiner. Yes, this has become common practice with AMGA guides: clove hitch to one locking biner. But for my money, such a nonredundant method relies too heavily on a single piece of gear that can easily hide flaws—and the gate might get torqued open by a bight of rope. A very, very slim chance, granted, but you don't want to take any chances, so use two carabiners, gates opposed, or better yet, a locking carabiner and a regular backup carabiner.

Two locking biners at the power point, with gates opposed. One locking biner and a regular biner is sufficient, but if you have two lockers on hand, it never hurts to be extra careful.

Overhand on a bight.

Finished overhand on a bight.

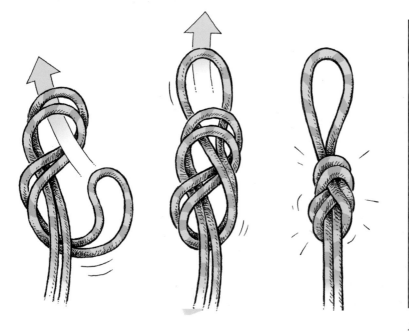

Tying a figure eight on a bight.

Finished figure eight on a bight.

Understand, however, that the climber should always be more concerned about rope/sheath damage from sharp edges and rough rock than the possibility of getting sap on the line.

Here, then, are some popular knots used for tying into an anchor.

Overhand on a Bight and Figure Eight on a Bight

Once you have arranged a belay anchor—a subject we will explore in great detail in Chapter 5—you must tie into it. Since you are already tied into the end of the rope, you must use a knot intended for the middle of the rope—a "loop knot." For this purpose, two knots, the overhand on a bight and the figure eight on a bight, provide the strength and ease of tying that make their use exclusive as the main tie in to the anchor—the power point. The overhand on a bight is the simplest knot imaginable, but once weighted can be a bear to untie. The figure eight on a bight is usually better—strong and easy to untie once weighted or shock-loaded.

Some climbers initially clip off with a clove hitch, the advantage being the ease of getting things perfectly adjusted. Though a properly tied clove hitch will work fine here, to me the clove looks weird as my one and only tie-in knot, so for purely psychological reasons, I, and many others, go with the figure eight.

Clove Hitch

A tie-in knot that is quick and easy to tie, is easy to adjust for length once tied, and unties easily is naturally a knot welcomed by climbers. The clove hitch is such a knot. Some climbers believe the trade-off for all this utility is that clove hitches reportedly slip at around 1,000 pounds of load, although tests have shown that a clove hitch will, in fact, not slip in a dynamic rope (it can, however, slip in a static rope, making the knot a poor choice for hauling gear or jugging lines). Clove hitches can also work themselves loose, so be sure they are kept tight at the bottom of the biner. The reliability of a clove hitch can be improved by using a pear-shaped locking biner.

Knot Strength: Climbing Ropes vs. High-Tensile Cord

The few knots we use in climbing all have limitations, but in terms of knots tied into the lead rope, strength is rarely, if ever, one of them. Lab tests prove that knots generally weaken the material with which they are tied. But the materials used in climbing rope have to my knowledge never failed because a clove hitch, an overhand, or a figure eight compromised the strength of the rope so much that it broke solely because of the knot. There is so much overkill built into a kernmantle rope (in working condition) that the strength differentials between the few knots we use are moot points.

On the other hand, some knots tied into high-tensile cord greatly reduce the overall strength of the cordage and should never be used. Independent tests show that high-tensile cord, when tied into a loop with a figure eight on a bight, loses about 40 percent of its strength at the knot. With a tensile-breaking strength of around 5,000 pounds for 5.5mm high-tensile cord, this still would hold a good 3,000 pounds—but why use a material in the weakest possible way? The fix is simple: Always tie high-tensile cord with a triple fisherman's knot and leave it tied that way for miscellaneous uses, which guarantees no significant loss of strength in the material.

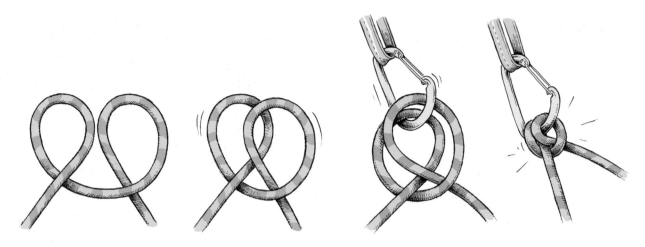

Tying a clove hitch.

Finished clove hitch.

An esoteric point here about clove hitches: The load-bearing strand of the rope coming from the clove hitch should be aligned near the spine of the carabiner and away from the gate, or you sacrifice nearly one-third of the carabiner's strength should the gate come open. Traditional wisdom says that an anchor should not be arranged exclusively with clove hitches, that the wise climber uses a figure eight somewhere in the anchor system. But testing indicates that this "traditional wisdom" reflects what I mentioned earlier about the look of the clove, not its performance. Many climbers feel that the best use of the clove hitch at the belay is to use it as the power point (with a locking biner for adjustability), then back it up with an overhand on a bight or figure eight on a bight to a bomber piece in the anchor system.

That much said, the clove hitch can be a little tricky, and every novice needs to experiment with a short piece of rope/sling and a biner to get the clove hitch "wired." Because you can easily tie the clove incorrectly, it's essential to know how to properly tie it before doing so in the field. Half an hour of fiddling, and the clove is yours for life.

The Belay

Belaying—the technique of managing the rope to safeguard a climber against a fall—is the most important responsibility climbers routinely face. We will look carefully at each aspect of the belaying system, but first, here's a brief overview.

The belayer passes the rope through a belay device and clips it into a locking carabiner attached to the belay loop on his harness. He feeds out or takes in rope as needed to keep the climber safe. The belayer locks the rope off if the climber falls, holds the climber on tension if necessary, and might lower the climber back to the ground at the end of the climb. A belayer keeps excess slack out of the rope, but doesn't allow the rope to pull down on the leader. He also doesn't "hoist" a toproped climber up the route. The responsible belayer double-checks the leaders and his own harness buckles, the anchor setup, belay device, locking biner, and tie-in knots before either climber leaves the ground (much as a pilot will quickly go over a checklist). The belayer is responsible for the safety of the person climbing. He must be proficient, and he must stay focused on the climber. The belayer should situate himself in a secure stance so he can't trip over his own feet and, say, pull the leader off. Finally, he should make certain the rope is properly stacked in the rope bag and will flake out smoothly, without any snags that could stop the leader in an awkward position on the cliff.

When belaying a leader, the belayer feeds out rope through the belay device, or "belays" (belay devices will be discussed more fully later). Both his anchor and location are generically called "the belay" or "belay station." You climb in stages called "pitches," which usually refers to the distance between belay stations, something less than a rope length. A pitch is rarely a whole rope length, since you often stop short at a ledge, a good stance, or a crack that offers a convenient place to build a belay anchor and then belay. A bombproof anchor is far more important than stretching out a lead simply

Belaying the leader on **Crimson Cringe, Yosemite.**

Belaying requires attention to the task. Keep your eyes on the climber and be ready to feed out rope as she advances, take in rope if slack develops, or apply the brakes in the event of a fall.

exceptionally rare that both the belay and anchor should fail, and it's into the beyond if they do. That is why extreme vigilance is always paid to both the anchor (discussed shortly) and belay.

The mechanics of belaying are basic; consequently, some climbers pay less-than-perfect attention to the task. Don't fall into this dangerous trap, for a belayer literally holds his partner's life in his hands. A cavalier attitude toward the importance of the belay or the anchors will get someone killed in a hurry. The process is fundamental, and the technique is simple and reliable. Still, 40 percent of all fatal climbing accidents in Yosemite are due to mistakes and failures in the belay chain. Consequently, the importance of a sound belay system cannot be overstated.

Belaying Mechanics

There are two ends of the rope: your end, which you are tied into and which is tied off to the anchor, and the "live," or "business," end, which goes to the person climbing. The rope is fed through a belay device and locking carabiner attached to the belay loop on your harness. The live end going to the climber is handled by the "guide" hand. The "brake" hand holds the rope on the other side of the belay device. When the climber is leading away from you, the guide hand feeds the rope out, pulling it through the belay device; when the climber is ascending up to you, the guide hand pulls in the slack as the climber ascends. As the rope is reeled in, it passes through the belay device to the brake hand, which is also pulling in slack. The brake hand pulls the rope away, and the guide hand pulls it toward you; always keep the rope snug through the device.

Belaying a climber leading away from you is fairly simple: The guide hand shuffles out the rope in little tugs, the paid-out rope moving smoothly through the belay device and the brake hand on the other side. Taking the rope up, or belaying a climber "in," is a little tricky at first, and involves a three-

to make it longer. If you pass obvious belay stations, you often end up wasting time constructing an anchor in a poor crack or at an awkward locale.

Belaying is the technique of not only paying out the rope, but also holding it fast should your partner fall. The entire protection system depends on the certainty of both the belayer and the belay anchor to do their job—to stop the climber should she fall, and to remain fastened to the cliff. It is

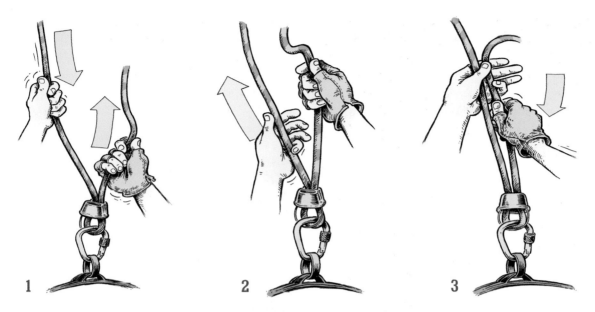

Taking in rope while belaying. The guide hand is on the left and the brake hand is on the right. 1. Grasp the rope firmly with both hands and feed it through the device as shown. 2. When the guide hand reaches the device, slide it back up the rope. 3. Clasp both ends of the rope above the brake hand, allowing the brake hand to slide down without ever actually releasing its grip from the rope.

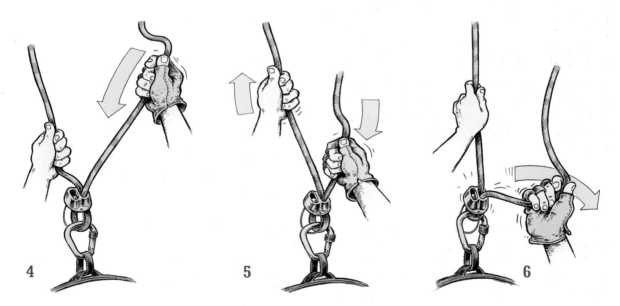

Feeding out rope and braking. 4. Grasp the rope tightly with both hands. 5. Pull rope out with the guide hand while feeding it in with the brake hand. 6. The braking action: Use the brake hand to bend the rope across the belay device as shown to stop a fall or hold a climber's weight.

part sequence. The guide hand is extended away from the waist. It clasps the rope and pulls it in. Simultaneously, the brake hand is pulling out, clasping the rope and pulling it away from your body as it passes through your belay device. That's the first stroke: The guide hand pulls in, the brake hand pulls out. At the end of that stroke, the guide hand is at the belay device, and the brake hand is extended out from the device.

Part two requires the brake hand to momentarily hold fast while the guide hand slides back out along the live end. When the arm is fully extended, the guide hand—still holding the rope on that side—reaches across and grabs the brake-hand rope above the brake hand.

Part three involves the brake hand sliding back

to the belay device, and the process is repeated: Guide hand pulls in, brake hand slides back. This procedure sounds complicated but is very simple to perform. It is the best way to belay. Always observe the absolute rule: The brake hand never leaves the rope. Not only does it never leave the rope, your fingers are always curled around it, ready to clench hard when necessary.

A fall is checked by bending the rope across the belay device with your brake hand, which collapses the belay device onto the locking carabiner and locks the rope fast. When you try to belay the rope in, never letting your brake hand leave the

Rope position for feeding out slack or taking in rope.

Brake position.

clenched position, you'll see there is only one way to do so—the way just described. While there are no recognized tests to prove it, it's widely believed that a palm-down attitude with the brake hand will be able to sustain more force than having your hand palm up (experiment with the feel of the brake hand locking off the rope, and this will immediately be clear). For that reason, most belayers are taught to keep their brake hand palm down when belaying.

The ability to stop a falling climber depends on several factors. You must not be caught unaware—many falls happen unexpectedly. Your attention must remain focused on the climber, whose life you are entrusted with. When a climber falls, your brake hand must quickly bend the rope across the belay device (extending the brake hand at a 45-degree angle away from the device), causing the friction to increase and the rope to automatically lock up. Properly performed, most falls can be held with little effort. In time, this reaction becomes instinctive. To efficiently arrest a fall, you must be properly braced, anticipating both the impact force and the direction of pull caused by the falling climber. But all of this is of little value if you are not properly anchored. To say it again: The anchor is the backbone of the safety system. It, beyond anything, must be secure!

On sport routes and toproped climbs, the belayer often lowers the climber back to the ground at the end of the route. A retreating leader may also need to be lowered to the ground, or to the belay. To lower a climber, first lock the rope off by bending it across the belay device. Next, lean back, or "sit into," the rope to give the climber tension. Place both hands on the brake side of the rope and slowly but fluidly lower the climber to the ground. When the climber reaches the ground, slowly ease her onto her feet. (For a more detailed discussion of lowering, see Chapter 8, "Sport Climbing.")

While this description provides the basics and is a good review for the novice, far and away the best and most efficient venue to learn belaying fundamentals is in a climbing gym with an instructor watching your every move and backing you up to avert mishaps. Today, most everyone learns to belay in a class. The controlled environment and chance to practice in a toprope situation minimize the learning risks to almost zero (they are never zero). Because the gym climbs are short, you'll tend to climb many more routes inside than you would outdoors, so you'll find yourself belaying quite a bit in the gym. After belaying a few hundred times, which you can accomplish in a couple weeks at most any gym, the process becomes very natural, and you'll know the mistakes to avoid.

The Belay Site

When you start a climb, remember to make sure the site (belay station) is safe and, if at all possible, protected from rockfall, dropped gear, a falling climber, etc. Ideally, the belayer should be located close to, if not right at, the base of the rock and should always be tied taut to the belay anchor. If there is any slack between belayer and anchor, a long fall can jerk the belayer off his feet and thrash him around until he comes taut to the anchor. The rope, meanwhile, can be ripped from his hands, resulting in disaster. Every fall generates force in one direction—the direction of pull, an issue we will investigate shortly. Always station yourself in a direct line between the direction of pull and the anchor. If you don't, the force of the fall may drag you there anyway, and you might forfeit the belay—and the leader's body—during the flight. Remember ABC: Anchor-Belayer-Climber.

To clarify, consider these examples: You're tied off to a tree 10 feet away from the cliff, but you're belaying several feet to the side of the start of the climb. If the leader falls, you can plot the ideal direction of pull as a straight line from the tree to her first anchor. If you're not also in line with that pull—because you are some ways off to the side—the impact will, perforce, drag you in line. If you

A well thought-out belay site. The belayer's leg is braced to prevent him from getting jerked around. The setup also follows the Anchor-Belayer-Climber (ABC) order of arrangement. Note how this belayer is using both hands as "brakes" to hold the climber's weight on the rope.

are in line but have tied the anchor off with slack, you will probably be dragged toward (or even up) the cliff until the rope comes taut to the anchor. In both instances the leader has fallen that much farther. The belay is of little value while you are bouncing over the ground, and it's perilous to get banged against the cliff, for the sudden force can jar your brake hand off the rope. If you're set up correctly, catching a fall is usually a routine event.

If you must arrange your anchor on the cliff, try to rig it directly below the start of the climb (remembering our credo about the site being safe from rockfall, dropped gear, a falling climber, etc.). This puts the direction of pull straight up, which is far less awkward than having to compensate for a belay coming in from the side and forcing the belayer into an oblique angle. The location of the belay stance is of key importance when you are belaying from the ground and are anchored to protection that is placed in the cliff (as opposed to, say, being anchored to a tree some ways back from the cliffside). Since a fall will draw you toward the cliff, many belayers like to keep one leg braced against the wall, acting as a shock absorber in the event of a fall. If you're belaying safely on the ground, and your partner does not significantly outweigh you, you may want to forego the anchor so you can get out of the way of potential rockfall or dropped gear.

Belay Devices

Many types of belay devices are currently available. Most work by creating friction on the rope so the belayer can easily hold the force generated in a fall. A belay using a device has commonly been called a "static belay," as the rope is locked tight in the device in the event of a fall. Since most belay devices are clipped to the front of a harness, the term "static belay" is an overstatement. First, there is some rope slippage in the device, and second, you'd have to be a 20-ton Roman statue to keep your torso from moving with the pull. The main value of

a belay device is that it requires very little strength to hold even the longest possible fall, and there's little chance of it ever failing or the belayer suffering abrasions or rope burns—if the whole system is properly rigged.

When the disparity of weight is substantial between belayer and leader, belay devices really shine over the long-outmoded hip belay (which is explained later). For several years I did most of my climbing with Lynn Hill, who I outweighed by more than a hundred pounds. I fell countless times, and she always caught me effortlessly and never got a scratch.

The first belay device was the Sticht plate, invented by a German engineer in the early 1970s. The plate is a 4-ounce aluminum disk with one or two channel holes machined through it. A bight of rope is passed through one of the channels and clipped through a locking carabiner attached to your harness. (Two regular biners with the gates opposed will also work, though not as conveniently.) The plate has a keeper loop that, when clipped into the carabiner, keeps the plate from floating out away from the waist. Though once popular, the Sticht plate is now rarely seen in the United States.

The popular modern belay devices are variations of a channeled cone or pyramid shape, are feather light, feed rope a bit more smoothly than a flat plate, and have more surface area for heat dissipation. A bight of rope passes in and around a locking carabiner and back out the device. During a fall, the device locks the rope off at the biner. The amount of working friction depends on what slot in the unit you are using (the narrower the slot, the more friction), as well as the angle of the brake rope.

All standard belay devices create friction when a bight of rope is passed through a slot in the device and clipped into a locking carabiner connected to the belay loop on your harness. Such devices also double for rappelling. The Black Diamond ATC

ATC (Air Traffic Controller).

ATC Guide (in autolock mode).

Reverso.

Grigri.

(Air Traffic Controller) was the device of choice for many climbers for many years. As the diameter of ropes got thinner—presently as thin as 9.2mm—newer devices came along, including the Reverso 3 and the ATC Guide. While most sport climbing is done on thinner ropes, fat lines are still used in the gym and for toproping, as well as for multipitch adventure climbs. It is therefore essential to know what device, in what position (some devices are set up to work with various-size ropes), works best on what size rope.

Some climbers (very rarely) belay with a figure eight rappel device. It is acceptable to belay a toproped climber with the rope arranged in the figure eight as you would for rappelling, but this setup does not provide enough friction for belaying a leader. The smaller hole on most figure eights is designed for a bight of rope to be passed through and clipped into a locking carabiner, like you would rig a belay plate. This is the only safe way to belay a leader with a figure eight. It is not advised, however.

Someone was bound to create a device that automatically locks up the rope in the event of a fall, whether your brake hand is on the rope or not. The Petzl Grigri, Trango's Cinch, and the Salewa Antz (rarely seen these days) are such products, and have been in common usage for years. These devices come with extensive instructions about their safe usage, and they all require practice by even an expert climber to become proficient with them. These self-locking belay devices are excellent when you're being belayed by a novice. They're also great for sport climbing, when the climber is spending a lot of time hanging on the rope to work out moves. All these devices must be properly rigged, however, or the climber can hit the deck if he falls. For the majority of advanced climbers "working" a grim sport route, the Grigri is the device of choice. The literature that comes with the Grigri says to never use the device when climbing with gear (trad climbing), so don't.

Munter Hitch

The Munter hitch is a handy alternative to devices because it only requires a large-mouthed, locking biner attached to your harness. Knowing the Munter hitch could prove to be essential if you ever drop your belay device. When Swiss climber Werner Munter introduced this hitch to climbing, the UIAA conducted extensive tests and gave it the thumbs up. It steadily caught on after that, but over the last fifteen or so years has fallen out of favor with most American climbers, though it is still popular in Europe. See illustrations on next page.

During a fall, the brake hand goes out, and the hitch locks on itself. Always use an oversize pear-shaped biner with a locking gate whenever using the Munter hitch. The mouth on a regular, or even a D, carabiner is not wide enough to keep the hitch from binding when you switch from taking in to feeding out rope, or vice versa. Most climbers who have tried the Munter hitch have found it to work quite well. The action is good, the setup instantaneous, and you don't have to carry a device, even if it only weighs an ounce.

The drawback is that the rope often gets excessively kinked, so the hitch cannot be recommended over the more functional cone- or pyramid-shaped devices.

A word of caution: Because the rope is continually running through the biner, the action of the Munter hitch can unscrew the sleeve on a locking biner, so crank the sleeve tight before belaying, and keep an eye on it.

Hip Belay

With the advent of modern-day belay devices around 1978, the hip belay became obsolete almost overnight. However, it is essential to know how to belay with little or no equipment in case you accidentally drop your gear, or when team members are flying over supereasy terrain and you don't want to keep yanking rope through a device. Hip belays were the primary method for decades, and the

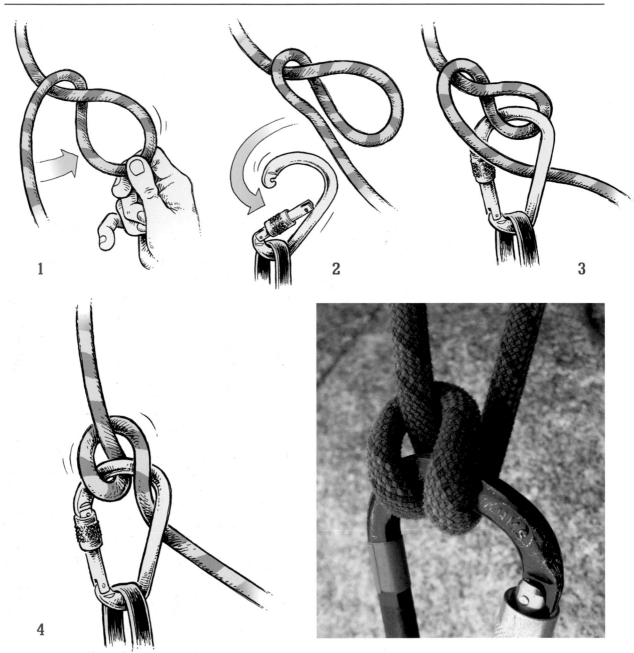

1. Twist rope. 2. Hold in place. 3. Clip as shown. 4. Pull up and out.
In this example, the belayer's brake hand is placed on the strand going down right.
The upward strand goes to the climber. Finished Munter hitch, lower right.

technique works well when performed correctly. A belay device substantially increases the margin of safety, however.

Hip belaying is similar to belaying with a device, with your body substituting for the device. As before, you have two ends of rope: your end and the live end, which goes to the climber. The rope is wrapped around your waist and grasped firmly in each hand. The live end is handled by the guide hand, and the brake hand holds the rope on your other side. Feed the rope out with your guide hand, pulling it around your waist and through the brake hand on your other side. Take the rope in, using the same sequence that you do with a belay device. The

Hip Belay

1. Grasp the rope firmly in both hands. Here, the brake hand is on the left when you are looking at the photo (climber's right hand).

2. Feed rope out around your waist.

(Steps 3, 4, and 5 on next page.)

guide hand pulls in while the brake hand pulls out, and the guide hand extends and grabs both sides of the rope. Finally, the brake hand slides back, and the guide hand drops the brake rope. Again, the absolute rule is to keep the brake hand on the rope.

When using the hip belay, there is a remote chance that the rope can be lifted over your back—if the guide hand is somehow jerked loose from the rope. A "guiding" biner solves this. Clip a biner into your harness near the guide hand. The live end is then taken up or paid out through the biner, so even if the guide hand comes loose, the line still goes around the back to the brake hand. You will quickly learn that the guide hand is no

Hip Belay (continued)

3. Pinch the rope with the guide hand.

4. Slide the brake hand back to your waist and repeat.

more than a guide and does little to stop the fall. It's the friction around the waist and the brake hand coming across the opposite hip that accomplish the brake.

When the pull is straight up, many climbers pass the rope under their butt instead of around their waist. Even with the guide biner, the upward pull will often draw the rope up your back, which is quite sensitive and fairly lean. So your bottom—with the rope running under it—is a better and more secure cushion when belaying for the upward pull. In any event, always wear a shirt, and keep it tucked in unless you want some galley slave scars.

On paper, the hip belay sounds strenuous and painful, and it's easy to envision a long fall sawing you in half or striping you with bone-deep rope burns. Neither should happen. Much of the impact force is absorbed by the rope, which stretches quite a bit; by the equipment the rope is running through; by the belay anchor; and, finally, by the belayer. And the friction afforded by your back or bottom, plus the natural dampening effect of your body, is such that—if the system is rigged and executed correctly—arresting even long falls is usually routine.

Beginners frequently develop a penchant for belaying one way, always using the same brake hand. Situations arise that will require you to belay with one hand or the other, so practice belaying both ways from the start.

5. When braking, pull the rope across the front of your waist like this.

The Secure Anchor

What does a "secure" anchor actually mean? Basically, our gear and our methods must be "good enough," but we can never demand that "good enough" be an absolute. Otherwise, we'll waste everyone's time overbuilding anchors and exasperating our partners with arguments chasing the unreachable goal of total safety. In practical terms, "better" means "stronger" only if what you have is not "strong enough."

When Does "Good Enough" Become Too Much?

"Good enough" means an anchor that will unquestionably hold the greatest forces a climbing team can place upon it. It's standard practice to factor in a safety margin of at least one fold, meaning the anchor is built to withstand at least twice as much impact as that generated by a factor 2 fall (explained shortly). Understand that an anchor that can hold Neptune in orbit is not "better" than a "good-enough" anchor because the former is safeguarding against purely imaginary forces. And we should know that even this advice is impossible to follow at least some of the time. It's likely that at some

point you will find yourself hanging from anchors you only hope are "good enough." Once you start up a rock wall, there are no guarantees.

Importance of Strong Primary Placements

Over the last twenty-five years, ingenious rigging methods have been developed. These methods take practice to understand and master. Their purpose is to exploit every possible ounce of holding strength from a given anchor in order to make it secure. However, the starting point of any belay anchor is in setting bombproof primary placements. The means by which you connect the various components into an anchor array (the way the anchor is rigged) should never be relied upon to provide the needed strength not found in the primary, individual placements. That much said, let's take a close look at the forces involved when a climber falls, forces for which the belay anchor must be built to withstand.

Fall Forces

In terms of influencing rigging and anchor-building strategies, the lab-simulated factor 2 fall has for decades been the most important and definitive test. As we saw in our review of ropes, the test was originally devised to measure the number of severe falls a climbing rope would hold and the maximum force it would impart to a falling climber. To quickly review: A factor 2 fall is where a climber falls twice the distance of the rope he has out from the anchor. The lab test used 2.5 meters of rope and dropped an 80-kilo weight 5 meters, rendering a factor 2 fall.

Possibly because it is called a "simulated drop test," the common understanding was that the test somewhat accurately replicated a real-life, on-the-rock factor 2 fall and provided legitimate evaluations of forces on that account. Consequently a factor 2 fall, and the forces measured in the lab drop test, became the gold standard by which all anchors were measured. From Chamonix to Katmandu, a belay was not "good enough" if it couldn't withstand the forces that the drop test said were generated during a factor 2 test fall.

Static and Dynamic Forces

Imagine a leader hanging off a bolt on an overhanging sport climb. The force on the bolt will equal the climber's weight, and that weight is a static force because all the objects in the overall system are at rest. Static force loading is what you have all over your house. Your desk sustains the static force of your computer. Your chair sustains the static force of your body.

In climbing, dynamic force occurs when a climber's body speeds up during a fall and slows down when she is arrested by the belay. Dynamic forces quickly build to a peak and then taper off to static forces once the climber stops moving. It is critical to understand how peak forces are created, because when slings snap and anchors blow out, it is the consequence of peak forces. This is such a fundamental point that climbing's entire safety system should be viewed in terms of peak force management.

Dynamic Forces in a Fall

As pointed out by Craig Connally in his outstanding book, *The Mountaineering Handbook,* the simulated (in the lab) drop test does not employ the safety system used by actual climbers on actual climbs. Basically the drop test is an exercise in shock-loading a system that is entirely static save for the 2.8 meters of dynamic climbing rope. In real-world climbing, flex and give are present in many components of the safety system, and when those dynamic qualities are accounted for, along with rope slip in the belay device, the force numbers (and the implications of same) are substantially lower than those provided by a UIAA factor 2 drop test. Says Connally:

> The [lab test] calculations assume that the climber is an iron weight tied directly to the rope. A real climber is a flexible object attached to the rope by a conforming harness. Distortion of the falling climber's body will reduce forces about 5 percent, and harness distortion will absorb another 5 percent during typical falls. Lifting of the belayer's body may also reduce peak forces by a significant amount, maybe as much as 10 percent, if design of the belay permits. The overall consequence is that fall forces for short falls are less than those calculated [in the lab drop test] because of all these various factors that absorb energy and reduce peak forces.

Additionally, Chris Harmston, Black Diamond's quality assurance manager, reviewed field failures of

climbing gear for eight years. He never saw a Stopper rated at over 10 kN fail, and only saw a few carabiners fail in closed-gate mode. This is telling because a BD Stopper is among the most commonly used protection device in all trad climbing. It's certain that Stoppers have held countless worst-case scenario falls, and since not one has ever failed, it's almost certain that the 10 kN rating (2,250 lbf) has never been seriously challenged, and that actual forces of factor 2 falls are possibly quite a bit less than that.

Connally asserts that the "top piece," be it a component of the belay anchor, the first piece of pro off the belay, or the last piece high above, is subject to—at the very most—somewhere around 1,900 lbf (8.5 kN). Moreover, this calculation is based on the climber being an iron block. Swap out the iron block with a human body, and the forces might drop to as little as 1,520 lbf at the top end. This is far less than the force measured in lab drop tests, where there is no belayer, no belay device and no rope slip, no give and flex from the climber's body or from the rigging typically found in a real-world belay anchor. The obvious implication of all this is that the topmost pro is the most important in the entire roped safety system, since it always sustains the greatest loading (and the leader and belayer might both end up hanging from it).

Conclusion: The main task of the belay is to limit loading on the topmost pro, a process that is facilitated by rope slippage in modern belay devices. Further force reduction is provided by the other flex and give in a normal belay setup, not the least

of which is the belayer's body, providing a counterweight to cancel out much of the upward force. Clearly a belay and a belay anchor with these characteristics bears little resemblance to a lab drop test, where an iron weight (the climber) is not belayed at all.

The Top Piece

Even though the forces in a real-life factor 2 fall are less than those registered in the lab drop test, we never want to fall directly onto the belay anchor, no matter if the forces are 5 lbf or 5,000 lbf. The whole point of placing protection is for the pro, not the belay anchor, to arrest the fall. That is why we fashion the belay to function as a peak force load limiter to keep loading on the top piece as low as possible. And since we never want to fall directly onto the belay anchor, the most critical time is when we might possibly do so, when the leader is first leaving the belay and has yet to place that first piece of protection. After the first pro is placed, any fall force on the belayer will be up (not down), potentially reducing the static force (the belayer's weight) on the anchor. Conversely, fall force on the top piece will always be down (and maybe out), and that dynamic force will be considerable.

This leads to a basic safety credo: What deserves our most critical attention is the first placement after the belay anchor, the so-called Jesus nut (a term that generically applies to any and all protection devices, from pitons to bolts to nuts, etc.). If a leader falls and the Jesus nut fails, the belay anchor becomes the last line of defense by default and must

When you only have one piece of protection in above the belay—a "Jesus nut"— you better make sure it's solid, because if you fall and it does not hold, all the force of the fall will be onto the belay anchor—a factor 2 fall. Here Greg Loniewski has one piece in on **Absolutely Free** *(5.9), Yosemite.* KEITH LADZINSKI

Obviously, to properly judge the direction of pull, you need to know where the route goes. In the example above, when you were standing in the middle of a flat field, you could see the orange tree due north, so the direction of pull was obvious. But unless you're heading for a bolt or other fixed protection, it's sometimes hard to know exactly where the leader will place the first piece of pro—the Jesus nut—and you won't know till Jesus is in place. And until Jesus is placed and clipped off, you can't know the exact direction of pull. But by observing the rock above the belay, and by referencing the topo (if you have one), you can normally predict the direction of the next lead—perhaps not exactly, but usually within 5 or so degrees.

Climbs following prominent cracks and chimneys follow an obvious and certain direction; and the protection, and the direction of pull, can be extrapolated from the line of the crack. But move out of conspicuous crack systems and the direction of pull can become less clear, particularly on face routes that wander around blind corners or connect various features on an open face. While no climb can go every direction at once, a leader might wander extravagantly trying to find the easiest route, placing protection first on the left and then on the right. This means the direction of pull can also change.

On vertical crack systems, the direction of pull is either straight down, in the case of a second climbing up to the belayer, or straight up, when the leader leaves the belay on the next pitch and clips the lead rope through protection placed in the vertical crack. In most every other case, the direction of pull will be in a direct line between the anchor and the pro nearest the anchor, in whatever direction that may be.

When you're belaying someone following a pitch, the direction of pull is obvious because in the event of a fall, the rope will always come tight (consider the rope an arrow pointing to the direction of pull) in a direct line between you and the last piece of gear before the anchor. And you know where that last piece is because you placed it or clipped it. But as mentioned, when leading, unless you're heading for conspicuous fixed gear, you can't be sure where the first protection will be placed; therefore, you can't exactly predict where the direction of pull will come from. But with rare exceptions, the general direction is at least somewhat clear, if not dead obvious.

Direction of Pull and Anchor Building

Determining the direction of pull is crucial because a belay anchor is often built to safeguard against specific directions of pull, not against directions of pull that cannot occur on a given pitch. Anchors that protect against specific directions of pull are called "statically equalized" (aka pre-equalized) anchors. Anchors that protect against multiple directions of pull are called "dynamically equalized" (aka self-equalizing) anchors, subjects that by the end of this book will be ground into your very bones.

Barring routes with a lot of traversing, some climbers don't factor the direction of pull much into their anchors, especially when the primary placements are bomber and the route follows a relatively plumb line trajectory—which the majority of routes do. Here the anchor consists of bomber pro (especially the Jesus nut), a good stance, and the

This leader has traversed from the belay. If he falls, the direction of pull on his belayer (and the belay anchor) will be in a straight line toward the first piece of protection the leader has placed, which in this case is off to the belayer's right. The anchor must be built to withstand that direction of pull. Mike Brumbaugh on **Belafouche Buttress (5.11), Devils Tower, Wyoming.** KEITH LADZINSKI

rope—enough for some climbers to feel confident they can handle all loads in all likely directions of pull (mainly straight up and down). While optimum equalization might be absent in such anchors, between stout primary placements, rope stretch, flex and give in the rigging system—and using the body as counterweight against loading from whatever direction it might come—many climbers feel comfortable the anchor is good enough. Statistics would suggest they were right; however, it should be known that climbers generally are so cautious about setting a sound Jesus nut just off the belay that not one climber in fifty (if not a hundred) ever catches anything approaching a factor 2 fall.

In short, so few belay anchors are ever put to the test that just how good, or bad, most anchors truly are remains unknown. A huge tree is never going to fail. The same cannot be said about many hand-built anchors.

A question commonly asked: If we understand the directions of pull, why build an anchor to safeguard against direction(s) of pull that can never occur on a given climb? Isn't that a little like facing a solar panel away from the sun? Well, not exactly.

If we always climbed on bolted sport routes or in laser-cut vertical cracks, there would be little reason to ever build belays with a wide-loading axis, resulting in a multidirectional anchor. We could simply design the belay to target the anticipated directions of pull—with a few degrees to spare—and we'd be mint. But there are those climbs where this strategy is not nearly good enough. Several recent anchor failures bring another, seldom-mentioned factor into the equation; namely, swing.

Swing

Consider our earlier example, when the leader traverses straight left off the belay, places a piece, and falls. What happens when the piece rips out? The leader's fall will describe a 90-degree arc, and then some, and the direction of pull will come from various rapidly changing vectors in a phenomenon called swing.

With swing, gravity is forcing, at an accelerating

Direction of Pull

- Every fall generates a dynamic force that will pull on the roped safety system from a specific direction or directions.

- The direction of pull is described by a direct line between the belayer and the first piece of pro (when belaying a leader), or the last piece of pro (when belaying a follower) through which the rope runs.

- Lead protection and belay anchors must sustain loading from every direction of pull that is possible on a specific pitch.

- To accurately judge the direction of pull, you must know where the route goes.

- When the direction of pull is uncertain, a multidirectional belay anchor is required.

- When a swinging fall directly onto protection, or onto the belay anchor, is possible, the pro and the belay anchor must be built to sustain loading across the full arc of the swing.

- Knowing the direction of pull is to a climber what knowing the direction of a possible ambush is to a foot soldier: essential for survival.

The climber following this pitch has unclipped the last piece of protection placed by the leader. As long as that piece was still clipped, the direction of pull on the anchor in the event of a fall would be in a straight line toward that last piece. However, when the piece is unclipped, the direction of pull on the anchor will be in an arc below the belayer—and the belay better be built to withstand the swinging load.

1. Set the primary anchors in the crack.

2. Click the rope sling through the anchors.

3. Separate the sling into individual strands issuing from the anchors.

4. Adjust the sling toward the anticipated direction of pull.

5. Tie a knot (double figure eight) to form a power point.

Remember that you want an efficient anchor, not simply one that will bear the most impact. The placements should be straightforward to place and remove and should be as centrally located as possible—a nice, tight grouping, as opposed to an entangling web of tackle crisscrossing the station.

Personally, I like to place a minimum of four pieces: three in the downward direction and, if the situation requires, one upward placement opposing the primary anchor. Sometimes three are enough, and sometimes that's all you'll get. Anything less is a crapshoot. And accept that sometimes you'll be shooting craps. The rock will not always afford instant and bomber belay anchors—you won't always be able to plug in a couple cams and call it good. You sometimes have to work at getting anything approaching "good enough."

Once the primary placements are set, you must connect the various components together so they function as one unit. Especially when the primary placements are less than ideal, connecting the components is often the most critical, and tricky, part of the whole procedure. Several possibilities exist for connecting the anchors, a topic we'll explore shortly. For now, remember that, if possible, the belayer's body should remain in line between the anchors and the anticipated direction of pull.

Those are the basics. Now let's dig into the particulars.

Step-by-Step Belay Anchor

- On popular routes the belay stances/ledges are usually well established (though not always ideal). Belay there.

- Further narrow your belay site down to the most secure, ergonomic, and practical position.

- Locate suitable cracks or rock features to fashion a "good enough" belay anchor.

- Set the most bombproof, primary big nut or camming device you can find—preferably a multidirectional placement—and tie yourself off before yelling "Off belay!"

- Determine the direction(s) of pull for both the climber following the pitch and the leader casting off on the next lead.

- Simply and efficiently shore up the primary placement with secondary anchors.

- Try to set the secondary placements in close, but not cramped, proximity.

- If the rock is less than perfect in quality, spread the anchors out, using several features, to preserve redundancy.

- Using modern rigging techniques, connect the various components of the system together so they function as one unit to safeguard against all possible directions of pull.

- Consider tying into the most bombproof anchor with a clove hitch (to aid adjustability).

- When bringing up a second after leading a pitch, if possible situate your body in line between the anchors and the anticipated direction of pull. Remember ABC: Anchor–Belayer–Climber.

- Also remember KISS: Keep It Simple, Stupid. Avoid overbuilding.

Tying into the Belay Anchor

The standard method of tying into the anchor is via a figure eight on a bight clipped into the power point (explained shortly) with a locking biner or two biners with the gates opposed. Once a team gets established on a multipitch climb, however, the method of tying in depends on at least two factors: (1) the number of climbers on the team, and (2) whether or not more than one person is doing the leading.

Out in the field you'll see folks tying into the power point with a single clove hitch, two clove hitches, a clove hitch and a figure eight (to multiple power points), a daisy chain, a sling or two or three, an adjustable link of rope and a Ropeman ascender, and countless other methods. Some of these techniques are sketchy and downright dangerous, none so much as attaching yourself with a high-tensile-strength daisy chain, which creates a static connection that sacrifices the considerable give and flex offered by tying in with the dynamic climbing rope.

The aim of establishing a protocol on tying in is to facilitate the smooth and secure transition from climbing to belaying to climbing again. If, for instance, a two-person party is swinging leads, the process is fairly straightforward. If you are a three-person party with one person doing the leading, or if the leading and the following is done in no particular order, the belay can quickly become a hateful mess if you don't have a simple and reliable system for tying into the anchor. There are no hard and fast, standardized methods in this work because the configuration of belays is so varied. It will take practice to come up with your own efficient system. There are, however, some basic strategies that work in most instances.

Without a simple plan and the knack to simplify, a belay anchor can get terribly cluttered when two or more ropes are in use.

One good strategy is to back up your connection. If you tie into the power point with a clove hitch, tie into another point of the anchor with a figure eight on a bight. The most bomber piece is a good choice for this backup. If you're using a cordelette to connect the anchor pieces, another potential backup point is the "shelf" of the cordelette, which is the point right above the power point. This shelf also offers an alternative clip-in spot for whoever is leading the next pitch in a group of three or more. The practice results in one less tie-in at the power point, thereby opening it up for others to clip in, and it allows the leader to quickly unclip and take off on the next pitch.

Spreading the Load

A fall generates forces, and as far as is possible, we spread the load over several sound primary placements and reduce the possibility that the whole array will fail. And that is, and always will be, the primary function of a belay anchor—to hold no matter what.

This photo shows a decent technique for tying directly into an anchor using the climbing rope. This might be necessary sometime if you're short on gear. Note how the climber has used a combination of clove hitches and a figure eight on a bight.

Spreading the load between multiple placements. Tie into the doubled carabiners with a figure eight on a bight and you're good to go.

separate, redundant loops that offer no extension if one of the primary placements fails.

The problem with this configuration is the issue of equalization. Lab tests show that unless the cordelette is configured with perfectly equal-length arms (impossible in actual practice), it provides rather limited equalization between the primary placements. Instead, the bulk of any loading is

Rigging a Cordelette

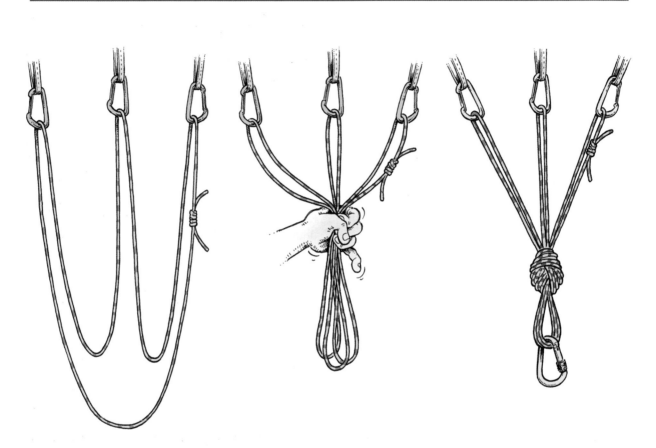

First, clip the cordelette into the primary anchors, then pull the loops of cord down between each of the pieces. Next pull the arms of the cordelette tight toward the anticipated loading direction (direction of pull). Make sure to align the fisherman's knot so it is below the highest primary placement in the system, free and clear of the power point knot. Secure the power point with an overhand knot, or if you have enough cord, a figure eight knot (as done here). Tie the power point loop about 4 inches in diameter, roughly the same size as the belay loop on your harness. Attach a locking carabiner and clip into the power point with a section of the climbing rope, not with a daisy chain or other device made of high-tensile cord.

Two-strand cordelette, locking biners at the bolts, with a double figure eight on a bight and triple biners at the power point. This rig is somewhat equalized for downward loading only. Any off-axis (sideways) loading will place most of the load on one or the other bolt.

This double-strand cordelette is being weighted with an oblique, sideways pull, producing slack in one arm (the right as you look at the photo) as the other arm takes all the force. A self-equalizing rigging system is greatly preferred when oblique forces are put onto the anchor.

each strand. The equalette can be used to connect two, three, or four primary placements and is especially effective in rigging vertically oriented placements, as found in a vertical crack. When rigging, keep the power point centered at the bottom by clipping the lowest placement first, then working up the placements from there.

To start, hold the right-hand limiter knot 2 to 6 inches below your lowest piece. (When rigged, an equalette will always feature a right- and left-side orientation). Imagine you are starting by tying into the "right side" of the anchor (as you face it). After clipping into the piece or set of pieces on the right, hold the left-side limiter knot even with the first

knot, and clip into the piece or pieces on the left. Adjust the strands so your knots end up evenly tensioned (clove hitches are very helpful there, if not required).

For a two-placement setup, connect each arm of the equalette to the placements via the loops in the cord, clove hitches, or overhand knots on a bight. For three placements, one arm will accommodate two placements (usually with clove hitches tied into individual strands of the arms), and the other arm will connect to one placement (via the loop in the cord, a clove hitch, or an overhand on a bight). For connecting four placements, each strand (four total) of the two arms will connect the placements via the

Three-piece anchor rigged with an equalette. Simple and stout.

Four-piece anchor rigged with an equalette.

loop in the cord or clove hitches. Be sure the load-bearing strands align with the spine of the biner.

The equalette can also be rigged using a double-length sling of webbing, though you'll find the 7mm cordelette easier and more versatile to work with, especially when tying clove hitches. Plus you have the added benefit of the stretch in the nylon cord to reduce peak loading on the anchor system.

Tests show that the equalette allows a high degree of equalization between the two arms, and it allows a ratio of equalization between both strands on each arm. While it is impossible (in a practical sense) to achieve anything close to perfect equalization between all four placements, the equalette achieves a degree of equalization—along with solid redundancy and minimum extension—to a higher degree than any system tested. This is not a big consideration with bombproof placements, but when the primary placements are average to poor, the equalette becomes a valuable asset.

Because the power point biners can slip side to side on the strands between the limiter knots, the system, when weighted, will dynamically equalize to accommodate a limited degree of off-axis loading. In those rare cases where horizontal forces can impact the belay, oppositional anchors are needed.

Tying the Equalette

- Use 20 feet of 7mm nylon cord tied into a loop with a double fisherman's knot, or 5mm high-tensile cord tied with a triple fisherman's knot.

- Form a U shape and grab the cord at the bottom of the U.

- Position the fisherman's knot about 18 inches above the bottom of the U.

- Tie an overhand knot on each side of your palm where you have grabbed the cord, about 10 inches apart.

Using the Equalette

- At the power point, always use two locking biners, with one locker connected into each separate strand of the power point (between the limiter knots). If you are forced to use one biner, clip one strand, twist the other 180 degrees, then clip the other strand to maintain redundancy. This is the same technique used to clip into a sliding X.

- Before using the equalette, make sure you have mastered the clove hitch.

- On multipitch climbs (with a two-climber team) where the first climber to the stance is going to lead the next pitch, each climber can clip into the power point with his own two locking biners. If the second climber to the stance is going to lead the next pitch, he can clip a locking biner directly into the two-locking-biner power point (biner to biner). This greatly facilitates secure and speedy turnover at the belay.

As with any comparatively new rigging system, it takes a few times working through a variety of anchors before you can rig the equalette quickly and efficiently. The hardest part of the system is getting used to feathering the knots to achieve equal tension in the arms and/or strands. But this is mastered quickly, making the equalette as fast to rig as the cordelette. And because you don't use as many knots with the equalette, breaking down the system is faster than breaking down a cordelette.

It is highly recommended that anyone new to building anchors should rig a cordelette at home, using a chair (with the legs as anchor points) or chairs. In this way you can get a feel for the basic constructs in a controlled setting and can learn how to rig the system and tie the knots just so. It takes time and practice, but most anyone can master the basics in a few hours, perhaps less.

Advantages of the equalette:

- It provides superior equalization over the cordelette.

- If you pull considerably off-axis on an equalette, two arms remain equalized. With the cordelette, any off-axis loading results in only one strand or arm being loaded.

- It has increased versatility. Given the same length of cord (20 feet), an equalette allows you to clip off four primary placements, whereas with the cordelette you can usually only clip off three.

- With practice, it is fast and easy to rig—and faster to break down—than a cordelette.

- The dual power point facilitates a fast and easy clip-in, even when weighted, resulting in smoother belay transitions.

- Clove hitches are faster and easier to untie than the overhand and figure eight knots used in other rigging systems.

- By leaving the limiter knots fixed in the sling, you gain all the function without the tedious and time-consuming repetition of tying multiple overhand knots at each belay.

The Quad

The quad is simply a doubled equalette, useful for those who toprope or belay off the ubiquitous side-by-side bolt anchors typically found at sport-climbing areas. And since so many climbers frequent sport areas, the quad is rapidly becoming a favored rigging device. Having a quad pre-rigged on a sling means you have a virtually indestructible, ready-made rigging system that almost perfectly equalizes two placements and is rigged as quickly as you can clip off four biners.

Two-bolt quad rig for a toprope. The quad is simply a doubled equalette.

Close-up of the quad's power point.

The quad is best rigged with 5.5mm high-tensile cord (for durability and compactness). First, form a loop by connecting a 20-foot piece of high-tensile cord with a triple fisherman's knot. Double that loop and form the doubled loop into a U. Tie permanent limiter knots, roughly 10 inches apart, in the bottom of the U (giving you four strands of cord between the two overhand limiter knots). Clip off the doubled ends of each arm to each bolt respectively, and arrange the power point via two lockers clipped into two or three strands between the limiter knots.

The quad is mega-strong and durable, and it provides great equalization, accommodates some off-axis loading, and is almost instantaneous to rig. For connecting two side-by-side bolts, the quad is unbeatable.

Composite Anchors: Cordelette, Sliding X, and Equalette

Before the Sterling Ropes tests, which redefined our use of the traditional cordelette rigging system and spawned the equalette, many climbers believed that the sliding X was best considered as a component and that the cordelette was the Whole Ball Game. In any event, because it is fast and requires nothing beyond a sling, the sliding X is the most efficient and flexible method of combining two primary placements to a cordelette, or an equalette.

As has been shown, horizontal loading would variously fall on single placements, introducing greater loading/cascade failure potential. In the past, it was here that we might have combined a sliding X with a cordelette so that if the leader fell from above the belay with no gear in, the whole anchor was equalized for a downward pull, but if the leader fell on the traverse, the two pieces connected by the sliding X would share the load. Now it seems that we have even more options, including an equalette, or an equalette combined with a sliding X, the latter configuration shorn up with one or more oppositionals set for upward forces, thus forming a

Belay anchor with cordelette and sliding X combo. While this setup—and ones like it—have been a mainstay for many years, incorporating new techniques such as the equalette will allow climbers to achieve even greater equalization.

super-multidirectional anchor. Whatever system or combination you choose, safeguarding the full range of the arc is the goal.

Another common composite-anchor situation occurs when a cordelette or equalette isn't long enough to equalize three pieces and remains pointed in the anticipated direction of pull. To fix this, simply equalize two of the pieces with a sliding X, then rig this with the cordelette or equalette to the third piece. In this situation it makes sense to use an equalette in place of a cordelette to achieve superior equalization.

What's Best for Beginners?

What, by and large, is the most appropriate system for beginners? Every instructor knows that beginners are sure to place sketchy gear (primary placements) and misjudge the direction of pull. For this reason, we suggest a self-equalizing system that will adapt to changes in load direction and that will exploit the collective strength of less-than-textbook placements.

Guide Tom Cecil says, "It is more protective to teach self-equalization to beginners. Using self-equalization as a strategy is like using training wheels on a bike. They allow the beginner to lean in any direction and still be held. Over time they learn to anticipate these forces."

Bob Gaines, owner of Vertical Adventures guide service, sees it this way:

The key in teaching novices is to stress the absolute importance of avoiding factor 2 fall situations. They must be taught to recognize the forces and place pro [the Jesus nut] soon and often above a belay. This helps ensure that the peak forces that novices encounter will occur at the highest piece of pro, not at the anchor. In most situations, when belayers are catching a leader fall, it is a good thing if the force generated by the falling leader is great enough to pull the belayer slightly upward, as the counterweight effect greatly reduces the force on the piece the leader has fallen on. Therefore, the best belay strategy is to be anchored against the upward pull with a bit of slack in the system, which provides some counterbalance shock-absorbing, but not so much so that the belayer is pummeled into the wall or extruded through the Jesus nut.

As far as toprope setups go, the direction of pull is basically straight down—easy to judge even by the novice. The biggest and most common mistake I see with novice riggers (aside from poor primary placements) is usually major extension potential and lack of redundancy.

That said, you are certain to hear arguments on the pros and cons of "fancy" rigging methods, just as you are sure to see very experienced adventure climbers tying off the anchor with the climbing rope. When the primary placements are absolutely bomber and you've enough experience and judgment to know they are, a rudimentary tie-in method is "good enough." The truth is, 95 percent of all discussion about belay anchors concerns methods required for only about 2 or 3 percent of the time, when the primary placements are sketchy. But if you get used to rigging anchor arrays with self-equalizing systems, you will get good and fast at the work, which is a key factor in adventure climbing, where time is a valuable commodity and dinking around is a liability.

The common knock against using the equalette, sliding X, and so forth is not that they don't work, but that they are slow to rig and are generally overkill. But overkill is not a bad thing if it can be accomplished in no time, and it might be a life saver for those exceptional cases where the anchor is very bad indeed, and a factor 2 fall is a possibility.

We've made it abundantly clear that the foundation of all belay anchors is the absolute holding power of the individual nuts, cams, bolts, etc., in the anchor array. Make sure these are bomber, and you'll almost certainly remain safe. It follows that the first and foremost skill to develop is gear placement; specifically, learning how to set solid placements. We've recommended many ways to accomplish this, including aid climbing 5.10 splitter cracks, experimenting low to the ground with a rack of gear and aid slings,

and jumping on placements till they blow (or not), along with following an experienced leader up a host of climbs to get gear placement dialed.

Next, the anchor and the entire rope system should be thought of as a peak force limiter. Such a system works best by making sure a fall is always caught by the top piece of pro, never the anchor.

Yes, the anchor should be built to sustain factor 2 loading, but if it ever comes to that, everyone should know that they will be facing what is probably the most dangerous scenario in all of climbing—winging straight onto the anchor.

Lastly, we have introduced self-equalizing rigging systems for those rare cases when you cannot secure bomber placements, and for situations where the anchor might withstand off-axis (lateral) loading.

This all may seem a bit much for gym-trained beginners, who come from an environment in which the reliability of the gear is not even a remote consideration. Imagine what they might think upon learning that what they have long taken as a given—the absolute trustworthiness of the system and the equipment—is no longer ensured when they venture outdoors. Says American climbing guru, Rich Goldstone:

> In the absence of certainty, the expert relies on redundancy. This can be a very slippery slope, however, since the opportunities for redundancy are endless and the party is, after all, supposed to get to the top of the climb in a finite amount of time. Nevertheless, the novice's best bulwark against their own inexperience is to incorporate as much redundancy into their safety chain as is practical under the circumstances they face. If this means carrying a little extra gear, so be it; don't let the light-and-fast experts, who know very well what game they are playing, cow you into carrying minimal gear when you have neither their personal skills nor share their risk choices.

As for redundancy, guide Tom Cecil teaches all beginners to employ a "carpet bombing" strategy and place as many pieces of pro as they can, a tactic

belayer is dragged upward in the course of holding a fall. For this to ever happen, the belay anchor would have to be set in vertical cracks and consist of nuts and, far less likely, cams—pro that might conceivably be plucked clean if the belayer were yanked a sufficient distance above the anchor. I've never read of an instance where a belayer actually got dragged above the anchor and where the primary placements in the belay anchor itself were plucked from the crack like cloves from a holiday ham.

We know that during a leader fall (held by pro above the belay), slight lift of the belayer's body and flex and give in the system act as peak force reducers, absorbing some of the fall's kinetic energy before the anchor is ever loaded. If nothing else, rope slip/stretch will likely preclude a meteoric hoist, even when little rope is out.

But that's with a belayer who weighs roughly the same as the leader. Get a leader who weighs twice as much as the belayer, and the lift factor becomes significant no matter the angle. Here the peak force reduction enjoyed by the body of a large climber is null and void. And so is the main argument against setting nuts for an upward pull: No matter the fall scenario, the belayer is not likely to be lifted far enough to threaten the anchor. My counter to this claim is that I (210 pounds) once fell at Tahquitz and pulled belayer Lynn Hill (105 pounds) 10 feet into the air. She held the fall fine,

and we were both unhurt, but an oppositional set at the belay anchor would have taken 20 feet off of my fall.

When Oppositionals Are Required

While there are instances—primarily on low-angled climbs—that climbers can argue against setting nuts to safeguard against upward pull, there are other times when upward oppositionals are compulsory. These include (a) steep hanging belays built from hand-placed gear, (b) whenever you are belaying below an overhang and the initial protection off the belay anchor (Jesus nut) is directly above or even behind (such as with a roof crack) the anchor, and (c) when a belayer is significantly lighter than the active climber. All three of these examples are where the rock is near, at, or past vertical; where a falling climber will basically be airborne; and where forces generated by a leader fall are great enough to start replicating the mega-hoist seen in our first two examples—the toprope scenario in the gym and in the Sierra Club cement bucket drop test.

Bottom line: A little "lift" at the belay is usually a good thing, acting as a counterweight and load limiter to the forces generated by a leader falling above. But whenever the potential of that lift exceeds a foot or so (the a, b, and c examples above), oppositional placements should always be incorporated into the belay anchor.

Summary

The anchor is the foundation of safe climbing. There is no mystery to rigging a sound one. If there is ever any doubt, double up the anchor. While three nuts are often adequate, it's not uncommon to see an anchor with four, even five nuts, all equalized. When the crack is thin, forcing the use of smaller protection, remember Tom Cecil's "carpet bombing" strategy, and place more rather than fewer. Trusting an anchor rigged completely from small units is petrifying duty, and should only happen in extreme emergencies, never out of choice.

Camming devices have proven their utility, but many climbers avoid rigging anchors completely from mechanical devices, particularly for toprope situations, where the weighting and unweighting can cause the cams to walk around. There's nothing like a bomber "passive" (nonmechanical) nut buried in a bottleneck. Come hell or high water, that nut's going nowhere. There are situations in climbing where you may take a calculated risk, but never with the anchor.

The limitations of attempting to cover every fundamental in one book is never so evident than with anchors, a subject that deserves 500 pages alone. We have two consolations: First, once you understand the basics, building your own anchors and watching how others build theirs—both of which are easy to do at any trad crag—will teach you faster and perhaps better than any manual can. Second, while I'm hamstrung for space in this manual, there are two more inexpensive books that deal strictly with anchors, also in the How to Climb series: *Climbing Anchors* and *Climbing Anchors Field Guide* (the latter being a great size for taking in your pack as a reference). These or similar texts, plus anything else you can read on the subject (particularly in climbing magazines), should be required for all beginners. The art of fashioning anchors is a lifetime study and continues to evolve with each passing year and as new equipment is introduced.

As the sport-climbing mentality continues to permeate the American climbing scene, the old ideals of self-reliance and adventure—the very bones of trad climbing—become less and less relevant. Just as sport climbing came from Europe, it might only be a matter of time before many popular American climbing areas copy the European practice of bolting most every belay anchor for convenience and safety. But even if this practice caught on tomorrow, it would take decades to outfit even a fraction of the tens of thousands of trad climbs nationwide. So in the interim, you'll be left to build your own anchors at most trad cliffs, and the fundamentals we've covered here are a good start to an exciting adventure.

The Art of Leading

Most veterans admit that climbing doesn't really start until you cast off on the lead. You can boulder around enchanted forests and follow a leader up the world's greatest rock climbs, but the moment you're the first on the rope, it's suddenly real in a totally different way. Everything is magnified because now you're playing for keeps. The decisions are all yours—as are the rewards and the consequences. Whether that first lead is up a razor-cut splitter at the base of El Capitan or on some sport-bolted slab in a scrap heap quarry, the feeling of command and the special demands are always the same. It's no longer just an exhilarating physical challenge but a creative problem-solving design requiring many intangibles with the penalty of injury, or even death, for a major oversight.

Because leading is a procedure involving equipment and an applied system, we can nail down certain objective realities, at least in a general way. But every leader is ultimately self-taught. We can open the way a bit, suggesting what skilled fine leading is about—and not about—and ever stressing safety, but more than that must not be expected from an instruction manual. A professional guide can take you a bit further in preparing for those first leads, but when you do take the sharp end, it's just you and the rock.

The First Lead

As has been discussed, a majority of climbers first learn how to lead in a climbing gym, which all offer beginner's leading seminars. Gym routes are set and obvious—many are color coded. Protection bolts are in place, and under these very controlled circumstances a new leader can jump out on the "sharp end" with a degree of security unknown in decades past. I highly advise getting the leading basics down in a controlled gym setting. Basic procedures like clipping the lead rope into protection, falling, lowering off, and so forth are simple maneuvers readily and securely learned in the gym. That way, once you venture outdoors, you won't have to learn everything about leading all at once.

For those first few leads outdoors, consider sticking with low-end bolted sport climbs, which require the leader to place no gear save the biners/quickdraws needed to clip the hangers. Since sport climbs usually start at 5.9 or easy 5.10, you will have to be pretty proficient to go this route. Just remember that when you segue from bolt-protected sport leads to trad climbs—where you not only have to route find, but also place all the protection, probably do some crack climbing, and build anchors as well—you'll want to make that first trad lead a very easy one indeed, no harder than 5.3 or 5.4. It's common to

Mike Doyal giving his all leading **Master Blaster** *(5.13+), Zion National Park, Utah.*
KEITH LADZINSKI

When contemplating your first trad lead, aim for a lower-angle moderate route. Here Heidi Wirtz tackles a Yosemite crack climb well within her abilities. KEITH LADZINSKI

see a gym-trained beginner trying to lead 5.9 trad and climbing himself straight into grief.

Again, keep it very simple for the first few trad leads, and boot the difficulty up incrementally. If there's any doubt about having the basic procedures dialed, pick a short route for your first lead and have a toprope backup in case your leading strategy goes bust. This requires two belayers—one each for the lead and toprope—but it's worth considering if there are lingering doubts and a guide is not available.

Most every trad area has a classic easy route or selection of routes that hundreds of beginning leaders have broken in on. Whatever you choose, be certain the protection is sound, that you are at least somewhat adept in the techniques involved, and that the route is straightforward, requiring no unusual shenanigans or special skills. A direct, easy climb—that's what you want. If the first trad lead proves too easy, no one's stopping you from hopping right back onto something a little stiffer. Once again, getting in over your head on your first trad lead is a deflating and potentially dangerous experience that may color, if not end, your climbing career. Take it slow. Cut loose only when you know what's happening.

Ideally, when the day of your first lead arrives, you will have taken a climbing course and had the fundamentals drummed into you by a competent instructor. You will have spent time placing nuts and building belay anchors, so when you grab the lead, you don't have nagging doubts about your ability to safely perform basic duties. You will have familiarized yourself with belaying, lowering, and basic leading (clipping bolts) at a climbing gym. You will have complemented your practical experience by reading this manual, or one like it. And you will have served at least a brief apprenticeship following an experienced leader up a host of climbs, becoming familiar with the nuances that a book cannot impart. You don't want to learn leading through trial and error—a first-time leader should know

the whole procedure well before stepping out as boss. But either way, you'll have to decide what it is you want to lead. That's where guidebooks play an important role.

Guidebooks

Picture a cliff, a quarter-mile long and 300 feet high. Folks first started climbing here in 1950, and the cliff has become a favorite for rock climbers. Since the first climber discovered the first way up the cliff, exploration has been steady, and now there are more than 300 different ways—or "routes"— up the wall. How do we know this? Since 1950 each route was recorded and later published in a guidebook, which was itself perpetually updated. A guidebook lists first ascents—the names and dates of the first people to climb a given route. At a modern sport-climbing area, most of the routes were probably established from the late 1980s up to the present, but the method of rating, naming, and recording the routes remains the same as in the "old" days.

Each route is named and given a tentative rating by the first ascenders, and by the time a route makes it into print, it's usually had enough ascents that the rating is at least somewhat objective, arrived at by consensus. All viable guidebooks have several master photos, or topographic drawings, with lines superimposed to show the various routes, or at least prominent features allowing you to find specific climbs by reference. A guidebook is indispensable to all climbers—from beginners who yearn for easy ground to experts who want to know where the hardest routes are, and everyone in between. It allows us to pick a route that best suits our taste and expertise. Many guidebooks have a quality rating, or at any rate, a list of recommended routes, so a visiting climber can spend a few days and know he's tasted some of the best the crag has to offer. A guidebook is particularly important for the beginning leader, who can use all the guidance she can get.

The early guidebooks used photos and written descriptions, but in the mid-1970s, the written

Left: Gear racked on a shoulder sling, sorted according to size. Above: Gear racked on a harness's gear loops, as it generally is for free climbing. This frees up the shoulders to hold long slings for quick and easy access, as shown.

clipped onto your rack depends on how you want them. Some climbers unclip the appropriate bunch, fit the nut of choice, unclip it from the bunch, and return the remainder to the rack. (The danger here is that you might drop the entire bunch.) Others know at first glance what nut they want and remove it individually from the sling or harness. (If you're wrong, it's better to have had the whole bunch in hand for an easy second try.) If you move wires individually, rack the carabiner gate out, so you can lift the nut out, instead of back and under. If you remove the whole bunch, rack the biner so the gate faces your body. Free biners and draws should be racked together, normally on the loop in front of the other pro. (Additional equipment will be explained later.)

There are other ways to rack gear, but perhaps more important than aping the most common routines is to discover what works best for you (likely what we've described) and to rack your gear the same way each time. Standardizing your modus operandi means you will become familiar with one method as your customary practice. That way, your hand will automatically know where to reach for a free biner or the wired nuts because they're always racked in the same way and at the same place. When you vary your racking methods according to whim, you must discover where things are with every climb. Not good. Stick to one method and get efficient with that method. At moderate climbing levels, efficiency is a virtue but not a necessity; when you start pushing your envelope, if you have to fumble around trying to locate gear, your common refrain might well become "Falling!"

Starting Out

You've picked a route and you know where it goes. In terms of a partner, always get an experienced climber to belay you for that first lead. She can give valuable coaching from below and can critique your lead once done. Moreover, you will know she can belay and can catch any fall you might take, which frees your mind to concentrate on the lead.

A standardized protocol of communication removes any doubt as to what the leader and the belayer are doing, are expected to do, are asked to do, and are warned to do (see Climbing Voice Signals sidebar). When you anticipate not being able to hear each other because of wind or river noise, for example, work out your own protocol in rope tugs before the leader starts the pitch. Maybe three sharp tugs from the leader would mean you can take him off belay, and two sharp tugs from the leader would mean you can climb. In such difficult situations, it is the responsibility of the belayer to be particularly sensitive to the rope so the leader has the proper amount of slack or tension.

Before you start up, clean the soles of your climbing shoes either by vigorously rubbing the soles together, or by rubbing the soles against your pant leg (standard). Modern rock shoes stick like fly paper, but not if there's a veneer of dirt on them. (Experienced climbers do not walk around in their climbing shoes, and only don them at the base of the route.) Next, study the rock above and spot any key holds, obvious features, or nut placements. Climb up mentally, imagining the required techniques. On easy climbs, the sequence is usually no mystery—just a matter of execution—so picture yourself doing the moves, then go after it.

The first section above the ground is crucial because if you fall there, you hit the deck. So climb no higher than you feel comfortable jumping off from, then set your first nut. Again, all gear placed to protect the leader is called "protection," or simply "pro." Make certain that the first pro is especially good and, if at all possible, multidirectional. From

Climbing Voice Signals

"ON BELAY?" The question the climber asks before he proceeds.

"BELAY ON" The response the belayer tells the climber when his belay is set and ready.

"CLIMBING" What the climber says to the belayer indicating the climber is starting to climb.

"CLIMB" The belayer's response that he's ready to belay the rope, proceeding to do so as the climber advances.

"SLACK" A command to the belayer to let out some rope, give slack.

"UP ROPE" A command to the belayer to take in the rope, pull up the slack.

"TENSION" or "TAKE" A command to the belayer to hold the climber on tension by holding the belay fast.

"LOWER" A command to the belayer that the climber is ready to be lowered.

"WATCH ME" commands the belayer to pay close attention, expect or be prepared for a fall.

"FALLING!" The climber is falling—a statement of fact.

"BELAY OFF" The climber's signal to the belayer that he has anchored himself and that the belayer's responsibility to belay should end.

"OFF BELAY!" The belayer's response to the climber that the belay has ended.

"ROCK!" Akin to yelling "Fore" on a golf course. Rocks are coming down; take cover.

"ROPE!" A rope is coming down; watch for it.

bottom to top you are always judging the rock quality, and it is crucial that the first piece of pro be set in solid stone. And make certain your belayer knows you're clipped in. The belay is worthless to the first pro because you aren't clipped into anything.

Now you're plugged in, and the system is operative. If the pro seems questionable, double it up—place two or even three nuts until you know something will stop your fall. At the outset, the leader must always calculate how far he has to fall to hit the ground, a ledge, or other feature on the route, and he should always have some pro in to preclude this. Up higher, once you have several nuts in—provided they're good—"decking out" is no longer a concern, but "rope drag" is.

Protection and the Direction of Pull

As a leader, you must continually assess the direction the rope will pull on all the protection below you should you fall. Until you can do this, you won't be a safe leader.

Beyond what we have already said about direction of pull, understand that very few climbs follow a straight line. Even cracks snake around, so to some extent the rope has to bend about according to the contour of the crack your pro is in. To ably predict the direction of pull, a leader must be conscious of the various forces on the entire system. When you fall, the rope becomes tight, and the transmission of force pulls all the protection toward the middle, toward an imaginary straight line between leader and belayer. Pro not placed directly in that line is subject to considerable sideways and upward pull, and can be wrenched free if you have not compensated for the oblique force. So when the route zigzags around, there are certain things we can do.

You always want the rope to follow as straight a line as possible, even if all your protection is from bolts (which cannot be wrenched free from sideways forces). The more crooks the rope makes,

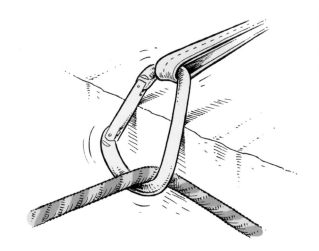

Stressing a carabiner sideways over an edge is dangerous.

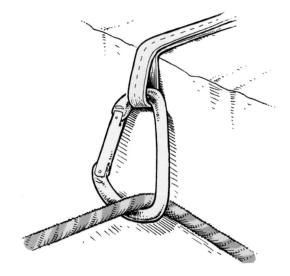

It's much better to use a longer sling.

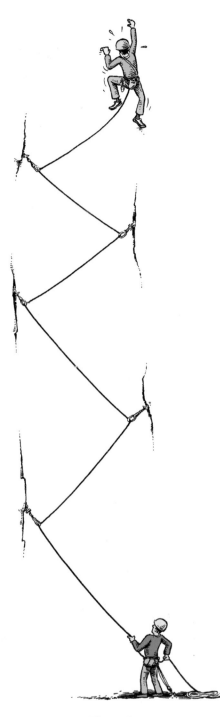

Not using runners.

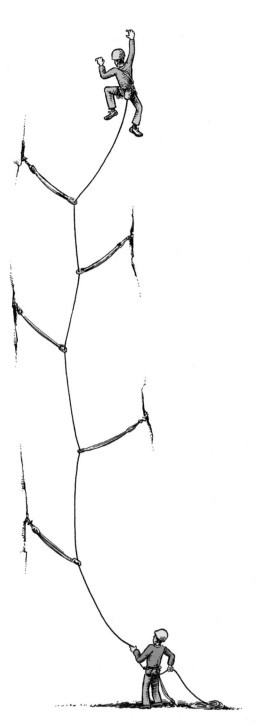

Using runners correctly.

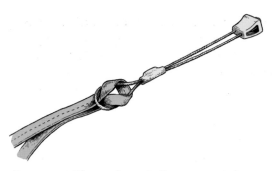

Incorrect. Never thread sling material directly into a wire; with a solid fall, the wire will slice right on through!

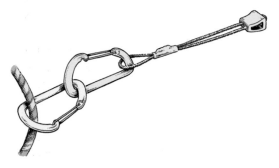

Incorrect. Never clip into an anchor that has any stiffness to it (like a wire) with two carabiners; a twist in the rope can pull the nut free or force the biners to unclip themselves.

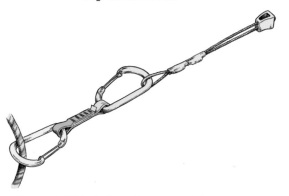

Correct. This is how to use quick-draws, with the rope-end biner gate down and out to easily accept the rope when you're clipping.

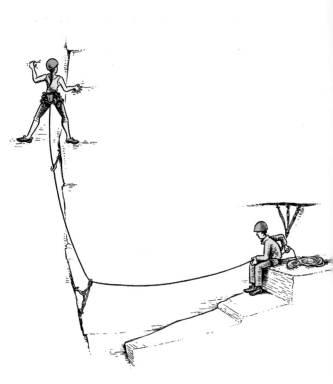

Use of a multidirectional anchor at the start of a lead to prevent the rope from lifting the protection from the crack.

the greater the friction (the "rope drag"), which is somewhat like the belayer holding you back. An experienced leader imagines a plumb line between the belayer and the end of the first pitch, and arranges protection so the rope follows that line as closely as possible. When protection is by necessity placed to the side of the plumb line, we attach runners to the pro that, in effect, extend the protection toward the imaginary midline. The drawback with runners is that they increase the distance of a potential fall to twice the length of the runner. For this reason, and because the runner is like a free tether and can move rather than being just a fixed point, it is very rare that someone will attach a runner bigger than the normal length worn over the shoulder. If the runner is well off to the side and a fall will still transmit lateral force on the nut, either set the nut with a firm downward jerk or place an oppositional nut beneath it to form a multidirectional protection (cams can often work as multidirectionals).

The theory is simple: You are not just trailing a rope but dragging it through your protection. Runners keep that drag to a minimum and the nuts in place.

When clipping into fixed protection or cabled nuts, even if they're placed in a direct line, it has long become standard practice to use quickdraws. To review, quickdraws (or simply "draws") are small sewn runners normally fashioned from 10mm high-tech webbing that harbor two carabiners, one for the pro, one for the rope. Draws are short, so they don't appreciably increase the potential fall, and they greatly facilitate the rope running smoothly. Moreover, cabled nuts are stiff and, when clipped off with single biners, can be lifted from the crack by rope drag. Draws prevent this. Some climbers prefer to rack their shoulder slings as draws by tripling the loops; this allows you to easily extend the draws to a full-size runner as required. Standard draws, however, are lighter and much less bulky.

If you're climbing directly above the last protection point, you'll want the rope running between your legs. If you're angling left or right off your last pro, try to avoid having the rope run directly between your legs. It's better to trail it over a leg because in the event of a fall, there is less danger of the tightening rope flipping you over backwards and increasing the chance of head injury. This rarely happens, but it's not unheard of.

When to Place Protection

There is no hard-and-fast rule concerning when to place protection or when to climb on. Experienced climbers place pro when they need it. To the beginning leader the experience is all new and he might not know when he needs pro; he is likely to think he always needs it. As we've seen, you definitely want sound protection at the start of a pitch and before any hard, or "crux," section. Anticipate the crux; place protection when you can, not counting on the hope that you can slot something 10 feet higher at the hard move.

Whenever you encounter an obvious bottleneck or are resting on a big hold, slot a nut—even when the climbing is easy. If the climbing seems manageable and you feel vigorous, go 10 or 15 feet between nuts and feel the thrill and freedom of the lead. But always be aware of ledges or features you may hit should you fall, and protect yourself accordingly. Avoid the temptation to "run the rope out," going long distances between protection, even if the climbing is clearly moderate. Once you are a good judge of your own prowess, the soundness of the pro, and the terrain encountered, do whatever you like. But the beginning leader will rarely want to go more than about a dozen feet between nuts, if that far. That's only ten nuts for a 135-foot pitch, which isn't excessive.

If one hand is holding you to the rock, clipping in can be trying. The universal method is to reach down below your tie-in, pull up a loop, and hold it in your teeth; reach down for more slack and clip in. Sounds odd, but there's not a leader alive who doesn't do this. Sometimes fixed protection is found in awkward positions and can be very grueling even to clip. This is especially so on bolted sport climbs, where clipping is an art and is often as hard as the leading.

As mentioned, bent gate carabiners, though great to clip a rope into, should only be used for that purpose. Never use them to clip into a bolt, fixed pin, or wired nut. Even quickdraws can bind and open the gate all too easily. Watch them.

Route Finding

Good climbing requires you to follow the line of least resistance, not wandering onto more difficult rock on the flanks. Route finding is part instinct and part experience. Study the topo and compare it against what you see. Locate salient features such as bushes or roofs, and know where the hard parts are in relation to them. The topo should tell you this info—for example, that the section above the mulberry bush is hard, that the crux is after the crack peters out. Get yourself prepared before you start by memorizing all the given information.

If you wander off route, look for the signs of climbing: chalk and boot marks, fixed protection, and broken flakes or holds. On popular routes, the texture and color of the rock is often smoother and lighter than the bordering stone because hundreds of shoes have paddled over every hold, probably for many years. With crack climbs, the route is often obvious. Face climbs are more nebulous.

Cruxes: The Hard Parts

Even easy climbs normally have "cruxes," sections harder than the rest. You will recognize them because the holds will suddenly run out; the crack will thin, widen, or get shallow; or the angle will bulge. Don't climb mechanically, but with all your savvy. Recognize the crux before you are on it. Set a good nut, or several nuts. Study the holds or crack and plot a likely strategy, but once you have committed yourself to it, improvise if your theory is wrong and forces you into sketchy movements. And climb aggressively. Use whatever works best and easiest, which sometimes might be an improbable sequence.

If a fall seems possible, or likely, make certain your pro is solid and observe what, if anything, you

will hit if you come off. If everything checks out, alert your belayer and go after it. No leader wants to fall, and you don't start up something without some hope of succeeding. The fact that success is not a given defines the challenge in climbing. But the fear of falling prohibits your best effort, and if everything checks out, the fears are probably groundless. Falling has become an integral part of modern climbing. Good protection and realistic judgment keep the sport sane.

Move On

A common leading error is to try to stop in the middle of a crux section to place protection. It's almost always better to place solid pro first, then gas it through the crux. Stopping at mid-crux can burn you out in a flash. However, on sustained climbs without a definite crux move or section, you'll have to stop in strenuous, sometimes awkward positions to set protection, and developing the skill to know just when and where to stop is what partially defines a competent leader.

The aim is fluid, efficient movement, not dinking around needlessly, clogging up the route and wasting everyone's time, including your own. Some beginners feel that a slow climber is a cautious climber, when in fact he's an inexperienced and inefficient climber. Time is a resource that like water, food, and sunlight, cannot be wasted if you ever hope to succeed on routes of any length. So from day one aspire to climb using the least amount of a limited resource—time. Don't rush, which is worse than dinking around and leads to form breaks, panic, and mistakes. If you find that you simply cannot get up to speed on the lead, practice toproping a climb without stopping. A pokey climber is almost always afraid. Work out the fear on a toprope and then get after it.

Cruxes often come in the form of roofs. Here Rob Pizem completes the first ascent of **Walking on Water** *(5.13a), Zion National Park, Utah.* KEITH LADZINSKI

Falling

Seventy-five years ago the rule was that the leader must never fall. The equipment was unreliable, and there was always the chance—though remote—of the rope breaking. Present-day gear is remarkably sound, and while no one yearns to fall, controlled falling has become standard practice for virtually all active sport climbers. Many leading climbers don't feel they have pushed themselves until they have logged some "air time." Indeed, you can never discover your limits unless you exceed them. Climbers routinely do, and the smart ones rarely get a scratch, even from 20-foot falls. This relaxed attitude is not due entirely to the gear, however. Climbers have become expert in calculating the risks and potential consequences, and people have learned how to fall.

There are two principal issues involved when you commit yourself to a potential fall: Is the protection adequate to hold the longest possible fall, and what will you hit should you fall? The belay is never in question because unless you're a lunatic, you don't climb with someone who can't hold your fall, however long or short it may be. If the pro is sound and the rock steep and smooth, it's fairly common to see a climber spend a whole afternoon falling off a difficult route. However, if the protection is dubious and there's something to hit, you very rarely see a climber carry on unless he is virtually certain he will not fall—and no one can know this with 100 percent certainty. It's not the act of falling but the consequences (what you might hit) that are the issue.

Climbing and protecting are separate skills, each of which keeps you alive, so for any lead—especially the first ones—don't challenge yourself in both at the same time. The beginning leader should avoid falling at all costs, but the possibility will arise, and both his and the expert's concerns are the same: the security of the pro and what he might hit if he falls off.

When you fall, you need to maintain body control, stay facing the rock, and avoid tumbling. On a slab, you slide down on your feet, both hands pressing off the slab, keeping your chest and head far away from the surface. Keep your legs bent and spread apart, catlike. The rope stretches considerably, so the jolt is less than expected. I once caught a partner on a 50-footer on a steep slab, which did nothing but wear his shoes out prematurely. He stayed relaxed and just slid down on his feet, balancing with his hands—like a high-angle slide. I saw another person take the same fall, freeze up, and start tumbling. He needlessly broke a wrist.

On vertical climbs, you don't slide, but plummet—and very quickly. Remember to keep your legs a little extended and bent so at impact they absorb the force like shock absorbers. Don't freeze up or go limp—that only invites injury. The screaming, rag-doll fall is worse still. The flailing arms will invariably smack something rock hard.

When you have traversed away from protection, a fall will swing you, pendulum fashion. The catlike stance is your only hope to avoid tumbling. Be prepared for your weight coming onto the rope, which can otherwise wrench you askew, even spin you like a top. Remember, pendulum falls are dangerous no matter your posture or agility. Slamming into a corner from 20 feet to the side is almost the same as falling 20 feet straight down and smacking a ledge on your side.

Even a long fall happens so fast that you don't have time to think. All the yarns about a person's life flashing before his eyes are baloney. You only have time to react, then it's over. Often it's the shorter, 8- to 10-foot falls that are the "wrenchers." Remember, any fall on a small amount of rope will be a wrencher since so little rope is out, thus restricting the dynamic qualities (the stretch) of the line. But whatever the length of the fall, if you avoid freezing up, stay relaxed, and face the wall, legs and arms bent, you'll usually not be hurt if your calculations were right.

Even as little as twenty-five years ago, falling was generally feared. As bolt-protected sport climbs and indoor gyms came into vogue, falling became a minor annoyance experienced by all. The danger

Falling is part of climbing. Assuming you have bomber pro, falling is not inherently dangerous. Keep your arms and feet in front of you to absorb the force of swinging into the rock. KEITH LADZINSKI

Before a crux section, arrange pro you are certain is sound so you can concentrate on the moves, not the consequences. Get on a foothold and scrutinize the face. Spot the best holds and break the section down to body lengths. Keep reducing each section down to the last visible hold, then construct a mental sequence and visualize yourself climbing it. If it's too strenuous to pause very long, size up the holds and cast off.

On strenuous leads, you have to be aggressive and really get after it, but try to never, ever abandon your form. Look at the baseball player who goes with a grand slam swing: Instead of trying to stroke the ball, he tries to murder it, and he usually strikes out. "Savvy," "alertness," and "controlled aggression" are all vague terms that apply to leading a hard face.

Learning to downclimb is particularly important to the face climber. If you know you can reverse a section, you minimize the potential danger and fear. Successful leaders will often venture out several times to gain the confidence to eventually go for it, getting more familiar with each effort and further reducing the hard section to the last, crux move. Hard face climbs and steep sport routes, however, are virtually impossible to reverse, and you'll eventually have to go for it in any event. But climbing up and down—if and when possible—can often help a leader settle in and muster the needed resolve. The specifics of downclimbing are covered in Chapter 7, "Getting Down."

Leading Crack Climbs

We have discussed the necessary techniques for climbing cracks—but the fact is that often the hardest part of leading a crack is not the climbing, but arranging the protection. Camming devices have simplified rather than eliminated this process. When the climbing is strenuous, the leader often finds herself hanging from a questionable jam and desperately trying to place protection. Here are a few tricks to remember.

On thin to medium-size cracks, don't plug up the best jams with protection. An experienced leader will often opt for a smaller nut or TCU that fits into constrictions between the bigger, better jams.

You will normally place protection above your hands. Sometimes, if the only good nut slots are where your fingers are, you will place a nut below your hands, slotting it just after you have removed your fingers. Try to set these nuts quickly, as often you are hanging on in a crunched-up position with a bent arm, which is far more strenuous than the straight-arm hang.

Be conscious that your feet don't get entangled in the rope. If your foot gets caught under both the rope and the nut, an upward step can lift the nut from the crack.

When the crack is parallel-sided and strenuous, go with cams, which are much faster to place and usually better.

Utilize all rest opportunities, and get a good nut in while you're there. Many renowned climbers have fallen to their deaths on easy ground that they didn't bother to protect. Arrange sound protection before any crux section of liebacking or jamming, and if it's safe, power over the section without stopping.

Hanging about in the middle of a crux section to arrange added protection can result in a fall you wouldn't have taken if you'd powered through. Conversely, if the protection is sketchy and your strength is dwindling fast, you'd best think hard about pressing on. The lead is no place to push things if you're soon to be out of control. Better to lower off and regroup.

Husband your energy. Don't use brute strength unless you need to—and sometimes you will, especially on precipitous sport climbs. Stay relaxed and try to get into a rhythm, a groove. Never thrash. Understand, of course, that we all occasionally do desperate things on the lead. The secret is to know when you're desperate and not make this mode of ascent your personal style. Everyone has desperate moments, and boldness can sometimes deliver us (and other times run up our insurance premium). The key word here is "sometimes." No one can climb precariously for long and not pay the devil for it.

Setting the Belay: Additional Thoughts

Once you have completed the first lead, you must rig an anchor to belay the second climber up. As we've seen, there are countless different possible belay constructs, all dictated by what the climb affords. Always stop at an obvious ledge or belay spot. Try to rig the anchor directly above the line of ascent so you can belay in line with the direction of pull. If you're on a ledge, tie yourself off with enough slack so you can belay at the lip of the ledge. This facilitates easy rope handling and communication, and keeps the rope from running over a potentially sharp edge. You'll usually choose to sit, facing out and down, but you can stand if you have a good brace. Just make certain you are tied off taut to the belay. If not, a fall will drag you straight over the lip. Not good.

Redirected belay. The rope runs from the belayer's device up through a carabiner clipped to the anchor, then down to the climber.

Direct belay, where the belay device is clipped directly to the anchor. This method is preferred by most guides today.

If you are a party of three, it is easiest for the third climber to climb past on a second rope that is trailed by the second climber. At the belay the third is tied off, and the free end is trailed again on the following lead. If the third climber wishes to lead a pitch, he is simply put on belay and clipped through the anchor, then off he goes. If for some reason he wants to go second, you are looking at some weird rope shenanigans, untying and switching knots, which is more hassle than it's worth but possible using the aforesaid techniques. If the route wanders, it is the second's job to clip the third's rope through key nuts to check any drastic sideways falls. The third climber must then remove the pro his rope has been clipped through.

Double Rope Technique

In decades past, most Continental and many British climbers led on two 9mm ropes. For several reasons, however, the technique never caught on in America. Managing a single lead rope is far easier. There is less weight for the leader to drag behind him, and the belayer's task is easier as well. Since American climbs tend to follow straight lines, the single rope has remained the standard (and it keeps getting skinnier every year).

The following list explains the advantages of using double ropes:

1. When a route wanders, a single rope will zigzag extravagantly through the protection, and a hundred runners can't eliminate the rope drag. By using two different-colored 9mm ropes, you can clip one line through protection on the left and one on the right, each rope running somewhat parallel and straight—or at least avoiding the drastic jags of a single rope.
2. When the climber leading on a single rope pulls up a loop to clip in, he's adding distance to a potential fall at twice the length of the pulled-up loop. With double ropes, if the top pro should fail, or if the climber falls just before clipping in,

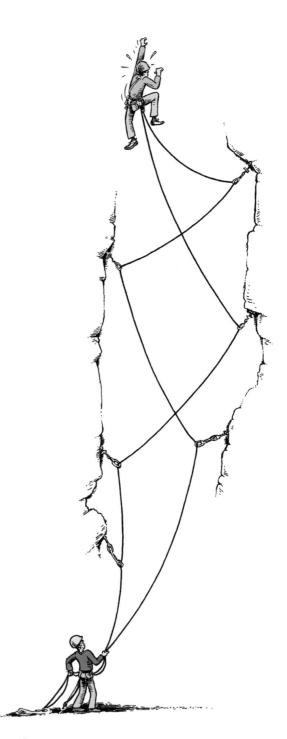

Poor double-rope technique.

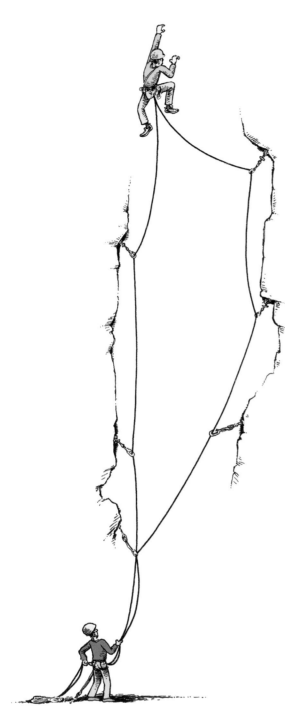

Proper double-rope technique.

the extra loop is not added to the fall since the other line is clipped in below and he will come onto it first.

3. When the protection is poor, you can stack or duplicate placements, distributing the force of a fall between two nuts and two ropes, reducing impact on both.

4. On horizontal traverses, a single rope must go sideways with the line of protection. With double ropes, provided that the leader was able to climb above the traverse before belaying, one of the ropes can be left unclipped from the traverse protection so the rope runs up and across to the belayer instead of dead horizontal—much better if the second should fall.

5. Perhaps the most important advantage is for those who climb regularly on sharp-edged rock like limestone, quartzite, or gneiss, where it is possible that a single rope could be cut during a fall. I have only heard of one fall that resulted from a severed rope, but for those climbers frequenting areas where it is even conceivable, double ropes are a solution.

6. Lastly, the second rope is immediately available for descent without trailing an extraneous second rope.

As the leader places pro, she will forewarn the belayer which rope she is going to clip in, saying "Slack on the yellow," for example. And herein lies the single biggest disadvantage with double ropes: their eminent potential for snarling and snagging—not only on rock features, but on themselves. A hip belay with double ropes is tricky business, requiring the lines to be fed out or drawn in alternately. With the belay devices, it's often hard to keep both lines running smoothly and ordered in a tidy pile. The lines can likewise become crossed in or behind the device. These problems are manageable with experience, so make sure you have some before belaying on double lines.

See additional double-rope illustrations on next page.

so your integrity will never be questioned. Most climbers find it more rewarding to climb several routes within their ability than to spend all day falling up one over their head. If you stick with climbing, you will discover all this for yourself; and if you find yourself hanging on the protection, no need to tell the priest. Just realize you're not climbing as well as you might be.

Free Soloing

By definition, you are free soloing any time you climb without a rope, regardless of the difficulty. The common usage, however, refers to a climber scaling a fifth-class climb where a rope and equipment are usually employed. Yet the true free soloer has only a pair of shoes, a chalk bag, and the prowess he brings to the cliffside. Since the penalty for a fall is almost certain death on a route of any length, even experts will question the sanity of the campaign. To the person not given to risk taking, even the most passionate explanation will ring hollow. Remember, free soloing is rarely a reckless practice—rather, it's a very calculated, conscious act. And it's a matter of degree. The chances of a 5.14 climber falling off 5.10 terrain are remote, but it's possible. Yet the nervy aficionado will sometimes push the envelope ever closer to his all-out limit till he is virtually doing a high-wire act above infinity, where a moment's lapse in focus, an imprecise toe placement, a fractured edge, and the Grim Reaper appears.

To the novice witnessing this firsthand, it seems the purest madness. Why do it? You should certainly not attempt it to find out why. The few who regularly practice free soloing are inevitably experts who by and large know exactly what they are doing and intuitively know exactly why. Moreover, while present-day free soloing has pushed the envelope further than ever before, it is rare for anyone to on-sight free solo anything beyond mid-5.11. The majority of hard soloing takes place on routes the soloer has previously climbed with a rope. Rehearsing a route removes all the mystery, and consequently much of the doubt and fear he would otherwise feel by walking up to a grim climb and soloing it cold, or "on-sight."

What the free soloer craves is either the raw intensity or the joy and freedom that comes from mastery. If he craves notoriety for his feats, he is motivated by selfish values and might pay for his vanity. The reasons to free solo must come from the heart and be monitored by an icy, analytical mind. Anything else courts disaster. We all climb, among other reasons, because it is exciting. So when the free soloer ups the ante to include all the marbles, you can imagine how the thrill is magnified. Foolish? Perhaps, but an element of folly runs through the skein of any climbing. The free soloer has simply pushed things to their ultimate expression. His rewards, in terms of intensity of experience, are the greatest. And so are the penalties. Amazingly enough, very few free soloing accidents ever occur (though when they do, an obituary soon follows). This is a clear testament that the practice is undertaken by experts in a very measured and sober way. Free soloing and deepwater soloing are both present-day expressions of the adventuresome spirit that was so prominent in 1950s, '60s, and '70s rock climbing, but largely co-opted for the sport-climbing revolution. This spirit can be marginalized but never defeated—and never understood by those requiring an explanation.

Ultimately, free soloing is a distinctively personal affair, and even daily practitioners discourage the practice, as they should. There is certainly no reason for the recreational climber to ever even consider it.

*Peter Croft has been one of the country's leading free soloists for many years. Here he is on **Loose Lips (5.11a)**, Joshua Tree, 1987.*

Climbers must also know how to improvise a descent for those unavoidable retreats. Sport climbers need only know how to retreat from a bolt in the middle of a pitch. Those who do longer routes must be capable of, and prepared for, a multipitch retreat. As I've already said, not one single climber has enjoyed a 100 percent success rate on long climbs. In most cases, the more long routes a climber has bagged, the more times he has also found himself descending a route for reasons ranging from falling stones to ebbing desire. He lives to again climb the high crag simply because he knows how to safely retreat.

Walking down should be the first option if the walk-off is easy, though frequently climbers will lower or rappel instead for convenience. Walking down is normally simple business, though not always. Be mindful not to cut down too soon to avoid getting "cliffed," where after an hour of bushwhacking, for example, you come to the edge of a 1,000-foot vertical wall. Then it's back the way you came, which is sometimes impossible (if you've already made a few rappels) and usually hateful and exhausting. Use good judgment to find the path of least resistance.

Downclimbing

Should rappelling prove unsafe or impractical, you will most likely have to downclimb. This most often happens when you climb up a face or a formation and downclimb off the lower-angled flanks or the backside. Competent downclimbing is essential to descend gullies, slabs, chimneys, or any stretch of rock encountered once the climb is over. Unless the rappel route is very straightforward, most experienced climbers will opt to climb down off a crag if a simple, realistic route is available. And even when the rappel route is a quick and easy task, climbers will still climb off. It's often faster, and their fate is in their own hands, not dependent on equipment.

Downclimbing can be as fun and challenging as climbing up. Almost without exception, downclimbing is done without a rope since the terrain is usually fairly easy. If you haven't made the descent before, you probably have little or no knowledge of the terrain below, so be careful. Hopefully you at least scoped the descent from the ground so you have some idea where you're headed.

The downclimbing route must be free of loose or rotten rock. If it isn't, no one should be in a position to be hit by rockfall. It is generally best to keep the party close together so falling stones cannot build momentum and the first one down can forewarn those behind of danger spots. If you do knock a rock off or if you notice anything falling, yell "Rock!" even if you think there is no one below. If you are in the line of fire, you have two options: duck and take cover, or glance up and try and dodge. Often there is not time enough to do both. If "Rock!" is yelled from far overhead, it's probably best to take a glance and react accordingly—at least in theory. The idea is to get into a place shielded from the projectile, hopefully under a roof or at least into a deep crack where the chance of getting struck directly is greatly reduced. If you're on an open face, your only hope is to take a look and try to dodge what's coming down. Rope, haul bags, parties above, wind, rodents—all of these things can dislodge rocks. And whenever rocks or anything else has whistled past, always check your partners and then the rope.

Per downclimbing: Don't be afraid to pull out the rope and rappel or belay if things get too hairy. Never solo down anything you don't feel absolutely confident about. Likewise, never coerce your partners to "down-solo" anything they aren't comfortable with. Instead, be the first to offer a rope to your partners, or get ready to buy a shovel.

If you're the stronger partner, go down first to find the most logical route and to spot your less experienced partners through the dicey stretches (provided you have a good stance). Again, try to stay close together so any dropped rocks can't gain

1. *When down-climbing, you'll often reach down low to grab a hold.*

2. *Cross-stepping is more efficient than shuffling the feet between holds.*

3. *Note how the upper hand grabs an edge while the lower hand pushes as the climber lowers her weight.*

4. *Stretch the leg down to the next foothold, then get repositioned and do it all over again.*

wrecking ball speed before nailing someone, so both climbers have ready assistance if someone gets into trouble, and so the team doesn't get separated.

If you rope up to downclimb, the weaker climber goes first with a toprope, placing protection for the stronger to "down-lead" on (hopefully the weaker partner knows how to place good protection). Rappelling is almost always a safer and quicker option than down-leading, though.

On lower-angled downclimbing, face out so you can see where you're going and lean back to the wall with one or both arms as needed for balance. As the angle steepens, you'll reach a point where it becomes easier to turn in and face the rock, peering past your hip or between your legs for directions. A little experience and all the nuances will become clear.

The ability to downclimb safely and quickly is a handy and often crucial skill. You can outrun approaching storms, avoid unnecessary rappels, and, provided you use common sense, have a fun time doing so. If you start down the wrong gully or shoulder, though, it can get nasty. Against my better instincts I thrashed down a manzanita-choked gully east of Basket Dome in Yosemite Valley, and Lord Jim with a chain saw couldn't have reversed it. Five hours and a thousand weeping punctures later, we finally gained the valley floor, and I've been careful what I head down ever since.

Rappelling

A million postcards feature a colorfully clad climber "roping down" the sheer crag, bounding in arcs, meters off the wall, a waterfall cascading in the background. To the layman, the image embodies everything quixotic about climbing, though there is no climbing involved. Beginning climbers are anxious to try it, though this zeal usually falters as they backpedal toward the vertiginous lip.

Old climbing manuals were quick to state how experienced climbers hated rappelling. In reality, most climbers don't really mind rappelling, though they avoid it if possible. There are ropes to uncoil and anchors to set, often leaving gear behind, and the spooky task of absolutely trusting the gear, rarely with any backup. If the rappels are long and involved, including many anchor transfers and a lot of eerie dangling on the equipment, even the best climbers will walk a long way to avoid the hassles. But any way you stack it, if you're going to climb, you're likewise going to have to rappel—and a lot.

"Abseil" (European) or "rappel" (American)—call it what you want, it all involves using friction to descend a rope. Statistically, rappelling is climbing's second most dangerous process, close on the heels of leader accidents. A climber's bulk is continuously stressing the equipment, and if any link in the weighted chain should fail, the result is final. Equipment failure, anchors pulling, knots coming untied, and a host of human errors—usually avoidable—have caused many rappelling tragedies. Consequently, assiduous attention must be paid to every aspect of the procedure.

Rappel Fundamentals

When rappelling, your hands have separate jobs. The uphill, or guide, hand is used mainly for balance and should never death grip the rope. It can't stop you, and you're only instinctively trying to duplicate the friction that the rappel device is creating. The other hand, the brake hand, determines your speed. Most climbers keep their brake hand well below their hip, with the rope slicing over it. When they want more speed, they move the rope out and off the hip; to slow down or stop, they wrap the rope back around the hip. The prime rule of rappelling is never let go with your brake hand, lest you slide out of control down the rope. The brake hand feeds the rope through the rappel device. If you're right-handed, you'll probably want to brake with your right hand, gripping with the right palm facing down.

Once you are set up and ready to go, make

789008581

MONEY ORDER

STATE REGULATED

REPUBLIC BANK
OAK BROOK, ILLINOIS

CC020

9020060287

4400 W. ARMITAGE AVE. - CHICAGO, IL 60639
TO VERIFY - CALL (773) 342-0995

Open 24 Hours - We Never Close
Abierto 24 Horas - Nunca Cerramos

FROM Enrique Alvarez Jr.

PAY TO THE
ORDER OF Karina Garcia

*****THIRTY FIVE AND 00/100 U.S. Dollars******

12/2/2012

EM   9020060287

$35.00******

NOTICE TO HOLDER: DRAWEE NOT LIABLE ON STOP PAYMENT.
• NO REPLACEMENT FOR 30 DAYS FROM PURCHASE. RE-ISSUE FEE APPLIES.
• PURCHASER AGREES TO INSERT NAME OF PAYEE AND IS SOLELY RESPONSIBLE FOR FAILURE TO DO SO.
NO REFUND WITHOUT YELLOW RECEIPT

NON-NEGOTIABLE

Rappelling.

When rappelling, keep your body at about a 45-degree angle relative to the face, knees extended but slightly bent, brake hand close to the hip, and head looking down. Keep your feet out in front of you and "walk" down the rock.

certain any gear or clothing is well clear of the friction device and cannot get entangled no matter what you do. Long hair must be securely tied back. Anything loose can be drawn into the brake system, and it happens so fast that a whole shirttail or head of hair can be snatched into the brake with only one downward step. Extraction is very involved, often dangerous, and, in the case of hair, always very painful. In most cases, when something has been sucked into the braking device, it becomes locked so tight that the climber is incapable of freeing himself, and a rescue with shears is necessary.

The crux of rappelling is often getting started,

particularly if you must descend over a lip. Once the rope is weighted, backpedal to the brink. Keeping your feet there, let out some rope until you are leaning well back, with your knees bent and feet wide apart. Don't move your feet down too soon. Stability is gained by having your weight pressed straight into the wall, requiring you to maintain a near perpendicular angle relative to the wall. Much less and your feet will skid off and you'll smack the wall—face first. After you have leaned back far enough and feel your weight driving into the wall, slowly pedal back, letting out rope and maintaining your perpendicular attitude. The moment you are established on the wall, bend your upper torso in, but keep your legs perpendicular to the cliff. Keep your feet spread apart at shoulder width for a good foundation. To see where you're going, slightly twist your upper torso toward your brake hand so you can look down.

Don't bound down the rope like a paratrooper; rather, walk down the cliff. The aim is a smooth descent, for several reasons. Heroic bounding or jerky action moves or stresses the whole system unnecessarily. Too much speed heats up the friction apparatus and can singe the rope's sheath, making it brittle and stiff to the touch. Inching down is pointless, though many beginning climbers think it is safer. Snailing down the stone wastes everyone's time and usually means you are over-gripping with the guide hand. Small steps, fluid action, fixing your gaze below to see your way, and always keeping your legs perpendicular to the cliff are the fundamentals of a safe rappel. Steady, fluid movement—that's the goal.

A beginner's first few rappels should be accompanied by a belay from above. If there is a problem, the climber is still on belay, which can give a trembling beginner enough confidence to try again. Usually just a couple of belayed rappels is sufficient to get the knack, and you can dispense with the belay.

A technique for belaying someone after you go first is the fireman's belay, where you hold onto the bottom of the rope. If the rappeller loses control, you pull the rope tight to stop his descent. This method doesn't back up his rappel device, however, nor does it allow you to check his rappel setup.

If you need to stop while rappelling to untangle the rope or take a photo, wrap the rope around your leg three times to free your brake hand. Be sure your brake hand is ready to take the weight when you unwrap the rope to continue your rappel.

Overhanging, Free Rappels

An overhanging, free rappel is when the rappeller is hanging in space with nothing for the feet. Two hands can be used to apply the brake and control speed. If you want extra friction to slow the descent, run the rope between your legs, then underneath one leg and up to the brake hand. The added friction of the rope running under the leg is considerable, and provided your rappel apparatus is giving adequate friction, you can easily stop by folding the rope over the top of your leg. However, try to maintain a smooth, steady descent; if you go too slowly, you'll tend to twirl on the rope. Maintain the same posture you would while sitting in a chair. A little tension from your guide hand will keep your upper torso upright.

As you come back in contact with the rock, extend your legs out like antennae, and slowly ease back onto the wall. Never race down a free rappel and suddenly stop. The quick deceleration generates enormous stress on the whole system and unnecessarily elongates the rope, which will abrade over even the smoothest lip.

Brake Hand Backups

If for some reason you are doubtful about controlling your rappel and are forced into making one—without a belay—you can rig a backup with either of two knots that bind on the rope when weighted but can be slid along the rope when not. The traditional knot is the Prusik, but it must be tied with 7mm or 8mm accessory cord. Webbing will not work effectively as a Prusik, but it can be combined with a carabiner to form a Bachmann knot, which serves the same purpose. Rig the Bachmann or Prusik on the rope and attach it with a sling to a locking biner on your waist. When rappelling, cup the guide hand loosely over the knot, sliding it down as you go. Make sure the sling is not too long. If you do go out of control and the knot jams tight, it must be within reach to loosen, or you're stuck. And remember that unless the knot jams tight the moment you start sliding, it will never jam but will burn through.

Overhanging, free rappel, using two hands for the brake. You can create additional friction to slow the descent by running the rope between your legs and up to the brake hand.

A system many guides consider better and safer is to rig a friction knot below your belay device and clip it to your leg loop to back up your brake hand. An Autoblock (a variation of a Klemheist knot) works adequately. Unlike a Prusik, the Autoblock will still move when directly weighted. Wrap a few coils of a loop of cord around the rope, then clip it back to your leg loop. It's good to have a cord pretied to the right length for this safety trick, though you can use a standard sling as well. Make sure the Autoblock has enough wraps that it easily grabs the rope. To rappel, hold the Autoblock with your brake hand and slide it down the rope. Notice the greatly increased friction of the rappel setup. If you need

to stop to untangle the ropes, the friction knot will hold you, freeing your hands. And if something like a falling rock causes you to let go of the rappel line, the friction knot will tighten so you don't go zipping down the rope.

That much said, I find the Prusik is easier to control and, ironically, tends to bind less. With the more elaborate friction knot/Autoblock/leg loop setups, there's a lot going on, suggesting the simpler Prusik as a viable first choice. Some instructors require beginners to rappel using an Autoblock backup. Fact is, most beginners have their hands full just completing their first few rappels, let alone while feathering a complicated friction knot that

A Prusik used to back up a rappel.

Tying a Prusik knot.

The Bachmann knot, an alternative to the Prusik, for use with flat webbing.

can bind fast and leave them dangling in untoward positions. The instructor's got to get the lead out and simply belay the novice down the line, which is easier, faster, and safer in the end. Start fiddling with Prusik, Bachmann, and Autoblock systems once you are fluent with rappelling. Till then, get a toprope belay.

The Line of Descent

The first question is: Where are you rappelling to? If you're simply heading for the ground and can see that the rope reaches, your task is relatively simple. If you have to make more than a single rappel to reach the ground or your destination, make certain

of several things. Are you descending to a ledge, a stance, or what? Do the ropes reach, and if so, what will be the next anchor? Do you have the necessary gear to rig an anchor? Many times rappel routes are established with fixed anchors; other times they are not. Numerous climbs end at a place from which you can walk off. If not, the way down often rappels the route just climbed. You know the topography, the ledges, the anchors. No mystery to it.

If you want to descend a virgin stretch of rock that requires numerous rappels, you have no way of knowing if there are adequate ledges and anchors. Even if you have inspected it with a telescope and can spot a big ledge, you still have no idea how good the anchors might be. Unless you carry a bolt kit, you are committing yourself to a real crapshoot that could leave you stranded. Forget about such an expedition.

For normal sport climbing, you need to know the place you're headed for, that there is an anchor or the possibility of getting one, that the same is available below—all the way to the ground—and that your rope will reach every rappel point/anchor in turn. Most guidebooks supply this information, but more often than not your judgment about a situation is what will get you down safely. At popular crags, ask around (specifying the length of your ropes) if you have any doubts about the descent. When in total doubt, rappel an established route, preferably the route you've just climbed—if you have to rappel at all.

Because every detail must be correct, it is critical that you double-check every aspect of the safety chain before leaning back to rappel. Double-check your harness buckle (and your partner's), the anchor and the rope's attachment to it, the rappel device and locking carabiner(s), and the rope-connecting knot. Just remember BARK—buckle, anchor, rappel device, and knot. Also, don't forget to inspect your gear often to be sure it's in good condition. Especially make sure your harness, belay loop, slings, and rope are in good shape. Occasionally check your biners and belay/rappel devices for wear or notches. Retire any gear as soon as you have any doubts about its condition.

Rappel Anchors

By now we know for certain that a bombproof anchor is the foundation of sane climbing. Every year, climbers—if not entire teams—are killed because of failed rappel anchors. Most all of these accidents were avoidable and were the result of human error. It's almost unique for a rappelling accident to be a so-called act of God—trees inexplicably coming uprooted, or several bolts or pitons popping mysteriously. Many times accidents are the result of someone trying to save equipment and chance it with a suspect anchor. Is the anchor unquestionably sound? It must be. Go with an indisputable natural anchor whenever possible— a towering ponderosa pine, for instance. With a hand-built anchor, a minimum of two nuts, bolts, or pitons are obligatory. Three, even four, different points are sometimes called for, depending on the quality of the placements.

Look the rappel anchors over carefully. Again, at least two bombproof anchors should be established at rappel stations, and they should conform to the SRENE standard: solid, redundant, equalized, and allow no extension. To review: "Solid" refers to the comparative security of the individual nuts, bolts, etc. "Redundant" means that you have a number of solid anchors. "Equalized" refers to the process of spreading the stress of a rappel over the various component parts of the anchor. "No extension" means that if one of the anchors should pull, there is no slack in the system that would allow the rappeller's body weight to suddenly shock-load onto the remaining anchors.

If the anchors are anything less than bomber, back them up if possible, and make sure everything is well equalized and that there is no chance for much extension if one placement blows. Avoid the American Triangle (see Chapter 4, "Ropes, Anchors, and Belays"), especially if the anchors are suspect.

Occasionally, rappel anchors consist of a single tree or set of slings on a rock feature; climbers should back up these anchors whenever possible. Anchor failure will likely kill you and your partner, so don't be cheap with your lives. If you use a tree, it's usually best to run the rope through slings and

Rappel anchor—tree with slings and rap rings. Expect to see many such anchors on adventure climbs. Check the condition of the webbing carefully, and if there's any doubt, tie your own sling.

Modern fixed anchors like these are almost always combinations of lap links, chains, and rings.

two biners, gates opposed, rather than around the tree; otherwise, you might damage your rope and the tree, or your rope could get stuck.

Fixed Rappel Anchors

Inspect fixed rappel anchors as if your life depends on them, because it does. Rusty pitons and bolts are particularly suspect. When in doubt, back up the existing anchor or place your own. The cost of a good nut is a small price to pay to see your children grow up.

At popular climbing areas, bolt anchors are

often connected by a chain. Never simply loop your rope around the chain. If a link or bolt hanger breaks, the rope will slip right off the chain. That happened 1,000 feet up El Capitan, and three young men died. I never better understood the significance of the word grief as when I saw friends of the stricken three milling around the El Cap meadow, their faces long as doom and asking how come. There is no reason anyone should ever have to repeat their fate.

Many times, fixed anchor slings will come equipped with a heavy metal ring, like a medallion, through which you can feed the rope. These rappel rings are nice to pull a rope through and are usually quite strong—the cast aluminum ones are the best—but beware the welded steel ones. A new nylon runner threaded through the eyes or hangers of the anchor isn't given to invisible cracks or work hardening. Though I've never heard of one of these rings breaking, it is theoretically possible. But you will never hear about a new runner breaking on a rappel, unless it's running over a knife edge. The standard line regarding rappel rings is to never use just one ring. Always inspect them because they do wear out, especially if they have been toproped through. Never toprope through a rappel ring. More on this later.

Most often on fixed rappel anchors, the individual placements—be they nuts (extremely rare), pitons, or bolts—have a host of runners threaded through them from past rappels. If you're relying on fixed slings left by previous parties, check every inch of them to make sure they haven't suffered from too much ultraviolet radiation (sun-bleached) or have been chewed by varmints. Especially check the part of the slings hidden from view, and inspect any rappel rings or links. Add a sling if there is any question about the condition of the existing ones, and add a chock or two if the other anchors don't look positively bombproof. It's your life you're dealing with here, so don't get into the fatal habit of trusting whatever fixed gear exists.

The rope is retrieved by pulling it through the slings, and the process can cause enough friction to greatly reduce the strength of the slings and occasionally burn through them. Some years ago, a collection of old slings taken from rappel anchors were tested for tensile strength, and it's reassuring to know that many of these slings were stronger than expected. Figures indicate that if there are more than four slings in place, there is little chance of all of them breaking. However, wear from the elements, cutting on sharp bolt hangers, and friction burns all factor in to greatly diminish a runner's

strength, so the importance of backing up suspect slings cannot be overstated.

Wherever the anchor is, you are obliged to rappel directly below it. Gravity deems it so. A weight on the end of a string hangs directly below the string's anchor—the plumb line. After you have descended a ways, you can traverse around a bit, but a slip might set you on a dangerous sideways tumble. So if you have to rig your own anchor, do so directly above (or as close as possible to) where you plan to descend, and don't deviate more than necessary.

Setting the Ropes

Barring special circumstances, you will always rappel on a doubled rope, or ropes, which is retrieved by pulling it through the anchor slings. To facilitate this retrieval, the point where the rope runs through the slings is of vital concern. If you are on a smooth wall, it makes little difference. On a ledge, if the anchor is low, the slings should ideally extend just over the lip of the ledge so the rope is not bent over a sharp or angled edge. Even the smoothest rappeller will bounce on the rope, which will abrade over an edge, leaving a pile of sheath fiber on the rock. A sharp edge may even cut into the rope. Be keenly aware of what the rope runs over—avoiding, blunting, or even padding any hazards.

Make certain the rope is not running through—or even near—any notches, cracks, flakes, or knobs. When it comes time to retrieve the ropes, they will invariably get lodged in these features. And, of course, inspect the ledge for loose or rotten rock. The action of a rappel can dislodge them, and when you are pulling the ropes down, the free end can whisk loose rocks directly onto your head.

On a big ledge you can't extend a runner over the edge, since no one carries 20-foot slings with them. So if the anchor is located some ways back from the lip of the ledge, rig the anchor as high as you can above that ledge—say, at eye level. This reduces the angle at which the rope passes over the

Sport Climbing

Sport climbing has dominated the climbing scene for going on three decades. Sport climbing, by common definition, is climbing on routes protected exclusively by bolts, as opposed to traditional climbing, where the protection is provided by gear hand placed by the leader. Of course, there is considerable overlap between the two types of climbing. For example, some routes have "mixed" protection, where the leader clips bolts and places gear. Sport climbing has also come to include climbing competitions, indoor gym climbing, and low bouldering—basically any type of climbing that is perceived to be "safe," a term that should never be applied to any form of climbing, especially bouldering. Incidentally, more broken bones arise from bouldering than roped climbing. Every time you fall you hit the ground, and even with crash pads stacked high and wide, bouldering deserves a warning to this effect.

Most sport climbing strives to remove the risk inherent in climbing, allowing the climber to focus on technical difficulty. It requires less commitment than traditional climbing because there is usually little penalty for error. Generally, gear consists only of shoes, a rope, a harness, and a handful of draws; and if it starts raining or the vibes are wrong or, more likely, you pump out, you simply lower back to the deck. The vast majority of sport climbs are 100 feet long or less, and provided the leader has a 200- or 230-foot rope (both are standard gear), she simply lowers off the top anchors right back to her pack.

By engineering most of the potential hazards out of the equation—meaning permanent protection bolts are spaced roughly a body length apart—sport climbing has become increasingly accessible to the masses, many of whom decry the seriousness of traditional climbing. Nevertheless, most sport climbs are steep to overhanging, so falls are quick, hard, and often scary because you are literally plummeting through the air, as opposed to skidding down a lower-angled trad route.

While sport climbing is perceived as a safe endeavor, a casual attitude can still earn you a pine box. Diligent attention must be paid to every detail in the safety chain. Climbers tend to place blind faith in the bolt protection found on sport routes—and for good reason. Bolts hold tens of thousands of falls each year, with very few failures. But some failures do occur, mostly with old ¼-inch-diameter bolts—virtually never found on modern sport routes—which can shoot from the stone like nobody's business. Poorly placed larger bolts can, and do, fail. Sometimes the bolt is sound but the hanger is suspect. At any rate, inspect the bolt and the hanger before blindly trusting them. Since sport climbing is so reliant on bolts, it might be a good idea to go back and review the material on bolts in the anchors section (see Chapter 4, "Ropes, Anchors, and Belays").

Dave Graham on-sighting a 5.14 sport route at Terradets, Spain. KEITH LADZINSKI

and earmarks a nervous or inexperienced belayer. Zipping a leader down the route is also poor form and dangerous. Slow her down as she approaches the ground, and make sure she's solidly on her feet before you feed out slack.

The biggest fears in lowering someone are that you could drop her out of control or let the end of the rope pass through your belay device, causing her to fall to the ground. Both of these mistakes have often happened, and to very experienced climbers. The lowering anchors must be within a half rope length for your partner to reach the ground. If any uncertainty exists about the distance to the ground, tie a knot in the end of the rope so it can't whistle through your belay device if it is too short. Also, don't be too far from the touch-down zone in case the entire length of the rope may be needed.

A Grigri or a Cinch works very nicely for lowering; just squeeze the locking cam. It takes some practice to lower smoothly, however. If you're having trouble squeezing the cam, use the lever, but be especially careful not to pull back on the lever too fast or you'll drop your partner like a ton of bricks.

The Climber's Job

The most common situation for being lowered is from double or triple anchors at the top of a sport route. If you can't stand on a ledge at the top of the pitch to rig the rope for lowering—and you rarely can—clip into one of the anchors with a sling. Clip both anchors if you're a long ways above your last piece. If the hanger features chain links or other connecting hardware, follow these steps:

1. Pass a bight (loop) of rope through the anchors and extend the bight down to your harness.
2. Tie a figure eight in the bight and clip this knot into a locking carabiner on your harness tie-in point or belay loop.
3. Double-check everything, then dismantle your original tie-in knot. You're now connected to the rope through the locking carabiner and figure

eight knot. Pull the end of the rope through the anchors and give the signal to lower.

This system is quick and safe because you are never untied from the rope or off belay. If lowering requires the entire length of the rope, however, this trick may leave you a little short of the ground. Some people complain that this technique leaves you connected to the rope with only a locking carabiner, but that's all that's holding you at the belayer's end anyway. Back up this biner with another, gates reversed, if that feels more comfortable.

Another alternative, especially good if a bight of rope won't fit through the anchors or if you need the entire length of the rope to lower, is to clip into the anchors with a sling or two, then tie a figure eight in the lead line 4 or so feet from the tie-in point and clip into it with a locking biner. This clip-off will keep you backed up by the higher pieces in the pitch and will make it impossible for you to drop the rope, which would place you in an embarrassing, scary, and potentially dangerous situation. Next, double-check everything, untie from the end of the rope, pass it through the anchors, and tie back into it. Now untie the backup knot, disconnect the slings, and lower off.

A third option that is quick but not as safe is to clip into the anchors with slings, untie the rope from your harness, pass it through the anchors, and tie back into it. The main problem here is the potential for dropping the rope and becoming stranded.

The rope must pass through steel chain links, welded cold shut hangers, or carabiners to allow safe lowering. Conventional bolt hangers and aluminum rappel rings are not suited for lowering or toproping directly through, so in very rare instances, the leader may have to leave a carabiner or two to lower off such anchors, or rappel rather than lower.

When climbing, lowering, and toproping, the alert climber is always on the lookout for sharp edges that may cut the rope. If the rock is especially

A climber being lowered down a slab, maintaining the same body position as when rappelling: lower body at a 45-degree angle relative to the plane of the rock (this way the climber's weight is loading directly onto the feet and onto the rock); legs extended and bent slightly at the knees; upper body folded slightly up at the waist; head turned and scanning the terrain below.

is to invite injury. And totally blasting those muscles every third day will bring much better results than doing so every day, or every other day.

From this we can conclude that while it is desirable to do specialized exercises that closely ape the climbing movement—and focus on the muscle groups most involved—it is likewise important to round out the routine and physique with an equal amount of general conditioning exercises. Anything else results in an unbalanced machine, where weak antagonistic muscles are throwing the whole body out of kilter.

Of course, the best training for climbing is climbing itself. There is no substitute for mileage on the rocks for gaining strength, endurance, and fluidity of movement. For developing sheer power and technique, bouldering has no rival. Technique, power, and endurance can also be improved in a climbing gym. If there isn't one near you, there probably will be soon. For raw power, campusing on a fingerboard has proven to be remarkably effective. And for general conditioning, weight training is second to none.

Bouldering

Bouldering is essentially climbing a sequence of moves (a "problem") where a rope is unnecessary. The world's hardest climbing—in terms of individual moves and small sequences—has always been, and always will be, done on boulders. The controlled medium; the ease of trying, trying, and trying again; and the ferocious though mostly friendly competition that surrounds the practice make ideal conditions for the best climbers to try the hardest sequences imaginable.

The first time I saw a world-class boulderer in action, I was thunderstruck. I'd been climbing about three months, clawing up easy climbs made difficult because—in the spirit of the great mountaineers—we bore weighty packs and climbed in hiking boots. And before me was a man in shorts, varappe shoes, and a chalk bag, powering up overhanging rock like it was a jungle gym, ever controlled and graceful, with precision and explosive strength that was mind-boggling. The experience reoriented me in seconds. No more packs, off with the hiking boots—it was time to start bouldering.

Bouldering is such an engaging and stimulating endeavor that many climbers prefer it to roped climbing. A dedicated boulderer brings a lot of artillery to a roped climb. Strong fingers and good footwork, requisite for any difficult bouldering, are hers in abundance. But it's the experience of having done thousands of different sequences that gives her the real edge. It's doubtful that an experienced boulderer will encounter anything on a roped climb that she hasn't already done—in some fashion or another—on the boulders. Beginning climbers can master the fundamentals in several months, intermediate climbers can become experts in a year, and experts can maintain their edge with a couple of good bouldering sessions a week.

All bouldering is not low-level work, however. Highball bouldering, essentially free soloing, has long been a popular game of nerves and control among experts. Because of their tremendous skill level, serious accidents are rare among expert soloers. As a novice or intermediate climber, you will never want to climb any higher than a point where you feel comfortable jumping off. If you must assume an upside-down or awkward position, have a friend spot you. Make sure your spotter is alert and ready, with his hands up to prevent your head and shoulders from hitting the ground if you fall. And remember, if you fall off, you do hit the ground. Always clear the landing zone of problem stones or other detritus that could cause twisted or broken ankles—the most common injuries in bouldering. If you think bouldering is for you, invest in a crash pad. No serious boulderer is without one (two or three crash pads are often stacked beneath high problems). There are many models to keep you from bruising an ankle. If there is any doubt about the seriousness of a bouldering problem—that it's too high or the fall is ugly—rig a toprope.

Bouldering at the Buttermilks, a popular area on the east side of the Sierras, California.

Toproping

Toproping involves rigging an anchor above the desired climb. The rope runs up from the base of the climb, through the anchor, and back down— one end for the climber, the other for the belayer who is anchored on the ground. Toproping lets a climber ascend with protection from above. For many beginners, toproping will be the only climbing done at the outset. As such, it stands out as a method of climbing all its own. Moreover, there are many 20- to 40-foot-high cliffs scattered throughout the United States that are essentially toprope crags. There's loads of exercise and fun to be had at such areas and the fellowship is often better than the climbing.

Though toproping should be a fairly straightforward procedure, much depends on the circumstances. The actual setup, the rigging of the anchor itself, is of crucial importance, so a basic knowledge of anchor systems is required. Refer to those sections of this book, and also see *Climbing Anchors*, part of the How to Climb series, for a more thorough examination of this topic.

First on the agenda is selecting a toproping site. Many climbing areas have routes that have become designated toproping climbs. These are easily accessed from below via trail or third-class

Toproping is an excellent way to train for climbing.

Toproping a strenuous lieback flake.

Don't be afraid to toprope short boulder problems if it makes you feel more comfortable.

scrambling and oftentimes are fitted with bolt anchors. Less frequently, you must rig your own anchor or extend the anchor via slings, et al, to the anchor point below the lip of the wall you are climbing on (to avoid rope drag and wear).

To set a toprope anchor, you'll have to get close to the lip of the cliff. Use caution! Every year climbers are killed when they slip off a ledge while preparing their climb. If the ledge is sloping or wet and you feel uncomfortable, choose another site or get belayed into position to rig things up. Find a way to anchor yourself so you can concentrate

on the task at hand. And be careful of loose rocks that can bean people below. Have your partner(s) stand away from the base. When those below are at a safe distance, they're better able to make sure and verbally confirm that you're lining the rope directly over the climb.

Hopefully the route you've selected to toprope has a stout tree at the top. This makes for a quick and easy anchor. I generally carry two pieces of 1-inch tubular webbing (one 20 feet and one 30 feet in length), a couple of shoulder-length slings, and, of course, locking biners. (I also have a few

A double-strand cordelette arranged with an extender rope (usually 25 or so feet long) can be used for rigging toprope setups.

Extend your toprope anchor over any lips or ledges to make the rope run smoothly.

pre-tied cordelettes and a 50-foot piece of static line that I use as an extender line to get the anchor rigging over any lip. Such "short" static lines, which are very wear-resistant, are common tackle for those frequenting toprope areas.) Again, hulking trees are usually the best natural anchors, but boulders can work well, too. Just make sure they are stationary and there is no possible way for the slings to slip off the boulders. You can use nuts and cams to this end, but then you're getting into advanced territory. Know what you're doing.

The anchor slings must extend from the anchor to just over the lip of the climb, allowing the rope to run freely through the biners. Because anchors are sometimes well back from the lip, equalizing the anchor and extending it to hang in exactly the right place can involve some engineering, mainly in arranging slings of exactly the right length. Since you are probably not yet a good judge of what is bombproof and what is not, make sure that both your anchor and any extensions are ten times more secure than you think they need to be.

Whenever you must extend the anchor with slings, check for loose rock or other choss that may be knocked loose. Toproping involves continuous climbing and lowering on the system, meaning the anchors and any extensions will be under pressure and will no doubt move or shift around a little. This movement and pressure can send off anything loose directly onto those below.

At the top anchor point (through which the climbing rope runs), clip the rope off with two locking carabiners. They should be opposite and opposed. And always make sure the top anchor point is draped over and below the lip, if only 6 or 8 inches. Otherwise the rope will be running over the lip, and with all that weighted lowering, even a rounded, polished lip will abrade the rope. If the lip is pronounced, a single lowering can wear right through the sheath—if the anchor point is not below the lip. It is common to find big balls of sheath fuzz on top of popular toprope setups. Can I say it enough? Extend the anchor point below the lip.

The combination of stretch in the rope, friction on the top anchor, and a weight discrepancy between belayer and climber often necessitates a ground anchor. Sometimes it is difficult to find one. If the angle of the rock is less than vertical, it is less critical that the belayer be anchored, though it's always desirable. If the angle is steep or the belayer is much lighter than the climber, an anchor is essential. It's no fun for a climber on toprope to hit the deck from 15 feet up. For that matter, it's no fun for a belayer to be yanked off her feet and slapped into the rock. Both happen.

When climbing with a toprope, climb in line with the anchor as much as you can. Anytime you traverse out of the plumb line—to either side of the top anchor point—gravity will swing you back into the plumb line if you fall. The closer you get to the top anchor point, the more pronounced the swing. This means that as you near the top, be especially careful to climb directly up to the anchor point. If you're near the top anchor point and are

climbing off to the side, your swing will be hard and fast if you fall. If the route wanders and the person who sets the top anchor is experienced, she can place directionals on rappel (rare). Directionals are cams or nuts that keep the rope more in line with the direction of the route and help control the amount of swing a falling climber takes. As the climber ascends, he unclips the directional and then reclips it while being lowered. Like everything else, directionals need to be bomber, unless you want to pendulum more dramatically than you would have without the directional in the first place.

Most beginning toprope climbs are on slabs or moderately angled face climbs, or follow lower-angled cracks. However, there are occasionally overhanging toprope climbs that follow huge bucket holds and are technically quite easy—like working up a ladder or a giant jungle gym. The potential problem here is that if you fall off, you'll swing out into space. Unless the angle is quite overhanging—rare on a beginning toprope climb—you can usually get reestablished on the rock by simply kicking your legs, which will get you swinging, hopefully toward the rock. If you can't get back onto the wall, lower off and try again.

Whenever it's possible that a toprope fall can swing the climber out into space, the ground belay must have a sound anchor. Otherwise, as we've seen, the weight of the dangling climber can lift the belayer off the ground (particularly when the climber outweighs the belayer by more than 20 pounds). Also, in those rare instances when the beginning toprope climb is quite overhanging—a proper jug haul—the climber will swing way out away from the wall if she pings. It is crucial that you know what you might smack if you come off. Climbers routinely bang into tree limbs and even high boulders at the base, which can result in injuries, so scope any possible obstacles and rig the toprope somewhere else if necessary.

Lastly, a toprope fall should be no longer than the stretch in the rope. Remember that the more rope out, the more stretch, so belayers should be extremely vigilant when a climber is just starting out on a toprope ascent. If the toproped climb is a long one—say, 50 feet—that means that there's more than 100 feet of rope in use. With just a little slack in the line, a falling climber can easily stretch the rope and fall 5 feet, or more. Again, on a long toprope climb (anything over 40 feet), the most dangerous time is at the outset, when the rope will stretch the most and when the chances of hitting the ground are the greatest. If there is any doubt or if the climber feels a bit "iffy," consider keeping a little tension on the line as the climber starts the route. Even 10 pounds of tension on a toprope can reduce the fall to mere inches. This, of course, assumes that you are toproping on a dynamic lead rope. In the gym, all topropes are set up with static (no stretch) lines. Some climbers who routinely toprope have static ropes for that purpose and thus eliminate the issue of rope stretch.

Beginners and experienced climbers alike benefit from toproping. It's a relatively safe way to hone technique, as you can concentrate solely on the choreography of ascent rather than finding and placing sound gear. Many experts climb on toprope, often to wire a difficult and dangerous climb in preparation for the redpoint.

Perhaps the best teacher of all is the firsthand experience you will get from frequenting popular toprope areas. Watch and learn. Pick out an experienced climber and ask her questions about the rigging and so forth till you understand every aspect backwards and forwards. Once you understand several basic principles (spelled out in Chapter 4, "Ropes, Anchors, and Belays"), you can globalize those basics to fit most any circumstance. But there's nothing like seeing these principles carried out in real life. Most experienced climbers will gladly give you a quick breakdown regarding how and why they do things. Seek and ye shall know.

Climbing Gyms

Indoor climbing is one of the fastest growing sports today. Originally indoor climbing took place in a dank basement or cluttered garage. Home walls were a last resort to keep in shape during the winter or a stretch of bad weather. Soon climbers realized the benefits of climbing indoors—training at any time, user-friendly holds (for the most part), customized problems, predictable weather, gorgeous hard-bodied women and lecherous men with no jobs, rapid skill gains, and lots of fun.

Modern climbing gyms are state-of-the-art. They feature giant overhanging walls, slabs, roofs, arêtes, crack systems, toprope and lead climbing, air ventilation systems, and gymnastics mats to cushion a fall. Many feature specialized training areas—bouldering walls and system or campus boards. The safe and controlled environment of rock gyms makes them a great place to learn the basics and meet future partners. And the sheer number of routes and armchair convenience mean you can get in much more climbing than you would in a normal outdoor setting.

Cast out of epoxy or resin and sand, climbing holds have evolved to pretty well simulate pulling on actual rock. The wide variety and availability of modular holds give gym route setters almost limitless creativity in the setting of masterpiece routes. In fact, route setting is an art in itself.

Climbing walls are great places to hone footwork and general technique. Most gyms hold climbing competitions as well as a number of clinics throughout the year. The clinics are usually small, theme-based classes taught by established climbers. Get involved and you'll get better: A little friendly competition can push a climber to excel.

Tendon-nagging injuries happen most often indoors, so take heed. While the shape and texture of holds is generally finger friendly, watch out for tweaky "crimp fests" (a series of crimps on microholds) on vertical and less-than-vertical walls. Such

Working the plastic at Rockreation climbing gym, Costa Mesa, California.

routes can be difficult, and it is essential to warm up sufficiently before launching off onto the wall. If you're just getting started with indoor climbing, or if you haven't done it lately, start off slow and be sure to take rest days; finger tendons are quite delicate, and you're likely to end up on the sidelines with a strained digit if you crank too hard, too fast.

You can quickly get strong climbing in an indoor gym, and this leads to another climbing gym problem: the transition from indoor to outdoor climbing. People who have climbed exclusively indoors and then try to climb at the same level outside are sometimes in for a rude and possibly perilous awakening. Climbing outdoors, especially on trad routes, is serious. You have to deal with weather, rockfall, holds breaking, and route finding, and most importantly, you must demonstrate a sound knowledge of protection, gear, anchor systems, and self-rescue techniques. As mentioned, I recommend going with an experienced friend—or better yet, a certified guide—for your first few excursions out of the gym. They will instill in you a proper respect for the serious nature of outdoor climbing.

All told, climbing gyms are a great place to learn technique and develop strength quickly. Perhaps best of all, they have become a positive social hangout for climbers. While I could write another fifteen pages on climbing gyms, the most relevant advice is that any moderately serious climber should check one out. The what and the how of it all quickly become obvious once you walk in and rope up. You simply look around, and adapt to what the good folks are doing.

Specific Training Techniques

Hangboards and Campus Boards

Hangboards, introduced in 1986, are wooden or molded-resin boards (usually about a foot high by 2½ feet long) that are mounted up high like a pull-up bar. The board features various holds resembling those on a climb, from good jugs to rounded nothings, and the usual routine involves pulling up on the holds, as well as free hanging for timed intervals. There are a half-dozen styles commercially available, and each comes with suggested workouts. Most all gyms have several hangboards wall-mounted for easy access.

There is no doubt that hangboards can increase finger, hand, and forearm strength and that the carryover value to climbing is high, but the jury is still out on whether they cause more injuries than benefits. It is probably a matter of the routine. Increasing stress beyond normal climbing levels, especially free hanging for long periods on the board's punier holds, virtually ensures injuries. One danger is that the tendon connections at your shoulders—if you are hanging fully extended—have less strength than you can develop with your fingers. This means that as you hang to exhaustion on your fingertips, your body weight naturally sags to the tendon connectors at your shoulders; it is these connectors that risk separating. Adding weights (around your waist or ankles) will reduce the time spent on your fingers, and that will tend to keep you off your shoulders.

Whatever routines you decide on, remember that if you push yourself to muscle failure, you need forty-eight hours to fully recover. So to optimize your results on any board, heavy workouts every third day are superior to those every day or every other day. Most importantly, start off slowly and gradually increase the intensity of your workouts. Everyone responds a little differently to hangboard workouts, so it's best to slowly learn what your body can handle.

A campus board is basically a sheet of plywood with 12- to 18-inch-long horizontal wooden edges screwed into the wood every 4 to 8 inches, in a ladder formation running from eye level to about 10 feet. The plywood is mounted on a wall at an angle of about 15 to 20 degrees overhanging, and the object is to "campus" up the beveled holds without

Doing reps on a hangboard.

strength dividends. Six to ten laps, with five-minute rest intervals between burns, is a standard workout at my gym. This is not endurance training but strength training, so the accent is on how hard you make it (by skipping holds, using smaller holds, et al), not on how many laps you can do at one go, hence the long rest period.

Of course, you could train finger endurance on a campus board if you had that in mind. There are a lot of instructions and recommended workout routines that come with these boards (and are posted in responsible gyms). Read up on them if you plan to include campus boards in your workout routine (this is specialized knowledge not germane to a general book like this).

Cross-Training

The practice of training for a sport by doing exercises outside the sport itself is nothing new. Called crossover training, or simply cross-training, it is used by all professional athletes: Skiers run stairs and lift weights; football players run, lift weights, brawl in strip clubs, and do stretching exercises to reduce the chance of injury; divers jump on a trampoline and lift weights; and swimmers lift weights, jump rope, and ride a stationary bike, as do baseball players, who also drink their share of beer. All of these athletes count on their routines to give them a sharp conditioning edge that will cross over to their keynote sport.

Weight Training

For years climbers scorned weight training, usually for the wrong reasons. Strength-to-weight ratio has long been deemed the aim of all climbing workouts, and most climbers are loath to add any size to their shrink-wrapped physiques—not knowing that a mere 5 pounds of brawn might increase their strength upwards of 10 percent. (Also, many people think you can throw on 5 or 10 pounds of muscle with a couple dozen workouts. In fact, an avid lifter is lucky to add a single pound of muscle every two

your feet. The normal campus board has a vertical line of holds at three different widths—decent (about an inch), bad (half an inch), and pathetic (smaller still). Many climbers train only on the larger edges to avoid injuries.

You need to get thoroughly warmed up before yarding up these units, and it usually takes a few weeks to get used to the strain, if you ever can. A beginner basically has no chance of doing much campus board work, but a fit athlete can work up to it quickly. To be sure, you will see your strength skyrocket if you can work consistently at this exercise and remain injury free. Training on a campus board every three or four days is plenty to see big

Stretching

With today's gymnastically difficult routes, flexibility is crucial. Being flexible will help you with side stems and high steps, and you will be able to keep your hips closer to the rock on steep terrain, allowing you to get more weight onto your feet. Good flexibility will also help prevent injuries. Traditional stretching exercises are good, and a few sport-specific stretches have also been developed—the photos here are just a few examples. Many rock gyms offer stretching and yoga classes to help improve your flexibility, as well as contact your inner sage. Yoga is also excellent for connecting your movement with your breath, a key aspect of hard climbing and graceful living.

to three months.) Correct weight training is tough duty, certainly more toil than joy, which makes it all the more unpopular.

Other misconceptions have kept many climbers off the iron. The first is the notion of excess bulk. As absurd as it is, people think that lifting weights automatically makes you huge. It's food, rather than iron, that increases body size. Controlling your diet controls size, and you can't eat a dumbbell. Second is the notion of the muscle-bound oaf who can't comb his hair for all the huge deltoids. If anything, correct weight training—which entails full-range-of-motion exercises and a lot of stretching between sets—increases flexibility. But you have to do things right.

This is not the venue to spell out specific workout routines. A comprehensive iron routine can be easily designed to focus on a climber's needs. There are hundreds of books, Web sites, and videos to show you what's what. The best routines take into account a person's physique and mentality and are so personal that little applies across the board. For the climber new to weights, it's best to start a normal, conservative routine and customize it as your knowledge increases. Perhaps the best thing about weight training is that it is very difficult to incur serious injuries. Soreness and tweaked muscles are part of any training, but in more than thirty-five years of being an "iron rat," I've never once gotten an injury lifting weights that has kept me out of the gym for longer than a week.

Freehand Exercises

Essentially calisthenics, freehand exercises involve all the Jack LaLanne–type routines (save towing the boats): push-ups, pull-ups, sit-ups, dips. It's pretty hard to get a well-rounded workout doing just freehand exercises, but they require little in the way of specialized gear and are certainly better than doing nothing. As with weight training, it is hard to injure yourself doing them.

Aerobics, jazz dancing, swimming, Nautilus machines, yoga (excellent for sport climbing), and untold other routines are also possible and popular. Anything that promotes overall fitness and flexibility can only help your climbing.

Cardiovascular Exercises

A strong heart and good wind are vital for strenuous climbs. Increased circulation helps in another respect as well: It brings more oxygen to your muscles, which means faster recovery and tissue repair. Any action sport, such as basketball or mountain biking, is good. Pure running or cycling are also good—just watch those knees. The king of all cardiovascular activities, however, is the jump rope. Its popularity in the climbing world can probably be attributed to the fact that it requires a lot of skill to be good. Single revolutions (skipping) on a rope marks beginning level; double revolutions between jumps, intermediate; and triple revolutions, advanced. The person who can consistently do triple revolutions on a jump rope has the heart of a lion and lungs strong enough to fill the sails of a good-size bark.

Injuries

As the technical envelope is pushed further, debilitating injuries are becoming more commonplace. Aside from the normal muscle tweaks and strains inherent in any physical endeavor, climbers are particularly prone to elbow and finger injuries, most of which involve some form of tendonitis. Having suffered these impairments on numerous occasions, I can assure you that ignoring the injury can result in pain so intense that straightening the arm or closing the fingers is impossible, and climbing is out of the question.

Concerning treatment for these conditions, I defer to climber/orthopedist Dr. Mark Robinson, who has conducted several studies involving climbing injuries and is in an experienced position to give advice. Here are some self-cures for tendonitis that Dr. Robinson recommends, and which provide a Western medical approach largely adhered to today.

1. Decrease activity until pain is gone and all swelling and tenderness disappear.
2. Wait two weeks more.
3. Start with easy strength exercises—putty, gum, rubber squeezers (two to three weeks).
4. Low-angle climbing on big holds (one month).
5. High-angle climbing on big holds (one month).
6. Back to full bore.

Dr. Robinson adds: "Anti-inflammatory medicines (aspirin, ibuprofen, etc.) can be used to control symptoms and speed the recovery process. They should not be used to suppress pain to allow even more overuse, since this will eventually lead to worse problems and a longer recovery period. Various mystical and pseudo-scientific remedies, such as copper bracelets, dietary modifications, herbal cataplasms, horse liniments, ethnic balms, etc., are at best unproven. Very few, if any, of them bear any conceivable relation to what is known to be the basis of the problem."

What the doctor is telling us is that he doesn't fancy homeopathic remedies, and that time and patience are key ingredients to a full recovery. There are certainly people with different opinions—and case histories to support a more holistic approach to recovery—but, in fact, the key to healing is probably common sense: If it hurts, lay off it till it doesn't hurt, and in the meantime do whatever works to reduce the pain.

Whatever your healing method, returning prematurely to high-stress climbing with an injury is as foolish as ignoring an injury in the first place. "The tissues of the musculoskeletal system are capable of remarkable feats of repair and restoration," Dr. Robinson assures us, "but these processes are slow." Furthermore, there is nothing scientifically proven to accelerate these processes, except the use of anti-inflammatory drugs, which simply eliminate the restrictions and allow the healing to proceed. Many folks, however, swear by herbs and other alternative therapies ("alternative" is generally a term referring to everything but prescription drugs), such as Epsom salts. (*How to Climb 5.12* and *Better Bouldering* in the How to Climb series provide in-depth information on injury and injury prevention.)

The tendency to race back onto the cliffside and crank our brains out the second the pain is gone must be curbed. Experts and horse sense assure us this can only exacerbate the injury. Do what you want, but it's my feeling that Dr. Robinson's advice is probably the sagest course to full recovery (provided you augment his routine with effective supplements, especially glucosamine and chondroitin).

Injury Prevention

We know that the medical experts and countless wounded sport climbers have told us that certain exercises virtually ensure injuries, and we should avoid these if we're in for the long haul. But aside from that, what can we do? Some support of critical tendons can be achieved by taping—simply tape the trouble spots around the fingers on either side of the main (second) joint, around the wrist, and around the forearm just shy of the elbow. Professional athletes, however, are more and more relying on two things to avoid injuries: stretching and warming up. Aerobics and yoga might not make you stronger, but they may keep you from getting injured.

A very important practice is to do a little stretching and some easy climbing before jumping onto a hard climb. Warming up is part of any sport and is essential for climbers, whose movements so stress the elbows and fingers. This is particularly true for bouldering and sport climbing. Get limbered up with a running sweat, then max yourself. And if you tweak something, stop before you make it worse.

Responsibilities and Staying Alive

Throughout rock climbing's evolution, the simple joy of being the master of your fate, of seeing success or failure as the result of your efforts, has—as in any great sport—remained the heart of the experience. In the great Western tradition, self-reliance and the ability to account for your actions were always among the virtues that climbing encourages.

But there are many more climbers out on the cliffs than ever before. The community of climbers—once a small, counterculture, "outcast" society comprised chiefly of young men from dysfunctional families—now impacts the outdoors in profoundly visible ways. Trails and trash are found at the base of wilderness cliffs, and the responsibility for this lies with all of us, of course. Part of the allure of rock climbing is that it is more than just a physical exercise; we are intrinsically bound to features that nature has provided us. The environment is fragile, and the promise to maintain it is an integral part of our outdoor experience. The following suggestions address some of these issues.

Serve yourself and others by picking up trash when you find it, whether or not you brought it to the cliffs yourself. Relieve yourself away from the bottom of the route. Make a practice of carrying a small plastic bag to carry out all toilet paper, and mindful that uncovered feces decompose faster,

keep such deposits well clear of established trails and paths. On longer routes, urinate away from where others must climb. Anything else is gauche and unacceptable.

Stick to established trails whenever possible. Although competent to travel over the roughest country in pursuit of the most direct line to a selected route, climbers should more often demonstrate their sensitivity to the effects of rampant erosion that are the result of zealous proliferation of access trails. Nesting birds should be respected and left as you find them. Remember that you are a guest of the crags and their inhabitants.

Codes of proper cliffside etiquette are, of course, no different than those most people try to practice in the greater world. There are, however, situations that are unique. Usually, the first party to arrive at the base of a route gets the route first. You might offer the route to a clearly faster party, but once on a route, you should feel under no obligation to let a party pass if for any reason you are not comfortable with them above you. Again, if they are obviously a quicker team, it is probably a nice thing to offer, but if, for instance, loose rock is an issue, don't feel compelled to let anybody by; they made their choice at the beginning of the route. Another frequent problem is that certain climbs are popular as end-of-

Sonnie Trotter staying alive on **Eurasian Eyes** *(5.13b), Squamish, British Columbia.*
KEITH LADZINSKI

the-day trade routes or are simply local classics and, as such, often have folks queuing up despite the fact that there are often a dozen similar routes to either side. "Camping" on a local favorite is questionable form, but so is breathing down a party's neck to hurry up and clear out. If a climb is taken, move on to something else—there's always something else. And if parties are waiting, pull down and move on.

As climbing moves well into this new century, one of the biggest problems confronting all climbers is access to the cliffs. The loss of access to climbing or bouldering areas is an issue that affects every climber, regardless of technical ability or stylistic preference. The responsibility for solving or preventing access problems rests with each and every climber. Minimizing environmental impact, being sensitive to behavior that could affect access, and taking responsibility for your own actions by not suing landowners, climbing gyms, or belayers if you get hurt will help prevent problems. Climbing is inherently dangerous, and if something goes wrong, trying to blame someone else can never reverse the damage. When a climber starts up a cliff, nothing is guaranteed and he is owed nothing at all.

When access problems do arise, the Access Fund can help negotiate, organize, and even litigate closures of climbing areas. In some situations they actually finance the purchase or preservation of climbing and bouldering areas. Your tax-deductible contribution to the Access Fund is a concrete way of giving something back to climbing and making a real difference in the effort to save the rich diversity of climbing resources in the United States. Send your donation (of any amount) to the Access Fund, P.O. Box 17010, Boulder, CO 80308; (303) 545-6772; www.accessfund.org.

Staying Alive

Rock climbing is potentially hazardous, and it is the task of the individual to learn and understand the proper techniques to ensure the safest possible participation. Though no substitute for professional instruction or years of climbing experience, this manual has hopefully helped both the novice and the expert to a greater knowledge of rock climbing's fundamentals and nuances.

In summary, I offer part of a longer essay on safety that appeared in an early Yosemite climber's guide. Prepared by the head rescue ranger, John Dill, the essay contains wisdom distilled from more than thirty-five years of seeing every kind of accident in every kind of situation by every kind of climber—from rank beginner to world-class hero. To one and all, says Dill, "State of mind is the key to safety. It's impossible to know how many climbers were killed by haste or overconfidence. Many accident survivors will tell you that, somehow, they lost their better judgment just long enough to get hurt. It's a murky subject. Nevertheless, these mental lapses generally fall under three categories: ignorance, casualness, and distraction."

Ignorance

Even the most conscientious climber can get into trouble if he's unaware of the danger ("I thought it never rained . . ."). There is always something more to learn, regardless of experience. There are two basic steps to fighting ignorance:

- Continue to read, and listen to climbers who have survived. Back issues of climbing magazines are full of pertinent articles. Case histories in the American Alpine Club's Accidents in North American Mountaineering, a yearly compilation of accident reports, will show you how subtle factors may conspire to catch you unaware. Such accounts are the next best thing to being there.

- Practice. Reading may make you aware but not competent. Regardless of the written word, which is sometimes wrong, you must ultimately think and act for yourself. Several climbers have waited to learn how to Prusik until it was dark and raining, the route was overhanging, and they were actually in trouble. They had read about it, but they still had to be rescued despite having the gear to improvise their own escape. Book-learning alone gave them a complacency that could have proved fatal.

Casualness

"I just didn't take it seriously" is a common refrain. It's often correct, though it's more a symptom than a disease—there may be deeper reasons for underestimating your risk. Ignorance is one; here are some more:

- Habit reinforcement occurs when nothing goes wrong. The more often you get away with risky business, the more entrenched your lazier habits become. Have you unconsciously dropped items from your safety checklist since you were a beginner?

- Your attitudes and habits can be reinforced by the experiences (and states of mind) of others. The sense of awe and commitment of the 1960s is gone from the big wall "trade routes," and young aspirants with no grade VIs or even Vs to their credit speak casually about them. Yet most of the accidents on El Capitan occur on easy pitches.

- Memory decay. "I'm not going up again without rain gear—I thought I would die!" A week later this climber has forgotten how scared he had been in that thunderstorm. Rain gear was now too heavy, and besides, he'd rap off the next time. Many of us tend to forget the bad points. We have to be hit again.

- Civilization. With fixed anchors marking the way and generous amounts of chalk telling of hundreds of previous ascents, it may be hard to realize how high the potential danger actually is.

Some say the idea of a fast rescue adds to their casualness. Maybe, but who wants a broken leg—or worse—in the first place?

- Overconfidence. "It'll never happen to me. I'm a safe, cautious climber." Many of those killed were described by friends as very cautious.

Distraction

Distraction is caused by whatever takes your mind off your work: fear, thirst, sore feet, skinny-dippers below—the list is endless. Being in a hurry is one of the most common causes. Learn to recognize when you or your partner are becoming distracted. Stop, get your act together, then proceed. Here are two examples in which being distracted has caused problems (often fatal):

- Experienced climbers have often been hurt after making "beginner errors" (their words) to get somewhere quickly. There was no emergency or panic, but their minds were elsewhere—on a cold beer or a good bivouac—or they were just sick of being on that route for a week (often called "summit fever"). Their mistakes were usually shortcuts in protecting easy pitches, on both walls and day climbs. As one climber put it, "We were climbing as though we were on top."

- Darkness once caught two day climbers for the first time. Unprepared, upset, and off route, they rushed to get down, arguing with each other about what to do. After several errors, which they knew to avoid, one climber was killed rappelling off the end of his rope.

The percentage of accident victims is minuscule compared to the hundreds of thousands of active rock climbers. But the dangers are real, and should you or a ropemate be so unfortunate as to suffer an injury, Ranger Dill has put forth the following concerning rescues:

> Despite the best of preparations, an accident can happen to anyone. Self-rescue is often the fastest

and safest way out, but whether it's the wise course of action depends on the injury and how well prepared you are. Combining with a nearby party may often give you the margin of safety you need, but do not risk aggravating an injury or getting yourself into a more serious predicament—ask for help if you need it. Sometimes a bit of advice, delivered through a loudspeaker, is all that's required.

If you don't have formal first-aid training (which is highly recommended), at least know how to keep an unconscious patient's airway open, how to protect a possible broken neck or back, and how to recognize and deal with external bleeding and serious blood loss (shock). These procedures are lifesaving, do not require fancy gear, and are easy to learn and perform. Note that head injury victims are apt to be irrational and very strong. Even if he's unconscious, if you have to leave him, make it impossible for him to untie himself.

The Other Sides of the Game

Climbing is a broad game of which rock climbing is only a part—a fundamental, popular part, but by no means even half the game. Big walls will always provide the most awesome form of pure rock climbing because the venues—towering monoliths like El Capitan in Yosemite Valley and Hidden Tower in Pakistan—are peerless for grandeur and intimidation. Huge sixth-class routes are steep, often unnerving trials that terrify and amaze even twenty-year veterans. They are sometimes three-quarters of a mile high, and a hanging bivouac at that altitude is an ordeal no climber is fully prepared for—or ever gets completely accustomed to. It's always a game of "keeping the lid on" when most everything around you, as well as your own instincts, tells you to clear the hell off and fast. But

the climber who paws over the lip of a big wall, still whole in body and soul, has experiences and memories that no other sport can hope to match.

Mountaineering, in its extreme form, is the riskiest of all the climbing games. Sudden storms, avalanches that sweep entire mountains, horrific rockfalls, hidden crevasses, and physiological disorders from altitude and cold are all out of a climber's hands and have drawn the curtain on hundreds of veterans. The old method of sieging the mountain, using armies of climbers, bottled oxygen, and countless other helpful strategies, has given way to "alpine" ascents, where a handful of climbers go for broke with little or no backup, are irreversibly committed, and survive only through personal prowess, iron will, and luck. Successful parties invariably return with tales fantastic and astounding, and the ill-fated (by no count the minority) have stories none the less remarkable, though often with a tragic twist.

There are a hundred different games that fall somewhere between the ace poised on a boulder in the British Virgin Islands and the ironman who has just soloed Mount Everest. Some make a specialty of ice climbing. There are peak baggers who have never seen a rope, solo climbers who rarely use a rope, sea cliff climbers, limestone climbers, desert climbers, gym climbers, sport climbers, snow climbers, ski mountaineers, and people who own thousands of dollars of gear and only talk a good game. Chances are that the modern climber, whatever his or her specialty, has mastered the fundamentals while rock climbing. It remains the basic form in acquiring the knowledge of rope management, physical movement, and the mental conditioning required and applicable to any mode of ascent. The competent rock climber can readily cross over onto big walls or big mountains and is qualified to make the transition quickly and safely. Happy climbing.

Dry tooling on mixed rock and ice is just another variation on the climbing game. Here Sam Elias makes his way up mixed terrain near The Fang (WI5), Vail, Colorado. KEITH LADZINSKI

Appendix A: Resources

One of the happier consequences of a wider participation in rock climbing is easy access to good information. What follows is a listing of some of these resources—there are many more that can be sought out by those dedicated to the task.

Magazines

Rock and Ice
417 Main Street, Unit N
Carbondale, CO 81623
(970) 704-1442
www.rockandice.com

Climbing
2291 Arapahoe Avenue
Boulder, Colorado 80302
(303) 225-4628
www.climbing.com

Alpinist
P.O. Box 190
Jeffersonville, VT 05464
(802) 644 6606
www.alpinist.com

Deadpoint
An online climbing publication.
www.deadpointmag.com
info@deadpointmag.com

Web Sites

The following Web sites have articles, photos, videos, gear reviews, forums, trip reports, and lots of other information related to the sport. In addition to these general interest sites, many localized climbing Web sites exist—just Google your area and "climbing" and see what you come up with. And don't forget the blogosphere—many climbers regularly update their blogs with articles, interviews, podcasts, photos, and videos.

www.rockclimbing.com
www.supertopo.com
www.mountainproject.com
www.8a.nu
www.trainingforclimbing.com

Organizations

Access Fund
P.O. Box 17010
Boulder, Colorado 80308
(303) 545-6772
www.accessfund.org

American Alpine Club
710 10th Street, Suite 100
Golden, CO 80401
(303) 384-0110
www.americanalpineclub.org

American Mountain Guides Association
P.O. Box 1739
Boulder, Colorado 80306
(303) 271-0984
www.amga.com

The American Safe Climbing Association
P.O. Box 1814
Bishop, CA 93515
(650) 843-1473
www.safeclimbing.org

Books

The How to Climb series from FalconGuides is a great resource for all types of climbing. Check out these books for complete coverage of the many nuances of the sport. More information is available at www.globepequot.com.

Advanced Rock Climbing, by John Long and Craig Luebben

Better Bouldering, by John Sherman

Big Walls, by John Long and John Middendorf

Building Your Own Indoor Climbing Wall, by Ramsay Thomas

Climbing Anchors (Second Edition), by John Long and Bob Gaines

Conditioning for Climbers, by Eric Hörst

Girl on the Rocks: A Woman's Guide to Climbing with Strength, Grace, and Courage, by Katie Brown. Photos by Ben Moon.

Gym Climb!, by John Long

How to Climb 5.12, by Eric Hörst

Knots for Climbers (Second Edition), by Craig Luebben

Learning to Climb Indoors, by Eric Hörst

Mixed Climbing, by Sean Issac

Rappel!, by Craig Luebben

Self Rescue, by David Fasulo

Speed Climbing (Second Edition), by Hans Florine and Bill Wright

Sport Climbing, by John Long

Toproping, by S. Peter Lewis

Training for Climbing (Second Edition), by Eric Hörst

Appendix B: Climbing Glossary

abseiling: Descending by sliding down a rope. See also rappelling.

adze: The flat end of an ice ax head.

aid: Means of getting up a climb using other than the actions of hands, feet, and body English.

aid climbing: Using equipment for direct assistance, which allows passage over rock otherwise impossible using only hands and feet; opposite of free climbing.

aid route: A route that can only be ascended using aid climbing techniques.

alcove: A belay ledge surrounded by vertical rock on all sides.

Alien: Brand name for a type of spring-loaded camming device (SLCD), the most popular type of anchor. See also Friends.

anchor: A means by which climbers are secured to a cliff; the point where the rope is fixed to the rock.

anchor matrix: The placement of anchors using various rigging systems.

arête: A narrow ridge or an outside edge or corner of rock.

arm bar: A means of holding onto a wide crack; also called arm lock.

arm lock: See arm bar.

ATC: Air Traffic Controller, a belaying device made by Black Diamond.

backstep: Climbing move; placing the outside edge of the foot behind, usually on a vertical hold.

bail: To give up on a climb or summit attempt due to bad weather coming in.

BASE jumping: A rapidly growing sport with professionally organized competitions and legal jumping sites all around the world. BASE is an acronym for the four categories of fixed objects BASE jumpers launch from: buildings, antennas, spans (bridges), and earth (cliffs).

bashie: A piece of malleable metal that has been hammered into a rock seam as an anchor; used in extreme aid climbing.

belay: Procedure of securing a climber by the use of a rope.

belayer: The person at the belay station securing the climber.

beta: Prior information about a climb, including sequence, rests, gear, clips, etc. Running or auto beta is when someone instructs the climber on how to do the moves as they go.

beta flash: Leading a climb without falling or dogging, but with a bit of previous knowledge on how to do the crux moves, such as seeing someone else do the climb.

bi-doigt: A two-finger handhold.

Big Bro: Specialized protection for wide cracks.

Big Dude: Brand name for a type of spring-loaded camming device (SLCD), the most popular type of anchor. See also Friends.

big wall: A long climb traditionally done over multiple days, but which may take just a few hours for ace climbers. See also wall.

bight: A loop, as in a bight of rope.

biner: See carabiner.

Birdbeak: A tiny hooked piton manufactured by A5 that has a single side and is intended to be hammered in if necessary.

bivi: See bivouac.

bivouac: An uncomfortable sleeping place in the middle of a route; also called bivi.

blast: To begin a big wall, after the line fixing is done.

bolt: An artificial anchor placed in a hole drilled for that purpose.

bomber: Absolutely fail-safe (as in a very solid anchor or big, big handhold); also called bombproof.

bombproof: See bomber.

bong: An almost extinct species of extra-wide pitons. Today large chocks are usually used.

bouldering: Climbing at the base of a cliff or on small boulders to practice climbing skills performed without a belay rope, having just a mat to fall onto. Climbers do "boulder challenges," where the solution is a series of moves that are repeated until it's accomplished.

bounce: To crater from an extreme height; usually lethal.

brain bucket: A helmet.

bridge, bridging: See stem, stemming.

bucket: A handhold large enough to fully latch onto, like the handle of a bucket.

bump: Using an intermediate handhold to shift to a higher hold without changing body position.

buttress: An outside edge of rock that's much broader than an arête, definitely mountain-size.

cam: To lodge in a crack by counterpressure; that which lodges.

Camalot: Brand name for a type of spring-loaded camming device (SLCD), the most popular type of anchor. See also Friends.

campus: To climb an overhanging section of rock using the arms only; a method of training grip, contact, and upper body strength.

carabiner: Aluminum alloy ring equipped with a spring-loaded snap gate; also called biner or krab.

ceiling: A section of rock that extends out above your head; an overhang of sufficient size to loom overhead; also called roof.

chalk: Standard equipment used to soak up finger and hand sweat on holds, although not allowed at certain areas.

chickenhead: A bulbous knob of rock.

chimney: A crack of sufficient size to accept an entire body.

chock: See nut.

chockstone: A rock lodged in a crack.

choss, chossy: Rotten rock that is prone to fracturing.

Class 1: Mountain travel classification for trail hiking.

Class 2: Mountain travel classification for hiking over rough ground, such as scree and talus; may include the use of hands for stability.

Class 3: Mountain travel classification for scrambling that requires the use of hands and careful foot placement.

Class 4: Mountain travel classification for scrambling over steep and exposed terrain; a rope may be used for safety on exposed areas.

Class 5: Mountain travel classification for technical "free" climbing where terrain is steep and exposed, requiring the use of ropes, protection hardware, and related techniques. See also Yosemite Decimal System (YDS).

Class 6: Mountain travel classification for aid climbing where climbing equipment is used for balance, rest, or progress, denoted with a capital letter A followed by numerals 0 to 5 (eg., 5.9/A3, meaning the free climbing difficulties are up to 5.9 with an aid section of A3 difficulty).

clean: Routes that are variously free of vegetation or loose rock, or where you don't need to place pitons; also the act of removing chocks and other gear from a pitch.

cliff: A high, steep, or overhanging face of rock.

cling grip: A handhold where you grasp an edge with your fingers.

cold shut: A relatively soft metal ring that can be closed with a hammer blow; notoriously unreliable for withstanding high loads; commonly found as anchors atop short sport climbs.

cordelette: Standard tackle that facilitates equalizing the load between two or more anchors. A 16-foot section of 6mm Spectra is tied into a loop and clipped through all the anchor pieces, then tied off to create a single tie-in point, forming separate and equalized loops.

crack: Type of irregularity on the stone.

crag: A steep, rugged mass of rock projecting upward or outward.

crimp: An upper body grip where the first knuckle is extended, allowing the fingertips to rest on a small ledge while the second knuckle is flexed.

crimper: A small but positive sharp edge.

crux: The most difficult move or sequence of moves on a climb, typically marked on topos with the difficulty rating.

difficulty ratings: See Classes 1–6, Grades I–VI, R-rated climb, V system, X-rated climb, and Yosemite Decimal System (YDS).

dihedral: An inside corner of the climbing surface, formed by two planes of rock, like the oblique angle formed by the pages in an open book.

downclimb, downclimbing: A descent without rope, usually when rappelling is unsafe or impractical.

drag: Used in reference to the resistance of rope running through carabiners.

dynamic: Lunge move or explosive leap for a hold otherwise out of reach; also called dynamo, dyno, or mo.

dynamo: See dynamic.

dyno: See dynamic.

edge: A small hold ledge or the act of standing on an edge.

edging: Climbing move; placing the very edge of the shoe on any hold that is clear-cut.

exposure: A relative situation where a climb has particularly noticeable sheerness.

flag: Using a limb as a counterbalance.

flake: Type of irregularity on the stone.

flash: Free climbing a route from bottom to top on your first try, but with the aid of beta.

footwork: The art and method of standing on holds.

free: See free climb.

free ascent: See free climb.

free climb: The upward progress gained by a climber's own efforts, using hands and feet on available features, unaided or free of attending ropes and gear. Rope is only used to safeguard against injury, not for upward progress or resting; opposite of aid climb; also called free or free ascent.

free solo: Free climbing a route alone from bottom to top on your first try.

Friends: The original spring-loaded camming devices (SLCDs) made by Wild Country. Sometimes used as a generic term to describe othe brand-name camming devices such as Aliens, Big Dudes, Camalots, Quad Cams, and TCUs.

frog step: A climbing move where you bring one foot up, then the other, while keeping your torso at the same level, forming a crouched, or "bullfrog," position.

gaston: To grip a handhold that is above and to the side of the body, with the hand in a thumbs-down position.

girth hitch: Method of looping a sling around a tree or horn.

gobies: Hand abrasions.

grade: A rating that tells how much time an experienced climber will take on a given climb; the "overall seriousness" grade (referring to the level of commitment, overall technical difficulty, ease of escape, and length of route), denoted by Roman numerals.

Grade I: A climb that may take only a few hours to complete, such as Class 4 scrambles and Class 5 climbs.

Grade II: A climb that may take three to four hours.

Grade III: A climb that may take four to six hours, a strong half day.

Grade IV: A climb that may take a full day.

Grade V: A climb that may take one or two days and involve technical difficulties, weather, and other objective hazards, such as rockfall or avalanche danger. A bivouac is usually unavoidable.

Grade VI: A climb that may take two or more days on the wall.

Grigri: An auto-belay device made by Petzl.

gripped: Extremely scared.

greasy: Adjective used to describe a slick surface.

hangdog, hangdogging: To "climb" a route, usually bolt to bolt, with the aid of the rope to hang and rest; not a free ascent.

headwall: A much steeper section of cliff, residing toward the top.

heel hooking: The attempt to use the foot as a hand, usually on a vertical climb, where the heel is kicked over the head and hooked over a large hold.

hex: See hexentric.

hexentric: Six-sided or barrel-shaped anchor that can be wedged into wide cracks and bottlenecks; also called hex.

highball: A term used to describe bouldering problems that are high off the ground.

horn: A flakelike projection of rock, generally of small size.

jam: Wedging feet, hands, fingers, or other body parts to gain purchase in a crack.

jug: A handhold that looks like a jug handle.

kneedrop: Climbing move where the knee is dropped low and the rump is right over the foot.

krab: See carabiner.

latch: To successfully grip a hold.

layback, laybacking: See lieback, liebacking.

lead: To be the first on a climb, belayed from below, and placing protection to safeguard a fall.

lieback, liebacking: Climbing maneuver that entails pulling with the hands while pushing with the feet; also called layback, laybacking.

line: The path of the route, usually the line of least resistance between other major features of the rock.

lock-off: A single handhold with enough strength to allow the other hand to shift to a new handhold.

lunge: An out-of-control dynamic move; a jump for a far-off hold.

manky: Of poor quality, as in "manky finger jam" or "manky protection placement."

mantle: Climbing maneuver used to gain a single feature above your head.

mantleshelf: A rock feature, typically a ledge with scant holds directly above.

mantling: The act of surmounting a mantelshelf.

micro-taper: Small taper mostly used for aid climbing.

mo: See dynamo.

mono-doigt: A one-finger handhold, as in "mono-doigt pockets."

mountaineering: Reaching mountaintops using a combination of skills (such as rock climbing and ice climbing).

move: Movement; one of a series of motions necessary to gain climbing distance.

Munter hitch: Belay method that requires no special device.

nut: A wedge or mechanical device that provides secure anchor to the rock; also called chock.

off-width: A crack that is too wide to use as a finger, hand, or fist jam but too narrow to get right inside and climb as a chimney.

on-sight: To successfully climb a route without prior knowledge or experience of the moves; also called on-sight flash.

on-sight flash: See on-sight.

open grip: A handhold where the edge or pocket supports your fingers out to the second joint (or farther) and your hand lies flat against the wall.

opposition: Nuts, anchors, or climbing maneuvers that are held in place by the simultaneous stress of two forces working against each other.

passive nut: Nonmechanical carabiner. See also nut or carabiner.

pegs: See pitons.

pinch grip: A handhold where the thumb pinches in opposition to the fingers on either side of a projection.

pinkpoint: To lead, without falling, a climb that has been pre-protected with anchors rigged with carabiners.

pins: See pitons.

pitch: The section of rope between belays.

pitons: Metal spikes of various shapes that are hammered into the rock to provide anchors in cracks; also called pins or pegs. These types of anchors were common in the 1970s, but not used today.

placement: The position of a nut or anchor.

pocket: A hole or cavity in the climbing surface used as a hold.

pocket pulling: An exhausting type of climb most often found on limestone, dolomite, and welded tuff formations.

pro: See protection.

protection: The anchors used to safeguard the leader; also called pro. (Until the 1970s, protection devices were almost exclusively pitons—steel spikes that were hammered into cracks in the rock. Since then, various alloy wedges and intricate camming devices have virtually replaced pitons as generic protection devices. These wedges and cams are fitted into hollows and constrictions in cracks, and when fallen upon actually wedge farther into the rock. In the absence of cracks, permanent bolt anchors are drilled and fitted into the rock.)

Prusik: Both the knot and any means by which you mechanically ascend a rope.

pulling plastic: Indoor wall climbing.

pumpy: Climbing adjective that indicates the continuous nature of the climb.

Quad Cam: A type of spring-loaded camming device (SLCD), the most popular type of anchor. See also Friends.

quickdraw: Short sling with carabiners at both ends that helps provide drag-free rope management for the leader.

rack: The collection of gear a climber takes up the climb.

rappel: To descend a rope by means of mechanical brake devices.

rap: Informal term for rappel.

redpoint: To lead a route from bottom to top in one push, clipping protection as you go, without falling or resting on protection.

rib: A narrow buttress, not as sharp as an arête.

ring grip: A handhold where fingers are nestled close together, with the thumb wrapped over the index finger.

Rocks: Brand name of passive crack protection developed by Mark Valance.

roof: A section of rock that extends out above your head; also called ceiling.

RPs: A type of micro-taper.

R-rated climb: Climb with serious injury potential; protection may be sparse or "runout," or some placements may not hold a fall.

runner: See sling.

runout: The distance between two point of protection; often referring to a long stretch of climbing without protection.

sandbagging: The "shameful" practice of underestimating the actual difficulty of a given route.

second: The second person on a rope team, usually the leader's belayer.

send it: An emphatic statement to someone encouraging him or her to hang in and finish a route without falling.

sharp end: The lead climber's end of the rope.

shred: To do really well; to dominate.

sidepull: Pulling on a vertically aligned hold to the side of the body.

signals: A set of commands used between climber and belayer.

slab: A section of rock or gentle angle, sometimes a relative reference when it's a part of a vertical wall.

slap: To touch a handhold but fail to latch it.

sling: A webbing loop used for a variety of purposes to anchor to the rock; used to sling gear on; also called runner.

smear, smearing: Climbing move; standing on the front of the foot to gain friction against the rock across the breadth of the sole in order to adhere to the rock.

soft ratings: Ratings deemed harder than the actual difficulty of a given route.

solo climbing: Climbing without the use of ropes or any other gear, where the focus is reaching the summit, not on moves. Falls most likely result in injuries.

Spectra: Brand name of a popular climbing rope that's stronger than nylon; also called Spectra cord, Spectra line.

sport climbing: Similar to traditional rock climbing but with the protection (bolts) already in place. Instead of using nuts and cams, the climber uses quickdraws (short slings with a carabiner on each end). Most sport climbing is face climbing and is only two pitches, or rope lengths. With the danger element removed, the emphasis is on technique and doing hard moves.

spotter: A person designated to slow the fall of a boulderer, especially to keep the boulderer's head from hitting the ground.

spring-loaded camming devices (SLCDs): Also called springs; see Friends.

spring step: A climbing move where you "bounce" off your foot to propel your weight upward.

stance: A standing rest spot, often the site of a belay.

static step: A climbing move where you press your weight on one leg while simultaneously bringing your other foot up to the next hold; generally the most strenuous and least efficient way to move.

stem, stemming: The process of counterpressuring with the feet between two widely spaced holds; also called bridge, bridging.

Stoppers: Brand name for protection that acts like metal wedges placed in cracks and attached to the lead rope to limit the leader's fall if she loses her footing.

stringing your nuts: Attaching a length of rope to hexes and tapers rather than using a swaged cable.

sustained: Climbing adjective that indicates the continuous nature of the climb.

taper: An anchor, typically in a boxy shape, that can vary from thumbnail-size micros to 1½-inch bombers. Variations follow four basic patterns: straight taper, curved taper, offset taper, and micro brass or micro steel taper.

TCU: See three-cam unit.

thin: A climb or hold of relatively featureless character.

three-cam unit (TCU): A type of spring-loaded camming device (SLCD) designed specifically for thin cracks. See also Friends.

thrutch: To strain excessively. To move up, as in "Layback or thrutch up a low-angle chimney."

toeing-in: To edge with the shoe pointing straight on the hold; especially useful in small pockets.

toprope, toproping: A belay from an anchor point above; protects the climber from falling even a short distance.

trad climbing: See traditional rock climbing.

traditional rock climbing: A roped climber ascending rock by placing passive protection (such as nuts and hexes) to ensure his safety. The climbing rope is attached to the climber through a sit harness; the other end is attached to the climbing partner, who feeds out the rope as needed through a belay device; also called trad climbing.

traverse: To move sideways, without altitude gain.

Tricam: Brand name for an anchor that creates a tripod inside a crack or pocket.

tweak: To injure, as in "tweaked finger tendon."

undercling: Grabbing a hold with the palm up, often used as a balancing tactic until a free hand can reach above to a better hold.

V system: The universal bouldering language, established in the early 1990s at Hueco Tanks, Texas. Ratings range from V0 to V14, with V0 being the easiest and V14 being roughly equivalent to 5.15a YDS.

wall: A long climb traditionally done over multiple days, but which may take just a few hours for ace climbers. See also big wall.

water knot: Knot used to tie a runner.

wired: Known well, as in "wired route."

work, worked, working: To practice the moves of a difficult route via toprope or hangdogging.

X-rated climb: Climb with groundfall and death potential.

YDS: See Yosemite Decimal System.

Yosemite Decimal System (YDS): The usual American grading scale for identifying technical difficulty of routes, where 5 denotes the class, and the numerals following the decimal point indicate the difficulty rating, usually according to the most difficult move. Subgrades (a, b, c, and d) are used on climbs rated 5.10 and harder. When the grade is uncertain, two letters may be used (eg., a/b), which is a finer comparison of technical difficulty than the more general plus and minus (+ and -) signs.

Index

About the Author

John Long is the author of more than twenty-five books, with over one million copies in print. His short-form literary stories have been widely anthologized and translated into many languages. In 2006 he won the Literary Award for excellence in alpine literature from the American Alpine Club. In 2009 *Rock and Ice* magazine named him the most influential climber of the last twenty-five years, not only because of his groundbreaking ascents on Yosemite big walls, but also because of his monumental contribution to American climbing literature: "His humanistic style, rife with hyperbole and buoyed by humor and heart, represents the very best American climbing writing."

PROTECTING CLIMBING **ACCESS** SINCE 1991

JOIN US
WWW.ACCESSFUND.ORG

Jonathan Siegrist; Third Millenium (14a), the Monastery, CO. Photo by: Keith Ladzinski